THE DUNKIRK EVACUATION: THE FRENCH PERSPECTIVE

THE DUNKIRK EVACUATION: THE FRENCH PERSPECTIVE

OPERATION DYNAMO AND THE UNTOLD STORY OF THE FRENCH SACRIFICE TO SAVE THE BEF

PAUL L. DAWSON

FRONTLINE BOOKS

First published in Great Britain in 2026
by Frontline Books
An imprint of
Pen & Sword Books Ltd
Yorkshire – Philadelphia

ISBN 9781036133801

A CIP catalogue record for this book is available from the British Library.

Typeset by Lapiz Digital
Printed and bound in the UK by CPI Group (UK) Ltd,
Croydon, CR0 4YY.

Printed on paper from a sustainable source by
CPI Group (UK) Ltd, Croydon, CR0 4YY

FSC www.fsc.org MIX Paper | Supporting responsible forestry FSC® C013604

The Publisher's authorised representative in the EU for product safety is Authorised Rep Compliance Ltd., Ground Floor, 71 Lower Baggot Street, Dublin D02 P593, Ireland.
www.arccompliance.com

For a complete list of Pen & Sword titles please contact
PEN & SWORD BOOKS LIMITED
47 Church Street, Barnsley, South Yorkshire, S70 2AS, England
E-mail: enquiries@pen-and-sword.co.uk
Website: www.pen-and-sword.co.uk
or
PEN & SWORD BOOKS
1950 Lawrence Road, Havertown, PA 19083, USA
E-mail: uspen-and-sword@casematepublishers.com
Website: www.penandswordbooks.com

CONTENTS

LIST OF PLATES

1. German soldiers pictured by the memorial to Georges Guynemer on the promenade at Malo-les-Bains after the end of Operation Dynamo. Guynemer was a top French fighter ace with fifty-four victories at the time of his death on 11 September 1917.
2. A street sign on the old D16 running into Dunkirk during or just after Operation Dynamo. Note the destroyed vehicle in the background. (Historic Military Press)
3. A German despatch rider liaises with other troops amongst abandoned British and French vehicles and equipment near Dunkirk during Operation Dynamo. (Historic Military Press)
4. British troops making their way into Dunkirk as the evacuation gathers pace. According to the original caption, as 'the stream of soldiers and trucks must not be held up', a 'French marine fills in a crater caused by a German aerial bomb'. (Historic Military Press)
5. British troops entering Dunkirk pass the smouldering wreckage of a lorry, a small part of the debris of war that came to increasingly litter the streets of the port. (Historic Military Press)
6. A French soldier passes the same burning lorry that can be seen in the previous image. (Historic Military Press)
7. A French Army Renault UE Chenillette light tracked armoured carrier is pictured having been abandoned in one of Dunkirk's side streets. (Historic Military Press)
8. Assorted French and British military vehicles, including at least two Universal Carriers and a Morris Quad, block a road into Dunkirk and its environs. (Historic Military Press)
9. Apart from the East Mole in Dunkirk itself, there were just the soft, sandy beaches, stretching for 16 miles eastwards from Dunkirk to Nieuport, from which to rescue the men – beaches at

places such as Malo-les-Bains, Bray-Dunes and La Panne. This image shows Allied troops on one of these beaches forming into long winding queues ready to take their turn to board small boats which took them to larger vessels. (Historic Military Press)

10. A remarkable shot of the beach at La Panne during a German air raid on 29 May 1940. It was taken from the decks of HMS *Oriole* by Sub-Lieutenant Crosby; he had turned and captured the very moment that a pair of German bombs fell on the sands and exploded. (Historic Military Press)
11. The graves of French and British troops, possibly killed during the loss of the paddle steamer *Crested Eagle*, are examined by German troops after the evacuation. This is the stretch of beach where *Crested Eagle* was beached and wrecked, the paddle-steamer being immediately out of view to the right. (Historic Military Press)
12. Abandoned Allied vehicles, including at least two Universal Carriers, at the top of the beach at Malo-les-Bains, to the east of Dunkirk, towards the end of Operation Dynamo. Note the harbour arm or jetty that can be seen in the background. (Historic Military Press)
13. An abandoned British or French gun on the promenade at Malo-les-Bains. In the background is the wreck of the French destroyer *L'Adroit*, which was bombed and sunk by Heinkel He 111 bombers in shallow water off Malo-les-Bains at 12:00 hours on 21 May 1940. (Historic Military Press)
14. French and British troops on board ships berthing at Dover, 31 May 1940. (Historic Military Press)
15. Abandoned vehicles and equipment litter the seafront at Dunkirk in the immediate aftermath of Operation Dynamo. The abandoned Thames sailing barge in the centre background is believed to be *Ethel Everard*, which had been towed across the Channel by the tug *Sun XII* in company with another barge, *Tollesbury*. The building in the distance with the round tower is the Malo Terminus Casino. (Historic Military Press)
16. Taken by a German soldier in the immediate aftermath of Operation Dynamo, this picture shows abandoned British and French vehicles on the quayside in the harbour at Dunkirk, with, in the background, the East Mole or jetty that proved so important during the evacuation. (Historic Military Press)

To Dr Phillip E. Judkins.
Thank you for forty summers of friendship and encouragement of my research. I hope this book is fitting tribute and acknowledgement of our friendship.

INTRODUCTION

History tells us that from 26 May to 4 June 1940, Operation Dynamo evacuated most of the British Expeditionary Force to safety from Dunkirk. British propaganda and mythos make much of this victory and that the fall of France was inevitable, and moreover that the French were 'cheese eating surrender monkeys' who simply let the Nazis walk into France with a few shots being fired, condemning the plucky BEF to near disaster. British propaganda also speaks of Blitzkrieg, a new type of warfare, which the Germans unleashed with superior guns and tanks, radios and military thinking that outclassed the Allies, resulting in a quick and inevitable victory. Writing in a *France 24* article in 2020 to mark the 80th anniversary, French journalist Stéphanie Trouillard commented that 'speed with which France crumbled and capitulated in the face of the May 1940 German invasion' was 'shocking, 80 years on'. Not only the British see France as doomed to failure, but so too the French. German propaganda makes the fall of Dunkirk the symbol of German superiority, the defeat inevitable, sudden and catastrophic. It is also undeniable that Operation Dynamo occupies a preponderant place in British memory which salutes its undefeated soldiers, and someone other than the British Army had to be blameable for the defeat.

In the same article in *France 24* a former professor of history at Saint Cyr Coëtquidan military academy, Michaël Bourlet, shifts the narrative from French incompetence. Having read hundreds of archive documents, he suggests that that there was little evidence of France being unready, particularly militarily, in 1940. He adds that 'The idea that the army was badly prepared, poorly motivated and ill-equipped against the invincible Wehrmacht is a myth constructed by Pétain's Vichy regime. Unfortunately, it's still used today, because it makes a good excuse: it's so much easier to admit defeat if you say you had a weak army facing a much stronger one.'

The paradox is startling: the cognitive dissonance between on the one hand Dunkirk happened because the French could not fight and the other, Dunkirk was a re-run of Thermopylae of plucky Brits versus the Blitzkrieg because of unstoppable Panzers. Which is it? Neither hypothesis is tenable, I believe. But was the defeat really that shocking an occurrence? How much of such claims is based on fact? Ignorance of the French defence and sacrifice that allowed Operation Dynamo to take place began in 1940. A brief analysis of British newspapers for Operation Dynamo barely mentions the French. For example, *The Guardian* of 1 June 1940 makes no mention at all of the French holding the perimeter. Thus, for 85 years, the sacrifice of the French Army has barely been mentioned in the creation of a necessary myth to explain victory from defeat and to blame someone else for the British Army's failure. The Dunkirk evacuation is often cited as a key moment in British history, but it has also been described as a myth of British exceptionalism, a narrative that emphasises the nation's unique ability to overcome adversity. While the evacuation was a significant event, the myth surrounding it has been used to promote a particular view of British identity and history, often overlooking the complexities and failures of the event. The emphasis on the 'Dunkirk Spirit' often overshadows the fact that the evacuation was a strategic defeat for the Allies. France also suffered immense losses, and the evacuation was only made possible by the efforts of other nations, including France and the Commonwealth. The Dunkirk myth, like other narratives of British exceptionalism, plays a role in shaping national identity, reinforcing a sense of British superiority and resilience through selectively remembering the past. Without the French sacrifice, the British Army would not have escaped at Dunkirk: yet for 85 years the French are seen as 'cheese eating surrender monkeys'. If the French gave up so easily, who saved the BEF? The British mythos does not work when tested with hard facts: but nationalism and xenophobia relies on emotion and not facts.

This has resulted in historical revisionism, increasingly so after Brexit in 2016, where the narrative of Dunkirk focuses more on the British experience than the broader Allied effort. The reality was, Britain's well-trained expeditionary force in France was beaten just as quickly and thoroughly as the French, and saved itself only by abandoning its French allies and fleeing across the Channel. In 2010, when discussing the 51st Highland Division in France after Dunkirk on the BBC's *Good Morning Scotland*, one historian commented 'the French fought on for another month, well it was their Country after all. You could equally well say the French fought on for another month, but the British fought on for another five years.' A gross oversimplification of the reality to pander to nationalist mythos. Free French forces, under General de Gaulle, participated in the Syria-Lebanon campaign and also fought alongside British forces in Libya and Egypt against Italian forces. The campaign in Syria and Lebanon was particularly important as it removed a potential German foothold in the Levant and consolidated Allied control. Again, the myth of British exceptionalism, and 'Dunkirk Spirit', that Britain shouldered the burden of war alone, does not stand up to hard facts. These actions of the Free French helped solidify the Free French movement and its claim to represent France on the Allied side. The Free French forces, though small in number initially, played an increasingly important role in the Allied war effort, particularly after the entry of the United States into the war and the subsequent expansion of the Free French movement. Yet, the perception is that France surrendered, and did nothing to aid the Allies militarily other than the Resistance, which was parodied by the BBC comedy *'Allo 'Allo!*, further cementing the perception of France at the time into nothing more than a joke.

It is hardly surprising therefore, that most accounts of the Campaign of France and the lead-up to Dunkirk are based on British observations of the French Army: filled with national pride and chauvinism, the British officers over emphasised the weakness of the French Army, and overstated the capability of the BEF. The reality was, the French had better tanks, better aircraft and better weapons than the BEF. Far from being demoralised, the French and Belgians contested the ground inch by inch. The Campaign of France was not a foregone conclusion for the Germans, a point increasingly made by a new generation of German historians who explore the campaign from German archives. The contest at Dunkirk being filtered through Anglo-German perception, while the French are largely ignored, like the Dutch and Belgians.

Yet the perception that the French were routed and surrendered within days of the campaign opening was not one shared by the senior German officers physically present in May and June 1940. General Heinz Guderian admitted 'Despite the major tactical errors of the Allied command, the soldiers put up an obstinate resistance with a spirit of sacrifice worthy of the poilus of 1916.' Erwin Rommel echoed this sentiment: 'The [French] colonial troops fought with extraordinary determination. The anti-tank teams and tank crews performed with courage and caused serious losses.' That France fell was a failure of the Allies: it was as much a Dutch, Belgian and British failure as a French one.

The fall of France in 1940 is surrounded by myths, particularly regarding the perceived weakness and cowardice of the French Army. These myths, often fuelled by British wartime propaganda and post-war narratives, ignore the French military's strength, the complexity of the situation, and the significant resistance offered by French soldiers. The myth of French cowardice is a distortion of the complex reality of the battle, the subsequent occupation of France and the Vichy regime's collaboration and wilful historical amnesia. The real injustice in this the 80th anniversary year of VE Day is not the failure to commemorate the French success over the Germans and the campaign's importance in the inevitable victory of the Battle of Britain, but the slur over the years on the courage of individual Belgian and French soldiers and airmen who fought like lions in the defence of their country and freedom. The narrative of French cowardice is a damaging myth, because it ignores the bravery and sacrifice of French soldiers and the strategic and logistical challenges they faced. The narrative of British exceptionalism that has grown up around Dunkirk needs to be balanced with a more nuanced understanding of the events and the contributions of all those involved. This book seeks to set the record straight. I must thank Dr P. E. Judkins for his forbearance in answering endless questions on Second World War radio technology and to Sally Fairweather for accompanying me on various research trips to collect the research material needed to complete this book.

Paul L Dawson, Forts des Dunes, 4 June 2025

Chapter 1

TO WAR

As September 1939 dawned, the French Army believed itself to be arguably the best in the world. The modernisation plan of 1935 had transformed the fighting capability of the army and air force. Yet, popular history and mythology of the Second World War implies the Wehrmacht had superior tanks, guns and aircraft throughout the war and the Allies were always 'playing catch up'. In fact, French armour development was a generation ahead of what the British Army had by 1937. On paper at least French tanks and aircraft were the best in the world.[1]

Aware of shortcomings in their own armed forces in numerical terms, the French sought a formal agreement with the British: France believed that their army alone could not defend their borders successfully without British military forces.[2] To that end, intelligence-sharing increased and staff talks began in March 1939.[3] Yet it was undeniable that both France and Britain had sought to avoid war at all costs as winter 1938 turned to spring: both nations were still re-arming and legitimately felt they needed to 'buy time' to complete the process before facing Hitler. To that end, perhaps naively, no combined planning had been conducted. Once Hitler occupied Czechoslovakia in violation of the Munich Agreement, this all changed. With war on the horizon, the French and British began formal discussions on how they would fight the inevitable war.[4]

In the wake of the fall of Czechoslovakia, the British government made a commitment on 21 April 1939 to provide an army of six regular and twenty-six Territorial divisions to aid the French, Belgian and Dutch armies, the British Expeditionary Force (BEF). This commitment came after an earlier understanding made in February that four regular army divisions of the Field Force would land in France to help the French, scheduled to reach the assembly area on the thirtieth day after mobilisation.

Until this commitment, no staff work had been done, there was no information about French ports and railways and no modern maps. After the invasion of Poland, the BEF was ordered to France on 4 September. Maurice Gamelin, generalissimo of the French Armed Forces, stressed to Whitehall the need for as much military aid as possible to guard against an attack through the Netherlands and Belgium as he believed France was not prepared, yet, for war.[5] The BEF was commanded by Lord Gort, who was described by one contemporary as 'utterly brainless and unable to grasp the simplest problem'.[6]

Seeking to avoid the mass bloodletting of 14/18, and to defend as much of Europe as possible from Hitler's aggression, despite having no formal alliance with Belgium, French prime minister Edouard Daladier and British prime minister Neville Chamberlain built into their event planning the provision of as much military help for Belgium as they could. Daladier quite rightly feared that German occupation of the Low Countries would threaten France's main industrial region in the north while Chamberlain stressed that it would threaten London and southern England, making the maritime approaches exceptionally vulnerable to air attacks.[7] Ironically, when war did break out, a memo to the War Office dated 4 September, revealed that the Allies had no formal plan.[8] Today we would call this 'blue sky thinking'. War had been inevitable since 1938, and Whitehall was under no illusion that the BEF could be nothing other than a junior partner alongside the French Army in war; yet at the same time, Whitehall was determined to have as much operational flexibility as possible. The net result of this was that until March 1939 extensive contacts which could have led to early joint planning were deliberately avoided by the War Office.[9] Discussion of French strategy is not covered in great detail or questioned in the records generated on the French Army by Whitehall. Silence on this must be inferred as agreement with it, and moreover an understanding of the principles behind it. France's defence strategy would have been understood by all contemporary observers of military affairs, including in Germany. The strategic picture that developed throughout the 1930s combined with the military and economic resources that France had at its disposal meant that French options would be limited in the event of war being declared. The Allies' amorphous goal was to hold on to as much of Europe as possible behind a front line redolent of 14/18 whilst France and England massively increased their defensive and offensive capabilities. The War Office in London appreciated that France had planned since 1937 for a long defensive war in which greater national mobilisation would compensate for Germany's initial economic and demographic advantages. What or where to defend lay in the hands of

General Maurice Gamelin, the commander of French armed forces and found himself made Supreme Allied Commander.[10]

Having declared war, and having no plan of operations to hand, Gamelin, the British Staff and the Cabinet in London set about devising what they hoped was a plan that would enable them not to lose the war.[11] French War planning for much of the 1930s was for the French army to fight in Belgium, and Holland to deny any *espace de manoeuvre*: the enemy could be 'bled white' on a continuous front through Holland and Belgium.[12] Thus, no need existed for a Plan B; Plan A would work as it had at Verdun.[13] Gamelin in 1937 preached the necessity of establishing a continuous and solid front line, and that the quicker it was established, the better it would be: motorisation aided the creation of the front. Gamelin understood that changes in technology allowed for a more rapid establishment of the continuous front and a long-drawn-out war of attrition.[14] The aim was to contact the German onslaught and allow the French army to complete its re-armament. Gamelin knew that based on production capacity, the Allies had the advantage over Germany, and as in 1914 and 1918 any German advance could not be sustained. The German high command knew this and planned accordingly. The concept of the continuous front was devised to prevent a repetition of the German breakthrough to the outskirts of Paris in August-September 1914. The Maginot Line was part of this, accompanied by much lighter and often unfinished fortifications consisting of lines of blockhouses and anti-tank obstacles set along the Belgian frontier to the north. That no second line of defence existed was in part political. Any secondary defensive line would be costly and drive through the industrial heart of northern France. To offset this, the development of mobile reserves, which bore a degree of similarity to what de Gaulle spoke of in 1934, would allow units in sectors regarded as static to be relegated to the lowest priority by the Command: one such was the Ardennes. In order to create the reserve, the economies in manpower along the static sections of the continuous front would be reduced and given over to A or B Divisions, freeing regular troops to fight in the Low Countries. Of the ninety-four mobilised divisions in the French Army in September 1939, just thirty were classed as A Divisions, i.e. those soldiers on two-year conscription and professional full-time soldiers. The majority were reservists, classed as B Divisions. On mobilisation, the reservists were either plugged individually into the skeleton companies of the active regiments or formed into ad hoc *unites de marche* for training. The problem was it did not provide the reservists with the opportunity to train in their combat formations.[15] In B Divisions, even officers as senior as battalion commanders were often reservists.[16] The concern in the French *Grand quartier général* (GQG), because of lack of training and limited experience of combat, was that these men's first exposure to combat would be their last.[17] Lack of training, or at least its limitations, meant that French operational doctrine was simplified compared to the BEF or Wehrmacht. A modernised strategic reserve, consisting primarily of armour it was argued, could easily be accomplished by a reorganisation of existing resources, and thus with a modicum of expense. The downgrading of the by Marshal Petain and Maxime Weygand , successive commanders in chief to fund the development of armour was with hindsight a costly mistake. France was severely hit by the depression of the 1920s, and lacked the fiscal capacity to develop armour and fund the completion of the Maginot Line and its secondary line across the frontier with Belgium. This is not to say the French were not unaware of the incomplete state of their defences, and sought means to rectify them. Brigadier Swayne with the BEF was concerned of the lack of depth to certain positions and on a visit to the Lille area in September 1939 noted 'To the North of Lille where the frontier faces North there are no defences but the river Lys, which itself constitutes an important obstacle'. Equally, just to the south of Lille he reported that 'the foremost line has only been completed' and that 'between Halluin and Armentières . . . there are three lines of barbed wire (old pattern) but some of this barbed wire is close to the A/Tk [anti-tank] ditch and is thus liable to be destroyed by artillery fire on the ditch'.[18] Concern over the lack of completeness of French defences mixed with British criticism of the perceived inactivity of the French army to complete the defences, became for a time a rare issue of tension between the two allies. In March 1940 Gamelin requested British army labour to assist in the construction of secondary defensive positions in certain parts of the French sector. The BEF was unprepared to help the French.[19] Gort did not believe that the incomplete nature of the French defences was sufficiently serious to justify British support to his ally.[20] He was badly wrong.

As we touched upon briefly earlier, since the early 1930s, the French high command devised a military strategy aimed at repeating a long war of attrition followed by an ultimate offensive sometime in 1942 or 1943. This was accepted by Chamberlain and his Cabinet. Allied strategy – often assumed to be solely French – was to fight a long defensive war in which greater national mobilisation would compensate for Germany's initial economic and demographic advantages. Whitehall understood that from previous planning dating back to 1932, the French Army had planned to fight Germany deep in Belgium maximising any Belgian contribution to the war and thus protecting the industrial north of France. Whitehall agreed. The initial campaign objective was therefore somewhat amorphous. British General Ironside admitted, Allied thinking lacked inspiration – which it did. He pithily remarked 'a war cannot, however, be won merely by trying not to lose it'.[21] The goal for the Allies, as in 14/18, was the defence of a static front behind which the Allies would re-arm, mass troops and then with overwhelming force, impose *bataille conduite* and defeat Germany.[22] French doctrine was to control all aspects of the battle, the doctrine of the *bataille conduite*. French doctrine was similar to that of Britain's: both sought to conserve manpower and *material*. To this end, French doctrine relied on a heavily centralised system of command and control over its forces. Where the doctrine of *bataille conduite* differed from the framework to which the British Army worked to, was that it was far more rigid with units advancing to a methodically set timetable and that encounter battles should be avoided at all costs. It is unclear to what extent the War Office in London was fully aware of the finer details of the *bataille conduite*, as there is an absence of discussion on matters of doctrine in Whitehall's surviving records on the French army. If, as should be reasonably expected, the War Office did understand the *bataille conduite*, its silence on the matter can be inferred to be the result of it being perceived as a sensible course of action. Both Britain and France had demurred from a bolder, less risk-averse framework for their armed forces to operate under. Allied doctrine called for the need to generate superior firepower from all available forces before commitment of armour: in doing so, command and control was also centralised away from subordinate commanders. French doctrine, correctly argued, that battles were to take place only after thorough preparation assuring advantages in men, materiel and battlefield position. The goal was to 'impose one's will upon the enemy while . . . maintaining a strict economy of resources'.[23] French doctrine in 1935 declared:

> The Commander exerts his will principally through the use of units held in the rear and of reserves . . . he controls their entry into the battle as well and directs their actions as reinforcements to feed and sustain the battle. He concentrates his final reserves in order to obtain decisive results in the area of his choosing. As he engages them, he works toward gathering together new reserves. He constantly replenishes his reserves with forces from the rear or gathered from another point of the theatre of operations . . . constantly aware of the need to reconstitute new reserves.[24]

This concept applied to both offensive and defensive operations. Even 'audacious solutions', explained the military manual of 1937 for the command of large units, 'should be executed methodically'.[25] The text further stressed:

> In general, and especially at the start of a war, it is important to fight methodical battles and to avoid battles of encounter. The latter, in light of the risks which they entail, do not lend themselves well to the employment of young or inexperienced troops. It is better, on the contrary, to only engage methodically on the battlefield, with all the necessary supporting firepower.[26]

This required, however, a slow process of coordination between different echelons of command in order to execute basic movement. This was in total contrast to what was argued successfully by the likes of Guderian in Germany, where junior commanders were expected to demonstrate their initiative and to exploit opportunities that presented themselves on the battlefield. That is not to say the French doctrine was wrong: doctrines which stressed independent tank armies were successful, but history tells us this success was for no more than 18 months to two years. El Alamein was a *bataille conduite* or methodical battle that defeated the inheritor of Guderian's principals. D-Day was *bataille conduite par excellence*. In short therefore, the Allies had the correct vision of how to win the war in the long term. However, in the short term, the French, like the Allies as a whole, were unable to execute their doctrine very well which was exploited by less risk-averse field commanders, like Guderian. In the long term, despite much early success, the Wehrmacht had a different problem: they had no plan, no vision, and no strategy to win the war. The French and British vision of strategic bombing was correct, even if they lacked the materials to execute this in 1940. The Luftwaffe remained a tactical air force. In short, the Allied plan of action was to hold the Western Front whilst reserves were massed for an offensive in 1942 or 1943: which in reality is what history tells us did happen. The goal for Gamelin was to ensure that the front was held, in essence, not to lose the opening the battle

In such a war of attrition, the German staff knew that if the Allies could contain their initial attack, then they would lose the war purely on industrial capacity. Therefore, for fighting in the West, the German plan relied on the speed and psychological shock of an attack concentrated on the enemy's weak point, the Ardennes. The German high command knew that they had only a few days to win a decisive victory: it was to be an all-out offensive.

As we said earlier, what or where to defend lay in the hands of General Maurice Gamelin, the French and Supreme Allied Commander, who had been given complete freedom of action by Daladier to draft the plan to defend the West.[27] However, whatever plan he generated had to be acceptable to Whitehall, who over time demanded the plan do more and more to defend British national interests. Gamelin has always been blamed for the strategy he devised – yes, as Supreme Allied Commander he did carry the responsibility the position came with – but much of his planning was to appease London. The British Chiefs of Staff Committee advocated an Allied advance into Belgium if the Germans invaded the Netherlands, even if the Allies encountered Belgian resistance to their movement. Why? Because British national interests were at stake. If the Wehrmacht took over the Low Countries they could blockade the Channel, the Luftwaffe could bomb and attack targets in southern England, and interrupt shipping. With the BEF in France, if the Allies held Antwerp and the Escaut estuary, it would be far easier to resupply it from these ports than via Calais. For London, it was of national importance to cordon off as much as Belgium and Holland from the Wehrmacht.[28] Any planning by Gamelin had to factor in the demands from London. The French military representatives who spoke with the British staff were warned in September that German occupation of the Flemish coast would create serious danger for Britain, at least this much of Belgium had to be occupied.[29] Mission creep in London's demands compounded Gamelin's obsession with Belgium.[30] The British may have questioned some of Gamelin's thinking, but never the move into Belgium.[31]

As one officer who served under Gamelin tells us, the impetus to move the Allied forces into Belgium was driven by fear that the German occupation of Belgium and the Netherlands would knock the British out of the war or at least force them to withdraw from the Continent. France in 1940 was too weak to 'go it alone' and thus Gamelin planned accordingly to fully embrace demands from London.[32] The plan of action was 'group think', its failure rested as much with Whitehall as Paris. In spring 1940, neither the British nor the French army had a strategic interest in adopting the Wehrmacht's risky 'one throw of the dice' mentality to doctrine. The Breda Hypothesis had one goal, to contain the initial German onslaught before settling in for the inevitable long war. An encounter battle, which is often spoken of in some histories of 1940 as the Allies' biggest failure to commit to, was not compatible with Allied strategy. Moreover, such a battle played to the strengths of the Wehrmacht and not those of the Allies. The problem was not that the Allies chose the 'wrong' doctrine. Allied strategy was wrong – but which commanders don't make errors? The single largest factor in determining the outcome of the Campaign of France was that the Allies failed to execute their doctrine. *Bataille conduite* called for tanks, aircraft and other weapons of war to be co-ordinated and ideally superior to the Germans.

Chapter 2

COMMAND AND CONTROL

Maurice Gamelin has, I believe, rather undeservedly been blamed by British and French historians for being incompetent, and judged as a man who should never have held command. Yet casting Gamelin almost as a Hollywood villain is to miss the point entirely. I believe there was no better man to lead France and the Allies in 1940: Gamelin's reputation rests largely on Vichy propaganda, which is undeserved. So, who was Gamelin, the man who would lead the Allies not to victory but stalemate?

Maurice Gamelin, aged 68 in May 1940, was a staff officer of some skill, but like most Allied officers he lacked any recent combat experience other than in colonial conflicts. The Allies lacked the training ground of Spain and Poland to evaluate equipment and ideas in combat and to refine them: Gamelin had to learn 'on the job'. This was something he was certainly highly capable of: indeed, from an early age Gamelin showed an aptitude for tactical and strategic thinking. After winning the national prize for philosophy, he continued his studies at the École du Louvre and then decided to take the entrance examination for Saint-Cyr military academy. Admitted in October 1891, he graduated top of his year in 1893. When Gamelin came back to Paris in 1897, he entered the prestigious École Supérieure de Guerre and finished second of his class of about eighty of the best future officers in the French Army. Charles Lanrezac, then second-in-command of the École Supérieure de Guerre and later a general in the early days of the First World War, noted Gamelin as an intelligent, cultivated and industrious young officer, bound to earn higher functions in the future. Gamelin joined the staff of the 15th Army Corps before commanding a company of the 15th Battalion of the Chasseurs Alpins in 1904. He received the applause of his superiors for his diligence at battlefield manoeuvres. In 1906 he published a philosophical study of the art of warfare. Critics of the time praised the book, predicting he would become an important military thinker in the near future. He was chief of staff under Joffre on the Marne from the outbreak of hostilities in 1914, where he earned the praise of his commander-in-chief. Aged 44, in 1917 he was given the command of the 9th Infantry Division with whom he distinguished himself on the Argonne, at Verdun, in the Aisne, around Noyon in March 1918 and halted the advance of German troops along the Oise. However, it was his skills as a highly capable 'pen pusher' and administrator, rather a man with grand strategy and vision for leading men in battle, that earned him his next posting to Brazil in 1919 till 1925, as head of the French military mission. On his return to France in 1925, the young General of Division was given command of the French troops in Syria as Deputy to the High Commissioner Jouvenel (September 1925 to February 1929), with the mission of repressing the Djebel Druze rebellion alongside General Sarrail. His success in supressing the rebellion earned him the honour of being elevated to the dignity of officer of the Légion d'honneur. On return, he replaced Maxime Weygand as General Chief of Staff of the army on 9 February 1931. This posting was ideal as Gamelin's organisational skill had been noticed and praised from his earliest days at St. Cyr military academy. Joffre wrote of him that 'he was for me the most precious contributor on my staff. At no time did I ever observe the slightest deficiency in his conduct or organisation.'[1] The British observed in January 1934 that Gamelin was:

> intelligent, practical . . . He gets on very well with English people . . . He is modern in his military views . . . being endowed with a lucid and elastic mind, he will probably evolve something really useful out of the present French military organisation without changing its basis.[2]

Gamelin was named president of the *Conseil supérieur de la guerre* (Supreme War Council) and army inspector in 1935 replacing Weygand, and was thus the natural choice to be named General Chief of Staff of the national defence (21 January 1938) with his headquarters at Vincennes in the mighty medieval fortress there. When war did come, he inherited event planning from his predecessors, Philippe Pétain and Maxime Weygand, and did very little to change French army thinking that dated from a decade – or more – earlier. This stressed the defensive along the Maginot Line with a degree of mobile army sweeping through the Low Countries to crush the German army against the Line. Exposure to the realities of the German offensive in Spain and then Poland exposed serious flaws in French thinking of the

1920s and early 1930s and in that of the British as well, for that matter. It was Gamelin's task to adapt French thinking in the light of lessons learned and to appease his politician masters in Paris AND London.

Wounded in 14/18, he had three large pieces of shrapnel lodged in his ribcage. Possibly suffering from syphilis, he was not a well man. His repeated attempts to resign his command, particularly after the 1938 Munich Crisis, was perhaps as much motivated by his declining state of health as weariness from command. From the time he had taken over the army in 1935 to his dismissal on 19 May 1940, he had submitted no less than ten separate resignation letters. One eyewitness noted late in April 1940m 'General Gamelin himself was looking worn and anxious'.[3] Days before this observation was made, he had attempted to resign on 13 April 1940.[4]

These attempts at resignation, as traditional history makes out, is proof Gamelin 'was not up to the job': however I believe his behaviour points to a man desperately searching for solutions to what seemed to him to be an increasingly irresolvable military problem, and not the actions of a man who believed he was 'out of his depth'. Gamlein, to the point of obsession, knew very well that the Allies' plan of action could not work if Belgian neutrality was respected. The continuous front had to be established before the Germans attacked: respecting Belgian neutrality meant the Allies could only advance into Belgium once the Germans had crossed the border, far too late to the Allies to put the agreed plan into action. His attempts to resign were probably an exercise in 'shifting the blame' to whoever took over, knowing he would be blamed for failure, especially by French politicians on the right.

The Allies having made their plan of action, which could never have worked in reality unless stronger political will was shown in London and Paris (and better still if someone had talked to Brussels!), it was up to Gamelin's subordinates to try and make the plan work. In command of what would be the battlefield for the coming campaign, was General Alphonse Georges who had his headquarters at the Château des Bondons. Georges entered the *École Spéciale Militaire de Saint-Cyr* and graduated third in his class in 1897. Seriously wounded while leading his battalion in 1914, he was then assigned to the general staff of the army, where he remained for the rest of the war, being a senior members of Foch's staff in 1918. Georges was appointed to the *Conseil supérieur de la guerre* in November 1932. He was expected to succeeded General Maxime Weygand as head of the French Army in 1935, but the job went to Gamelin instead. Georges was appointed as Gamelin's deputy, but they had a mutually hostile relationship. On the outbreak of war in September 1939, Georges became commander of all French field armies. This should have given him freedom of command: however, Gamelin was unable to be 'hands off' on how Georges was to command the defence of France. Gamelin had to constantly chase Georges to carry out orders, to remind him of his duties to train his men and complete defensive positions: Georges' command style was one of relaxed laissez faire over winter 1939/40. Was Georges 'the right man' for the job? Perhaps not, but who else was there? Did he feel slighted by Gamelin's promotion over his own? Clearly Georges exercise of command was of concern for Gamelin to feel he had to micromanage his subordinate.

Under Georges' command was the BEF. Whatever issues existed between Gamelin and Georges, it was Georges who had to fight the campaign from a plan that neither he nor Gamelin believed in.[5] It may have been this issue more than any that impacted the two men's relationship. Georges repeatedly told his superior the Allied plan was doomed: Gamelin had no option but to try and make the Allied plan work. Unless Whitehall agreed to a new plan of operations, Gamelin had to undertake the task assigned him. Georges rightly censured his superior for his dogmatic approach to the Allied plan of action, but what option did Gamelin have? He lacked the authority to cancel agreements made between London and Paris. He chose a pragmatic solution to 'make the best of a bad job' and in doing so, lost much of the respect from his junior officers and his reputation has been sullied ever since. Despite the breakdown of Georges' relationship with his superior, the relationship between Georges and Gort commanding the BEF was excellent as one British officer, Brigadier Swayne, recorded at one particular conference held between Gort and Georges:

> The conference was most successful and once again showed the goodwill and mutual confidence which was felt by both the French and British. The BEF is under the orders of General Georges who could therefore issue orders to them as to any other army, but General Georges is always at pains to discuss his projects with Lord Gort before issuing an order and to make any possible amendments to suit the conditions of the BEF whilst the latter is always prepared to do its utmost to fall in with the wishes of General Georges. In this atmosphere it is easy to come to an agreement which is satisfactory to all concerned. One receives the impression that everyone is prepared to discuss matters on their merits and that there is no question of mutual suspicion or of questions being dealt with on the basis of French v British. It is very different from the beginning of the last war and it is most encouraging.[6]

Also in Georges' remit of command came various French armies and groups. The *1re Groupement des Armée* guarded the north-east frontier of France, ready to move into Belgium and the Netherlands to oppose any German invasion of those nations. It was headed by *Général d'armée* Gaston Billotte. Like almost every French senior officer, he was a veteran of 14/18. He spent the bulk of the 1920s and 1930s in colonial posts in Syria, Tunisia, Morocco and French Indochina, before coming back to France in 1933 serving on the *Conseil supérieur de la guerre*. When war broke out in September 1939, he was 64 years old, and fast approaching retirement. He was given field command, for which his most recent experience was 20 years earlier. Commanding the *1re Armée* was *Général d'armée* Georges Maurice Jean Blanchard. Blanchard, a descendant of a Napoleonic general – his ancestor led the Carabiniers at Waterloo – was the deputy chief of staff for the French Army of the Rhine from 1927 to 1930 before being made chief of staff 1930 to 1932. In 1932 he was promoted to general, and commanded the artillery of the 2nd Military Region. From 1935 to 1938 Blanchard was commanding general of the 7th Military Region. In 1938 and 1939 he was a member of France's *Conseil supérieur de la guerre*, director of the *Centre des hautes études militaires* (Centre of Military Higher Studies) and Inspector-General for the Centres of Higher Military Education. Aged 63 when war broke out, like his superior officer he had no recent combat experience. This does not mean he could not rise to the challenge when it came: most Allied officers had no seen action since 14/18, or if they had, it had been in colonial conflicts. The lack of combat experience was endemic for the Allies, unlike the battle-hardened Wehrmacht and Luftwaffe.

Under Blanchard came the *Corps de Cavalerie* headed by General René Prioux, which was the closest formation France had to a Panzer Division. Prioux was 'cut from different cloth' to his superior. Seeing active service in 14/18 he was with the French Army headquarters in Morocco in 1919. He attended the *École Supérieure de Guerre* (War College) in September 1919 and was subsequently assigned to duties as an instructor there in 1921. By January 1923, he was in charge of the school's cavalry studies and was then promoted to lieutenant-colonel on 25 December 1923. He took part in the French military mission to Poland in 1929, of which he became commander in 1931. On 12 August 1932 Prioux was promoted to brigadier-general. In October 1932, Prioux was assigned as the commander of cavalry in Tunisia. By March 1936, Prioux was promoted to major-general and had been assigned as the chief of cavalry at the Ministry of War. Serving alongside Prioux commanding the *3e Corps d'Armée* was General de

Fornel de la Laurencie, *4e Corps d'Armée* of Aymes, *5e Corps d'Armée* of René Altmayer.

The *2e Armée* was commanded by *Général d'armée* Charles Huntziger, another veteran of 14/18. In 1933, Huntziger was named commander-in-chief of the troops in the French Mandate of Syria. He participated in the negotiations for the cession of the Sanjak of Alexandretta, then part of French Syria, to Turkey. He joined the Superior Council of War in 1938. He was aged 60 when war broke out. The commander of *7e Armée* was *Général d'armée* Henri Giraud. When war began between French and Germany, Giraud had not seen active service since 1920, and publicly disagreed with Charles de Gaulle about the tactics of using armoured troops. *Général d'armée* André Corap commanded the *9e Armée*. France's military leadership had not seen action in Europe since 1918. Almost to a man they were staff officers of ability: this is a very different skills set to commanding front line units at war.[7]

The French Air Force was divided between three different commands. General Vuillemin commanded the reserve forces and also the air assets assigned to co-operation with the various French armies, but from February 1940 this was devolved on *Général d'aviation* Têtu, who took his orders not from Vuillemin but from General Georges. Vuillemin was free to decide his own strategy, whereas Têtu, in theory at least, took instructions from Georges. Commanding the air force in the northern zone, taking orders from Vuillemin but not from Georges, was François d'Astier de la Vigerie. Gamelin commanded both Vuillemin and Georges, who then delegated to their immediate subordinates commanding different sections of the same air force. Failure of concept of strategy and communication was 'hard wired' into this organisational complexity

Were these men 'up to the job' of defending France? Only time would tell.

Chapter 3

COMMUNICATIONS

The French doctrine of the *bataille conduite* relied on excellent communications, yet the weakest aspect of the French Army, ironically, was communications. Only 0.15 per cent of military spending between 1923 and 1939 had been on radio and other communications equipment; to maintain signals security, Gamelin used telephones and couriers to communicate with field units, in stark contrast to the German Army.[1] Nor was the British Army any different to the French:

> By 1939 British army radios were still far from being completely reliable and there was much reluctance outside the tanks and artillery to rely on them as the primary means of communication. More often than not, therefore communications both in front and to the rear of divisional headquarters relied largely on cable. Furthermore, in practice the use of radios at the tactical level was limited to armoured and artillery units. Infantry divisions had so few radios that if they ever became dependent upon them for communications, each divisional headquarters would have to try to command three brigades using a single set. The unevenness of the distribution of radios across the army had important repercussions for all arms cooperation.[2]

The French were themselves aware that their communications systems had considerable room for improvement, but whilst serious attention was still given to the continued use of carrier pigeons by men like Marshal Pétain, little headway could be made.[3] A report in 1935 stated that 'Motorised, mechanised units lack suitable radio communications equipment'.[4]

These problems continued through to 1940, with insufficient attention being given to radio development. General Alombert, the *1re Armée*'s chief of staff, wrote on 8 September 1939 that there were shortages of all kinds of signals material and had equipment in 'urgent need of repair'. His chief signals officer, Colonel Coussillan, stated further that these problems needed to be addressed 'as soon as possible'.[5] The *1re Armée*'s headquarters and the *Ministre de la Défense Nationale* were repeatedly warned by the *Centre d'Organisation d'Artillerie* at Vannes that they faced a situation 'of extreme urgency' with a shortage of instructors 'essential for the proper functioning of the centre' to train communication officers with the army, adding that addition to various radio equipment that was 'urgently needed that had previously been requested but not supplied'.[6]

Inspector General of Tanks Keller, had warned in September 1939 that shortages of two-way radios in tanks was a major issue that had to be addressed, and quickly. Lack of equipment meant that their installation was limited to squadron and battalion command tanks. Each troop leader's tank had a 'receive-only' set; the remaining tanks, though often led by experienced sergeants, had to use visual observation to conform to their leader's movements. If the command tank was knocked out, it was impossible for a new lead tank to take over command. Thus, with predictable inevitability, the *bataille conduite* disintegrated into solitary tanks acting without any degree of co-operation. This restriction of two-way radios to command vehicles amplified the effects of an already top-heavy, top-down command system that characterised French military doctrine which did not stress officers taking personal initiative.[7] Moreover, this lack of two-way communication restricted the sharing of urgent battlefield intelligence.[8] Since French doctrine did not allow field officers to be tactically flexible, the outcome of the entire campaign relied heavily on the top French military leadership. This in turn relied on *very efficient* communications systems. The fast-paced warfare that the Germans imposed onto the Allies exposed the weakness of command-and-control systems that had not really advanced beyond 14/18 principals. Why? *Bataille conduite* imagines a static war à la 14/18, where the use of runners, dispatch riders and the civilian telephone network was perfectly acceptable. This thinking is understandable, as until the Polish campaign, the pace of warfare had not materially advanced since 1918. Incredibly, during the first ten days of the campaign, on average it took 48 hours from a battlefield commander reporting to the GQG for it to respond to the front-line units concerned.[9] In part this was due to the clumsy and impractical cypher system.

To answer Keller's concerns, or perhaps make them much worse, on 29 December it was admitted that due to budgetary constraints the rollout of the 1939 programme of replacement radio equipment, agreed in April, would not be achieved until the second quarter of 1940.[10] On

4 January 1940 Edouard Daladier expressed forcefully to the *Conseil Supérieurs de la Defence* that 'experience of the first months of the war it is absolutely indispensable for our army to review its means and methods of communications'.[11] An inspection was hastily conducted, and reported that the vast majority of French radio equipment was outdated, faulty, had limited range and was substandard to that of the Wehrmacht. It was not only the tank commanders who had issues: pilots reported that they needed an effective two-way means of communication rather than morse keys. The two-way radio telephones that existed barely worked.[12]

In the *Corps de Cavalerie,* one of the French Army' strongest formations, the lack of radios that actually worked was noted by the Corps headquarters as 'significant . . . that could seriously compromise the employment of troops or the functioning of services'.[13] That radio equipment was in need of repair in March 1940, or entirely missing, speaks volumes the French faced in trying to solve their communications problems.[14] The Army knew a problem existed, and tried to resolve it since late 1937, with a formal commission between the Allies being created in New Year 1938. Time was against the Allies in developing radio technology as effective as that of the Wehrmacht. While the French Army had some concerns about their signals and communications prior to the outbreak of the war, we should keep this in perspective. Complacency again played its part: or at least a sense of 'smug satisfaction' that the French equipment was 'good enough' until the Polish campaign transformed operating procedures and demonstrated the importance of communication between all arms. In a report on the French Army's telegraphy and signals in 1938, it was stated that 'the overall impression gathered . . . was very satisfactory . . . and serious efforts are being made at all levels to give them maximum efficiency'.[15] The report however judged that improvements were required 'with regard to radio equipment of the armoured and mechanical units' and that 'it is time for a considerable budgetary effort to be made to move on to the full realisation of both training and mobilisation'.[16] A report from July 1939 had concluded that despite much progress, nothing as yet had resolved 'the problem of creating radio links inside the large mechanical units'.[17] Progress was slow and on 5 April 1940 it was acknowledged that it would take at least three months to develop a prototype means of communication between French tanks as existed in German panzer divisions, and between 14 and 18 months to develop an actual production model. Could the British help, asked the *Conseil Supérieur de la Defence*.[18]

The British refused to co-operate: they needed all the two-way radios they had to equip their own tanks and fighters, and the President of the *Conseil Supérieur* was told on 31 May 1940 that it would be possible to develop comparable radio technology to the Wehrmacht, at the cost of 22 million francs, but nothing would be available for use until the end of 1941.[19] Tanks that could not communicate with each other and change the plan of attack and react to the battlefield as it evolved would be ruthlessly exploited by the Wehrmacht. Even though the French Army had broad deficiencies in radio equipment, on a tactical level this was particularly notable amongst French armour with a lack of radios which would allow tactical control and fast coordinated manoeuvre. That is not to say though that the French Army did not own effective radio communications equipment, it simply lacked enough of it. Missing or defective radios meant that tank commanders still had to wave little coloured flags from the turrets of their tanks to communicate very simple messages to their troop. It meant reliable radio contact with fighters and bombers was almost impossible. An army that cannot communicate cannot fight, let alone react to changing battlefield conditions. This had a major and fatal impact on the campaign to come.

As we hinted at before, another notable weakness in French signals and communications was a lack of fast, impregnable field signals security. This has been shown by one historian who noted that the French Army sought an especially high level of signals security which entailed coding and decoding of messages, orders and combat reports.[20] This created a 'bottleneck' in decoding the information and its onward transmission. Delays of two to three hours were 'hard wired' into the communications system.[21] In imagining a static war, of defence, in essence a replay of 14/18 such delays and reliance on the telephone network, the view from 1934–5 of French commander-in-chief Maxime Weygand was that the cost alone was too great, and a static front as imagined by Marshal Pétain, who downgraded the defensive capability of the Sedan sector, did not need mobile and rapid information exchange systems. Telephones had served their purpose on the Western Front for four years: why change a system that evidently worked? Yet, this all supposed the German OKW would 'play by the book' and be held in Belgium or on prepared positions along the Somme. What exacerbated this situation was the lack of communication between troops on the ground and to GQG. French awareness of the need to improve their strategic signals before war was declared is evident from the large construction programmes in the 1930s that laid thousands of miles of underground telephone cables across France and to its overseas territories. Gamelin in a note from 1938 to the French air and naval chiefs stated: 'the extension of the national network of long-distance telephone cables is of undeniable interest for the . . . needs of the government and national defence upon mobilisation . . . the minimal program is essential to these needs'. Furthermore, Gamelin stressed 'the urgency of the proposed extensions'.[22] The reliance on fixed telephone networks meant in a war of movement runners, couriers on motorbikes and pushbikes, or pigeons were necessary. The Allied armies, based on lessons of 14/18 and the unreliability of radio technology, concluded that telephone communications would be the primary means of movement. As well as being extremely vulnerable to aerial bombing, the telephone system also restricted the movement of the French and BEF's headquarters because they could only be established in locations where, they could connect to the telephone system.[23] German field commanders, as part of their command doctrine, were expected to be forward with their men and were enabled to do so by mobile communications. Limited in their mobility by the telephone network, conversely, the French chain of command failed to react to the tempo created by their German adversaries. The French officers behind the lines reacted only when reports were received by them, often hours later: their German counterparts could respond immediately because they had effective mobile communications. Because they relied on static headquarters because of the need to use telephone lines, the senior French commanders had almost no 'feel' at for the battle and once fighting began they quickly lost touch: we can make the obvious comparisons with the 'Chateaux Generalship' exercised by Allied commanders 14/18 for how Gamelin conducted the campaign.

In contrast the Wehrmacht used a lower level of security in its communications systems: in order to ensure that information was transmitted as speedily as possible to give a current situation report, the Wehrmacht opted to transmit orders and situation reports without losing time encoding and decoding them. Consequently, therefore, the Wehrmacht had a superior degree of operational efficiency compared to the Allies, despite the reduction in communications security. The Allies were operating in an information 'vacuum'. Guderian and his panzers had a constant flow of information that reflected accurately the situation within a few minutes. The Allied network meant that the information when it was received by GQG reflected a situation that no longer existed: planning the defence of France, or any combat operation, reliant on intelligence that is simply not reflecting the real world on the battlefield was totally impossible. When communications collapsed, as they inevitably did when the Luftwaffe bombed telephone exchanges and cut cables, or where information exchange systems were outpaced by the rapid operational tempo that the Germans imposed, the French GQG and other higher-level formations were paralysed. Lacking situational awareness, numbers of casualties, and real-time information on fuel and ammunition supply needs, GQG and commanders like Georges or Blanchard were totally unable to confidently or speedily make decisions and regain the initiative from the Wehrmacht. It was perhaps inevitable, and foreseen in 1939 that the French needed radios, lots of them, and ones that worked, that commanding a battle in almost information 'blackout' resulting lack of direction and control would lead inextricably to the disintegration of command and control and communications above divisional level. Indeed, once the fighting began, the situation on the front line was prone to rapid, if not constant, changes: in this scenario, local battlefield commanders were in the best position to assess what the enemy was doing, to assess what the immediate effects of the enemy action would be and respond accordingly since they could take the quickest decisions to adapt to the circumstances. Yet French military thinking was 'top down' since men like Georges, Billotte et al had the required perspective to manage and coordinate all the different soldiers and materiel on the front. But it relied, as we said on effective and speedy communications.

Yet the BEF was little better. It too was overly reliant on telephones and continued to have too few radio sets and trained operators to deploy with them, if the sets worked.[24] The establishment of the Franco-British Military Committee on Telecommunications in July 1939 exposed the weakness of existing systems. The aim was to:

> study all questions of common interest concerning telecommunications and to propose all measures which will ensure, in close co-operation, the best employment of the methods of communication according to the different situations which may arise during hostilities . . . To allot to the British and French signal services of all arms, the frequencies which they are to use, with a view to reducing, operating signals, etc . . . To exchange all military and technical information of common interest concerning telecommunications.[25]

In the event, it amounted to 'Arrangements for dovetailing the frequencies required by the British Field Force into the framework of the French army system. [For example] Landline requirements of the British army in France.' A research dossier was produced on the British No 8 Infantry Radio. French officers judged that:

it appears to be a well-designed device, without however presenting sensational performances. It is heavier and more complicated that the French ER 40 or ER 17 devices; handled by trained men, it can give good results; put in the hands of average operators, it may happen that the results obtained are much worse. It should be noted that most British devices have very good modulation, due to the good quality of the microphones used.[26]

Damning words, when we consider the French accepted as far back as 1935 that the 'ER17 are mediocre . . .They are unstable and unsuitable for operation in dense networks . . . The ER12 devices . . . give impure emissions interfering with neighbouring networks . . .The ER 13 . . . is an obsolete device.'[27] Nor was the much vaunted long-distance telephone network complete which was something the French were fully aware of. In February 1940 General Jullien, *Inspecteur Général Technique des Transmissions de la Défense Nationale,* urged that current development of radio and laying of telephone cables 'constitute a minimum program, the implementation of which meets imperative and urgent need for national defence'.[28]

Making matters worse for army-level communication back to headquarters were wider issues of manpower shortages in specialist signals posts was flagged up Colonel Goetschy, *Directeur des Transmissions* at GQG, who observed on 18 September 1939 that 'it appeared that the assignment of personnel from various specialties to the units of the special corps of military telegraphy provided for in the war manpower tables was not respected.'[29] Missing or faulty equipment and a lack of specialists meant the French GQG was operating more or less blind once action began, reliant on communication methods little changed from the army of Napoleon. Captain Miles Reid, attached to the headquarters of the French *1re Armée,* observed after the commencement of the German attack that:

A great deal of the difficulty can be attributed to the inadequate system of communications. An Army headquarters has no recording apparatus either with its immediately lower or higher formation. Everything is done on the telephone and incoming conversations are recorded in a 2d exercise book.

This book was in great demand and extremely difficult to see and (to me a foreigner) was frequently illegible. But the worst aspect was that frequently the book was removed altogether. On frequent occasions we had one telephone only provided for the operations section and access to this was practically surrounded with great difficulty.[30]

Reid's observations provide just a small, but incredibly important, insight into the difficulties that existed in the French Army's communications. Nor was this, again, solely a French problem. Both the BEF and the French had judged that telephone communications were the most economical means of communication; the lines were considered to be safe from damage because the main French trunk lines were carried by buried cables. Yet, many of these ran alongside main roads and were quickly cut by German bombing. What worked in peacetime, simply did not in times of war. No one in the BEF or French GQG had considered a plan B once the telephone network collapsed.[31] Moreover, the telephone system also restricted the movement of the BEF's General Headquarters (GHQ) because it could only move to where it could connect into the international telephone system to communicate with London. Thus, when the system collapsed, the BEF had to rely on radio communications to a much greater extent than it considered before 1940, and in doing so, discovered once the fighting had begun, that it had too few of the right sets and too few trained operators. Moreover, the BEF security procedures prior to transmission imposed lengthy delays.[32] The consequences of a failure in communications were made by liaison officer Miles Reid stating (after the fact) that once the Battle of France began:

> The French wanted continually to know the British position and vice versa. And . . . at times no one in either headquarters could give an exact static picture of the intensely dynamic scene . . . in the increased tempo of 1940 warfare it was quite impossible for one man to do both . . . The ineffectiveness of the telephone called for continual daily journeys backward and forward between 1st Army HQ and GHQ . . . At GHQ they felt my visits should be more frequent and at 1st Army they thought I should be there permanently.[33]

Once the campaign began, the Wehrmacht was moving at a speed that both French and BEF communications simply could not respond to. It also meant co-ordination between the BEF, French and Belgian armies was almost impossible. Writing after the fact admittedly, Brigadier L. H. Harris recalls the difficulties the Allies encountered as they withdrew through Flanders: 'Since leaving the Escaut the communications had been almost entirely by despatch rider. Lines would have taken too long to lay and, until the end we were still thinking we should be eventually taking up a stable defensive position and wanted to conserve our store for this.'[34] Indeed, Colonel de Cardes, an officer within the French liaison structures of the North-east Command reported on 19 May whilst trying to plan for the counter-attack at Arras 'from that date I lost all contact with the British and with the French liaison mission'.[35]

The importance of the breakdown of liaison between the French and BEF, as well as between various elements within each army during the course of campaign should not be overlooked. Indeed, a French liaison officer stressed that 'liaison is actually an element of combat'.[36]

It is clear, therefore, that on the eve of battle, the Wehrmacht had two clear advantages: better communications – at least in theory – and a doctrine that allowed local field commanders to act on initiative to unfolding battlefield situations rather than rigidly adhere to a fixed timetable, that could not react to events as they unfolded. If one part of the linear plan of operations was delayed or failed, the whole plan began to collapse. With the lateral thinking of Wehrmacht doctrine, problems could be overcome without recourse to the high command. This difference between linear A to B to C doctrine of the Allies and the Wehrmacht's ability to go A to D bypassing B and C entirely, was to prove critical in the outcome of the campaign. One writer commented: 'In modern war, communications are just as much a weapon as anything else with which an army is equipped; furthermore, they are the only weapon the operation of which directly affects the control of operations by a commander; without good communications, no commander can hope for success in battle.'[37]

Failure of communications would be a major contributing factor to the fall of France. The overriding conclusion one must make is that on the eve of war, the French command structure was overly complex and slow, hindering effective communication and decision-making. Once the German offensive began, the French struggled to react effectively and organise counter-attacks because of appalling communications.

Chapter 4

THE PROBLEM OF BELGIUM

The 'group think' between Paris and London on how best to fight a land war against Nazi Germany had, as we hinted at earlier, an insurmountable Achilles heel. For the plan of operations agreed by Whitehall to work, the Allied armies had to be in position in Belgium before the Wehrmacht arrived.

France and Belgium had had a collective defence pact signed in September 1920, but this was cancelled in 1936 as Belgium returned to pursuing a policy of neutrality following the occupation of the Rhineland by Germany in March that year. French doubts about the Belgian Army led to uncertainty about whether French troops could move fast enough into Belgium to avoid an encounter battle. France promised to come to Belgium's aid in case of invasion on 24 April 1937, which solidified French and Allied thinking of where the primary German strike was to come when it came.[1] Second, because of Belgian neutrality, the only information which made its way to the French high command about Belgian military intentions came from informal channels and secretive communications between Gamelin and Belgian Chief of Staff Édouard van den Bergen. It may not have been true.[2] None of this helped build trust between the various Allies or foster a sense of co-operation.[3]

Politicians in Whitehall, Brussels and Paris were all of the same voice: the French Army could not move into Belgium until the Germans had invaded. Belgium was a sovereign state and neutral, any violation was against international law. The insistence on obeying the letter of the law, when Hitler was flouting it so openly, was rather lost on the Allies who were fearful of German propaganda if they moved into Belgium.[4]

The Mechelen Affair (more commonly known as the Mechelen Incident) was a critical event in the Second World War. on 10 January

1940 a German Messerschmitt Bf 108 Taifun, piloted by Major Erich Hönmanns, took off from Münster heading for Cologne. On board was Major Helmuth Reinberger, carrying the highly confidential plans for *Fall Gelb* (Case Yellow) – the upcoming German invasion of Belgium, the Netherlands, and France. Hoenmanns became lost in heavy fog and mistakenly flew across the frozen River Rhine. Engine failure resulted in an emergency landing in a field near Vucht, in modern-day Maasmechelen, Belgium. The captured documents completely exposed the German intention to execute a modified version of the old Schlieffen Plan, concentrating their main strike through central Belgium. The Belgian military shared these findings with French and British authorities. Though the initial Allied response was mixed and plagued by distrust, the intelligence breakthrough heavily disrupted Germany's operational security. Fearing their strategy was entirely compromised, Adolf Hitler postponed the invasion and General Erich von Manstein successfully pushed forward an alternate proposal: the Manstein Plan. This shifted the main armoured spearhead south through the heavily forested, undefended Ardennes region, ultimately allowing the Germans to bypass and encircle the main Allied armies when the invasion finally launched. In the wake of the Mechelen Incident Gamelin hoped that he now had sufficient 'leverage' to use against politicians in Paris and Whitehall to allow the French and British forces into Belgium. The captured plans made it clear that the central thrust was to be through Belgium, and if that was to be held, the Allies HAD to enter Belgium when it seemed invasion was imminent. On the morning of 12 January 1940, Gamelin convened a meeting with his top operational commanders and the Chief of Military Intelligence, Colonel Louis Rivet. While Rivet expressed scepticism about the German plans being genuine, as did his counterpart in Whitehall, Gamelin saw the incident as a chance to pressure the Belgians into allowing French forces to advance into their territory It was feared that an attack, despite the freezing weather, was imminent.[5] Gamelin felt Belgian neutrality was a major impediment to operation planning, and hoped that the invasion scare could potentially push the Belgians to align with France and Britain, thereby granting France access to strategically important ground for a future attack. When the Panzers failed to roll, a diplomatic standoff resulted. Negotiations began on 14 January between Admiral Sir Roger Keyes, Churchill and the Belgian crown. What exactly was discussed is lost to history, but the French record of what was on offer stated that 'the King would ask his government to invite the Allied armies to occupy defensive positions inside Belgium immediately' if the Belgians received satisfaction in relation to their requested guarantees: the only guarantee we can be certain of was the assurances that the Allies would not open negotiations for any conflict settlement without Belgium's agreement. Daladier informed the British government that, as far as France was concerned, the guarantees could be given.

Both the Admiralty and Daladier were convinced the Belgians would receive a satisfactory response from the British government in relation to the guarantees, and would immediately invite the Allied armies to move into Belgium. Believing this to be the case, during the night of 14–15 January, Gamelin ordered the *1re Groupement des Armée* and the adjacent *3e Armée* to advance towards the Belgian frontier. This action was intended to heighten the sense of crisis and for the French army to be prepared if the German invasion did occur, allowing French forces to establish a strong defensive position in central Belgium before the arrival of the enemy. The problem was, no Panzers were on the move towards Belgium and moreover, it is undeniable that Gamelin, Daladier and Churchill via Keyes had been rather too optimistic in what Chamberlain, Eden and others would agree to. At 08:00 on 15 January, Gamelin was made aware of the British Cabinet's response to the request for guarantees: what Gamelin read made him believe that what was offered would be unacceptable to Belgium. Chamberlain agreed to everything and nothing, and stated they could not at the current time guarantee the requests made by Belgium. Gamelin telephoned Daladier in panic: he knew that the Allied army taking up position in Belgium was of critical importance. Three hours later Daladier, acting on the advice of the desperate Gamelin, told Pol Le Tellier, Belgium's ambassador in Paris, that unless the French had an invitation to enter Belgium by 20:00 that night, they would not only withdraw all British and French troops from the border but would refuse to carry out similar manoeuvres during future alerts until after the Germans had invaded. Alas, in this game of brinkmanship, the Belgian government called Daladier's bluff. Whitehall's watered-down guarantees kept the border firmly closed. Belgian Prime Minister Pierlot felt that Allied entry into Belgium would provide Germany with a useful excuse to attack as soon as possible, and he forced an embarrassed King Leopold to thank the angry Allies for their efforts while telling them not to cross the frontier.[6]

Undeterred, Gamelin entered into negotiations via Daladier at the end of February seeking the same assurances, but the Belgian government refused any discussion and collaboration with the Dutch and refused the French to cross the border.[7] Gamelin did not give up, and in a memo dated 12 March he opined that he was 'working steadily toward achieving' moving at least *7e Armée* into Belgium or at least co-operation with the Belgian Army.[8]

As we noted earlier, Gamelin was becoming increasingly desperate that the agreed plan of operations would fail even before it began due to a lack of political will in Paris and Whitehall. Is it any wonder he tried to resign?

Chapter 5

THE BREDA HYPOTHESIS

The Mechelen Incident further confirmed for Gamelin the lessons he had learned from observing the events in Spain and Poland, that the Luftwaffe was to be used in massive waves to decimate the bulk of French air power on the ground. The German fighters and bombers would then turn their attention to the advancing French columns.

To French observers, the Polish campaign had been decided by unstoppable waves of aircraft which, once established as masters of the air, devastated enemy military and civilian targets at will.[1] This fear led Gamelin to take ever larger risks in his war planning: 'German aviation acts with an extraordinary boldness. It conducts reconnaissance in a perfect manner, rendering all daytime movement impossible for fear of immediate aerial reaction. Action taken in the rear areas are informed by radio or by aerial signalling with exactitude, speed and precision.' Gamelin now sought to adapt French doctrine to effectively combat the Wehrmacht.[2]

For Gamelin the 'big takeaway lesson' from the events of September 1939 was that it had proven impossible for the Poles to attempt to move reserves from one area to another because of interdiction by the Luftwaffe, thus their defence plans quickly shifted toward improvised counter-attacks.[3] Gamelin was alarmed not by German armour but by the Luftwaffe. To defend the ground troops Gamelin ordered massive aerial reinforcement of the *1re* and *3e Armée* along the French left flank, further weakening the centre. Indeed, Gamelin referred to a German move into Belgium as 'the most dangerous' because it could have the fastest results in determining the outcome of the coming battle.[4] He was correct. As we noted in the earlier chapter, if the French army was not to be obliterated in getting to its allocated positions, the Allies had to cross into Belgium days or ideally weeks before the Wehrmacht attacked. Gamelin relied on blind faith that the Dutch and Belgians would co-operate. Indeed, Billotte commanding the *1re Groupement des Armée* told Gamelin the plan could only 'can only be imagined' to succeed 'if the Belgians and the Dutch formally commit to specific positions of resistance'. No such agreements had been made. General Georges wrote in the margins of Billotte's report, 'it's a wild adventure. The Dutch are not prepared to defend themselves. We have no agreements with the Belgians. Give up the dream!'[5] On 26 February Charles Huntziger, commander of the *2e Armée* stationed opposite the Maginot Line, confided to his diary after Gamelin refused to reinforce the Ardennes sector: 'Everyone has lost patience with Gamelin, who no longer acts with the slightest energy, not in Paris alongside the government, not in directing our military production, not in organising our air power.'[6]

The Breda Hypothesis was Gamelin's final gambit to increase his army's forward strength to its greatest possible level. For a man who was objectively risk-averse, Gamelin gambled he could create a continuous front from the Channel to Switzerland manned by British, French, Dutch and Belgian forces. The gamble was twofold; that the continuous front could be created, and more importantly that the Wehrmacht would not attack the Maginot Line or the Ardennes. In seeking to defend as much of Belgium as possible, the number of reserve forces available behind the continuous front would be perilously thin. It meant Gamelin had no reserve forces available to move rapidly to plug any break through. However, in Gamelin's defence, by extending the front line he aimed to preserve the majority of Belgian territory from being overrun: it would protect the south coast of England, as we said earlier, whilst simultaneously depriving Germany of some important Channel ports. Gamelin, like Whitehall, had to plan for a war of long duration to complete re-armament. If Belgium was held, in this context, in planning for an offensive in 1942, meant the Allies were that much closer to the industrial Ruhr region. Based on Gamelin's meticulous blueprint for stalemate, the Allied armies were to rush into Belgium and occupy pre-assigned defensive lines, and upon encountering the enemy, French units were expected to resume the practice of *bataille conduite*. The absence of any viable alternative option in 'case things went wrong' was, it seems, never a cause for concern. Whitehall's silence must be taken as agreement. Neither Gort or Whitehall raised any objections to Gamelin's thinking.[7]

Under the new plan, the *7e Armée*, which consisted of one DLM, two DIM (motorised infantry divisions) and three class 'A' infantry divisions, was assigned an assembly point twice as far from France as it was from Germany without suffering major airborne interdiction.

For Gamelin, sending the *7e Armée* forward in a mad dash to Holland was key to fortifying the morale of the BEF, as well as the Dutch and Belgian armies who would face the brunt of the Wehrmacht. These reasons alone, Gamelin believed, were more important than maintaining a strong strategic reserve, and one which he reasoned from what he observed in Poland, may not have actually been be able to join the battle when called upon, due to interdiction by the Luftwaffe. Unlike, it seems, Whitehall, few of Gamelin's subordinates were convinced.

In response to Gamelin, Giraud wrote:

> The operation planned for the VII Army would send it two hundred kilometres from the French border and only eighty kilometres from the German border . . . This manoeuvre wrongly assumes a strong understanding exists between the Belgians and Dutch to act in concert with one another . . . In addition the materiel devoted to this mission are greater than those we can spare while still conducting our principle manoeuvre to the Dyle River and Gembloux Gap . . . In conclusion, there is no reason to pursue these plans for the VII Army and instead to re-attach it to the First Army Group.[8]

Gamelin's own staff added weight to the censure of the idea:

> Such an operation . . . conducted so near to German aviation's zone of action, within very limited territory, upon soil which prohibits the digging of trenches and shelters, runs the significant risk of turning into a catastrophe.
> Conclusion:
> The operation contains serious risks which seem incommensurate to the benefits which we might anticipate.[9]

General Blanchard also expressed similar sentiments, believing that the French troops linking up with the Dutch and Belgians could never achieve this objective: 'We cannot then ignore the possibility of an encounter with the enemy before preparations are complete. The army would be thus taken in *flagrante delicto* and forced to deliver battle under unacceptable conditions, we risk an encounter battle of the riskiest sort.'[10]

Gamelin's belief in the feasibility of the manoeuvre defies logical analysis, especially when both Giraud and Georges condemned it.[11] But what choice did Gamelin have? He had to meet the demands of his subordinates and the politicians in Whitehall and Paris. Lord Gort, commanding the BEF, had explicitly asked Gamelin to embed the 7e *Armée* with the BEF because he believed his own armoured units were insufficient to match the Panzers. In order to appease Gort and Whitehall, to ensure Whitehall remained in the war and kept troops in France, Gamelin fatally acquiesced to Gort's demands. Worse, Gamelin had no meaningful or objective communication with the Dutch or Belgians about their support for the plan.[12] Gamelin relied on blind faith that the Dutch and Belgians would co-operate.

Blitzkrieg was based on overwhelming force being applied at a single point. Gamelin's plan, as his senior officers made clear, rather than strengthening the anticipated points of contact with the enemy, which it undoubtedly did, the incorporation of the strategic reserve into the forward armies was a decision which served only to weaken the French continuous front immeasurably. Yet Gamelin persisted, despite none of his senior officers have any faith in their commander and his operational planning. Minister of Armaments Raoul Dautry wrote, 'we must support the president in his desire to rid us of Gamelin. That general is incapable . . . of issuing a single order.'[13] During 16 March, Paul Reynaud tried to oust Gamelin, believing he was not sufficiently active in persecuting the war, but his support from Edouard Daladier ensured that he, remained in post.[14] Reynaud, who had become the Prime Minister of France on 21 March, spearheaded a renewed effort to prosecute the war against Germany and deepen the Anglo-French alliance. On 9 April, and again on the 22–23rd, Reynaud and Admiral Darlan travelled to London for emergency *Conseil supérieur de la guerre* meetings following Germany's invasion of Norway (Operation Weserübung). Reynaud became furious with Britain's reluctance to commit or delay their evacuation of Norway, going as far as to deplore the 'old men in London who do not know how to take a risk'. Reynaud made one last attempt to oust Gamelin on 9 May. The timing was appalling: in the midst of political crisis, the Germans attacked.[15]

Despite the French Army objecting to its commander-in-chief's plans, as noted earlier, Whitehall accepted Gamelin's plan of deploying the bulk of military assets into Belgium.[16] Again, the British were in complete agreement concerning what they considered to be the German intent of the principal thrust in Belgium.[17] Why did Whitehall and Gamelin brush away legitimate concerns?

The problem was Whitehall, Paris and Brussels refusing to allow the Allies to enter Belgium in case it triggered a German response. Therefore, moving the reserves into the front line was a way of avoiding their total destruction and, as importantly, assuaging demands by

Pownell and Gort. As we said earlier, Lord Gort, commanding the BEF, placed ever-increasing demands on Gamelin. Gort confided to Anthony Eden that:

> It is the shortage of war material, however, which is causing me the chief concern and I have drawn attention, on a number of occasions to difficulties that exist not only in war reserves but also in front-line equipment.

He noted moreover:

> I would specify in particular the serious shortage of tanks, of ammunition for certain natures of equipment and of many vehicle reserves and spare parts. To conduct a protracted defensive battle it is essential to have immediately available the approved scales of ammunition and reserves: without them many lives must be needlessly sacrificed and the successful outcome of the battle will depend as has so often happened in the past on the British refusal to admit defeat.[18]

As far back as November 1939, General Pownell argued that the due to lack of manpower in the BEF, the agreed plan of operations would necessitate it committing reserves in order to meet objectives and extend the front line, and requested from Gamelin that the mobile reserve, the *7e Armée,* was be incorporated into the front line on a temporary basis to provide the BEF with the reserves.[19] Gamelin had initially defined the *7e Armée*'s role as a mobile reserve for the French army, yet on 20 March 1940 Gamelin reluctantly confirmed his commitment to embedding his reserve in the front line.[20] In hindsight many modern historians believe that was the biggest error Gamelin made: with the best units of the French army in Belgium, German local success at Sedan could not be immediately challenged. Had this shifting of the reserve not occurred, the outcome may well have been different.[21] Yet in 1940 this was not how the order was perceived. On 6 April, the mission of the *7e Armée* was defined as 'to reinforce the Belgian National redoubt of Antwerp-Gand . . this is important to us as we shall have some French troops with which to make contact at the bridgehead of Gand . . . the 1st DLM is put under the orders of the BEF. Lord Gort specifically requested the 7e Armée to strengthen the BEF sector of operations.'[22] Clearly therefore, this was an example of 'group think' that has entirely been blamed on Gamelin: Georges the commander of forces in the north-east sector, along with Lord Gort commanding the BEF formulated a plan of operation, signed off by Gamelin, which all involved in the decision making process agreed with. Indeed, Gamelin felt he had no option but to move the *7e Armée* forward because 'we had to imagine the Belgians might not be resisting' and therefore needed as many men at the front as possible to resist the Wehrmacht. Because no one knew what the Belgians would do on contact with the Wehrmacht, Gamelin was all too well aware that he may need to 'plug the gap' in the line, and all he had to hand was the *7e Armée*. His thinking, based on experiences of Poland, was further influenced by Lord Gort. Gort admitted to Georges, that he believed the armoured units of the BEF would be unable to hold against a Panzer division and 'could not fight a running rearguard action to the Escaut . . . they could not be considered to be the equivalent of a DLM for this purpose'.[23] A *Division Légère Mécanique* (DLM) was designed to carry out the cavalry's traditional tasks of reconnaissance, screening operations, and forward delaying actions. Thoughts turned to establishing more heavily-armoured divisions, whose specific purpose was to break through the enemy lines as well as being capable of acting autonomously. The 1re DLM with the BEF used the AMR 35 as a light skirmisher and the Somua S-35 and Hotchkiss H-35 as main battle tanks, though the latter vehicle was not really suited for this role. The infantry component, 4e *Regiment Dragons Portés* (RDP) were equipped with the six-wheeled VDP Lorraine 28 all-terrain transport vehicle. A DLM was akin to a Panzer division. In essence, Gort was admitting his armour and was inferior to that of the French and the Wehrmacht, and the BEF needed 'stiffening' with French armour.

Gamelin probably acted as he did to assuage Lord Gort and Whitehall in the knowledge that he could have 160,000 men at the front in 72 hours: this assumed the rail network had not been damaged. With reserves well away from the front, they were safe from attack by the Luftwaffe. Gamelin had already issues instructions that in case the front could not be formed, the Escaut was to be the reserve line, between Wavre-Charleroi, the Aisne-Somme and if needed frontier of France. So, concerned about facing Panzer divisions with inadequate anti-tank guns and armour and perceived lack of manpower to sustain anything more than a combat of a few days, Georges reassured Lord Gort on 22 April that the BEF would have the *7e Armée* in support.[24] Days before the campaign began on 2 May, Gort was already imagining taking a subordinate role to Giraud.[25] The question is, why did Gort not ask for reinforcements from Whitehall? Gort admitted the BEF was 'not up to the job', and thus manoeuvred Georges and Gamelin to commit French reserves to keep the BEF 'in the fight.' Gort was adamant that the tanks under his command were few and obsolete; air support was totally inadequate; field artillery had not been provided with armour-piercing shells; reserves of ammunition were totally insufficient for the needs of the BEF. Gamelin's fatal miscalculation was, partly, to ensure Whitehall remained in the war.

Gamelin was correct that the Poles had been unable to move reserves, so he chose to move reserves to the front, yet, it seems he failed to grasp that the Luftwaffe would equally attack reserves moving as front-line troops to the Dyle. Ironically, Gamelin exposed more of the French army to interdiction than there had been before. In his favour, the intended positions along the Dyle River were closer to the French border – admittedly marginally – than they were to Germany but extended the length of the front line by 50km. In his favour, Gamelin would secure the Schedlt (Escaut) estuary to bring supplies into the combat zone by sea via Antwerp, and link with the Dutch along the line of the Escaut. Moreover, as Gamelin confessed to Edouard Daladier, he hoped that 'the Belgian government may be swayed if we offered the assurance of setting up our defence on the Albert Canal–Meuse line' to sway them from neutrality.[26] Gamelin's plan was the only option 'on the table', and a plan which appeased each Allied nation's fears. The French could move the dreaded front away from French industrialised zones, and for the British, it meant that they could concentrate their land forces on the Continent as close to Britain as possible and use their naval and air assets in support without compromising national security. In doing so, Gamelin had ensured the continued support of British forces, appeased his political masters in France and anticipated adding Belgian and Dutch divisions to the Allied forces so he could reach divisional parity with the Wehrmacht. The obvious defects were ignored. The Allies were going to war with a 'half-baked plan' that could not work.

Gamelin's thinking was based in French military doctrine that had been accepted since 14/18. This stressed the careful build-up of resources prior to commitment to action if an encounter battle was to occur: this is what Gamelin was working towards. He hoped overwhelming artillery, air support, armour and massing the best infantry into a single location would be sufficient to contain any German thrust. In thinking in this way, his centre was contained by the Maginot Line, leaving either an attack through Gembloux or the extreme flank in Switzerland. By massing his best units in the north, Gamelin probably hoped it would draw the bulk of the Wehrmacht to oppose it, weakening the German centre and southern flank. Yet Gamelin had no clear indication of where the Germans would deploy. He was 'working blind.' His strategic vision for imposing *bataille conduite* on the Germans was correct: the problem was making sure that the French got to the front line before the Wehrmacht did.

Chapter 6

CARRY ON REGARDLESS

Despite being aware that the Allied armies could not be established in Belgium until the Wehrmacht rolled over the border, rather than change his plans to adopt to the situation, and glibly assuming the German high command would stick to their event planning despite the Allies having a solid idea of what had been planned with the Mechelen Incident, following discussions at the Supreme Allied War Council on 28 March, and 9 and 23 April 1940 in London and Paris, the Allies agreed to 'carry on regardless' with the agreed plan. Many in Whitehall felt that the Mechelen Incident was a ruse to force the Allies to weaken the front in Belgium. For Whitehall it was 'better to wait and see'.[1] We tend to forget that whatever was devised by Gamelin had to be agreed in Paris AND Whitehall: the war was being run by committee, and the demands of both sides had to be met. Gamelin was not 'master of his own destiny'. Indeed, knowing very well to the point of obsession that if he was to defend Belgium and Netherlands from German aggression, Gamelin sought to enact the Breda Hypothesis which extended French lines of communication in the second week of April to ensure the French were in position before the Wehrmacht inevitably attacked.[2] His request was denied by the French and British governments. Had Gamelin been more forceful, had the French government not been in a state of flux then things could have been different. Ironically, Gamelin's event planning had been correct. As Heinz Karl Frieser points out, the original German plan was to advance exactly as Gamelin had anticipated, but Hitler had dismissed it out of hand as merely a variant of the Schlieffen Plan that lacked any original thinking. In the Allied case, however, strategic leadership never questioned the Breda Hypothesis. Preoccupation over Belgium turned to negligence: it meant that the Allies were completely unprepared to deal with the German plan to breach the Meuse in the centre of the Allied line and race to the English Channel, just as General Alphonse George had predicted.

But to go back a few weeks to mid-March 1940. Edouard Daladier had always been critical of intervention in Norway and Finland, believing that the defence of France had to be the priority. He therefore refused to send aid to the Finns, who were under attack from the USSR. After the news that the Finns had sued for peace, the French legislature denounced Daladier's actions; the government fell on 19 March. The government named Paul Reynaud Prime Minister of France two days later. Daladier had championed Gamelin and the Breda Hypothesis: Reynaud was 'cut from different cloth'. Yet, on becoming Premier and Minister of Defence, Reynaud could do little immediately. He had to form a new Cabinet, extricate the French forces from Norway and to face the reality of an imminent German attack. Édouard Daladier became Minister of National Defence and War, and Raoul Dautry as Minister of Armaments. The government's main focus was on preparing France for the expected German offensive, strengthening its defences, and maintaining alliances, particularly with Britain. Reynaud's government faced internal divisions regarding the best course of action against Germany, with some advocating for a strong defence and others for potential negotiations or an armistice.

It is undeniable that the experience of Norway had terrified the Allies. In an inter-Allied meeting with Gamelin on 26 April Churchill stated that 'we have severely underestimated the consequences of the enemy's aerial retaliation'. Such a comment could only confirm Gamelin's belief that he had to embed the reserve in the front line. The experience of Poland also solidified in Whitehall the need to occupy Belgium. If the south coast of England was to be protected from Stukas, the Allied army had to move into Belgium and occupy as much as possible of Holland. Others were more stark in their assessment. At the same meeting, Admiral Sir Dudley Pound confessed 'it is not possible to react effectively, confronted with the enemy's aerial superiority'. Reportedly, French Air Chief Vuillemin 'was silent and stupid as ever, kept quiet as we heard about the Luftwaffe's shocking efficiency in Norway'.[3] Gamelin agreed, stating 'the decisive factor in determining the outcome of the Norwegian expedition was the superiority of German aviation . . . The British were very afraid of the German air force'.[4]

Aware of the huge impact that the Luftwaffe could have on the deployment of the Allies into Belgium, Gamelin and many on the *Conseil supérieur de la guerre* were concerned that the French army could reach its positions and fight *à la bataille conduite.* Arguing that their national interests were at stake, the British Chiefs of Staff Committee in accordance with what Gamelin advocated, was for an immediate Allied advance into Belgium if the Germans invaded the Netherlands, even if the Allies encountered Belgian resistance to their movement.[5] When asked directed, Pierlot and the Belgian government once again refused: the reason given was 'independence-neutrality' which received overwhelming approval in the Senate. Gamelin could hardly invade Belgium to get his own way. However, in support of Pierlot, Prime Minister Neville Chamberlain and his counterpart in Paris Paul Reynard gave a rather different response to not supporting Gamelin. Having witnessed now the debacle in Norway, both men agreed that if the Allies moved into Belgium, it would leave their armies too vulnerable to encirclement: on this point they were quite correct. Countering this, Gamelin pressed to move forces into Belgium before the German attacked to ensure defensive positions were established. An impasse was reached. A further meeting was scheduled for May: this never happened as the Germans invaded.[6] Undeniably the last chance for full Allied-Belgian cooperation and the orderly positioning of Anglo-French troops was discarded as the Wehrmacht massed divisions and squadrons on Germany's western frontier. It could be reasonably said that this refusal led to Dunkirk and the fall of France. Yet neither Chamberlain nor Reynaud cancelled the Breda Hypothesis or sought amendment despite vocal criticism!

Chamberlain and Reynaud were correct: if the Allied army moved into Belgium too late to form defensive positions, the war was lost: then why proceed with supporting Gamelin's plan? Why then was not a new plan of operations created? Why had Chamberlain remained quiet? Lots of questions, but no easy answers as they are not recorded in The National Archives at Kew or the Archives Nationales in Paris. Terrified of London being bombed, the British Cabinet was still pressing to defend as much of Belgium and Holland as possible.[7] Although Whitehall had critiqued Gamelin's concept of the Breda Hypothesis, Whitehall never questioned the need to occupy Belgium.[8] Conversely, according to Colonel Jacques Minart, who served on Gamelin's staff in 1939–40, Gamelin's impetus to move his forces into Belgium was his fear that the German occupation of Belgium and the Netherlands would knock the British out of the war or at least force them to withdraw from the Continent.[9] Indeed, Gamelin in October 1939 had urged General Ironside to increase the number of British divisions being sent to the Continent, emphasising the 'necessity of the common effort which we must undertake in regard to effective strengths so that we may not find ourselves this coming Spring in a dangerous state of inferiority in face of the German forces'.[10] The fear of losing British troops was probably behind Gamelin ignoring the concerns of his own subordinates. Earlier in the year Georges had brought up the uncomfortable notion that the Wehrmacht might not actually attack Belgium in force, but send a smaller force as a feint, with their main effort in the centre of the French defensive line. He complained that the new modifications to the Dyle Plan stripped away his reserve forces and placed them far to the north. Gamelin, however, rebuffed Georges' critique, arguing that it was out of the question to abandon the Netherlands and that it was necessary 'to make an effort to at least give a hand to the Dutch and try to have a land communication with them'.[11] It seems incredible therefore that no negotiations with Belgium were entered into. Gamelin was right to urge the French to in essence occupy Belgium.

As April turned to May 1940, in accordance with Gamelin's instructions, Billotte and the *1re Groupement des Armée* was responsible for the defence of France from the Channel coast to the west end of the Maginot Line. The *7e Armée* (*Général d'armée* Henri Giraud), the BEF under Gort, *1re Armée* (*Général d'armée* Georges Blanchard) and *9e Armée* (*Général d'armée* André Corap) were ready to advance to the Dyle Line by pivoting on the right (southern) Second Army. The *7e Armée* would take over west of Antwerp, ready to move into the Netherlands, and the Belgians were expected to delay a German advance at the Albert Canal and then retire to the Dyle, from Antwerp to Louvain. On the Belgian right, the BEF was to defend about 12 miles (20km) of the Dyle from Louvain to Wavre with nine divisions and the First Army on the right of the BEF was to hold 22 miles (35km) with ten divisions, from Wavre across the Gembloux Gap to Namur. The gap from the Dyle to Namur north of the Sambre, with Maastricht and Mons on either side, had few natural obstacles and was a traditional route of invasion, leading straight to Paris. Since October the BEF's 3rd Division under General Montgomery and the French had been occupied with building defences around Lille.[12] In the sector occupied by the French *1re Corps* and 3rd Division 'there existed a single anti-tank obstacle in the form of a ditch defended by casemates constructed to receive anti-tank guns and machine guns' but it was not completed. General Bertschi commanding the defensive sector of Lille ordered as a matter of urgency the completion of this work, and a defensive line further forward as a preliminary stop line. The work was to be completed by the 48e DI and the BEF.[13]

Gamelin appealed again to move troops into Belgium on 1 May, supported by the British Cabinet.[14] Whitehall kept to its well-trodden message: if the Wehrmacht were to invade the Netherlands, the French

Army and BEF were to move instantly into Belgium.[15] The goal was to ensure that the Allied army reached its staging posts in Belgium before the Wehrmacht. It also assumed the Wehrmacht would not attack the Netherlands and Belgium simultaneously. In essence, the plan was nothing more than deployment orders, it said nothing of what would happen when contact was made. Gamelin was primarily concerned most about the need to 'complete his deployment' before contact was made with German forces.[16] The fatal flaw in Gamelin's thinking was his desire for the Allies to achieve parity regarding overall numbers of divisions vis-à-vis the Wehrmacht. Gamelin anticipated his forces to defend Belgian and even Dutch territory until sufficient Allied offensive forces could be built up, forcing the Germans into a long war of attrition to offset their advantages in manpower and mobile warfare. Moreover, Gamelin believed that the Allies would not have a superiority in force at any time before 1941 and would take no decisive action without it. As we said earlier, France was still re-arming in spring 1940 and was not prepared to go to war. Gamelin hoped to buy time by holding a continuous front as we mentioned earlier.[17]

As we have said many times before, as the last minutes of peace ticked away, incredibly as May 1940 began, no formal agreement was then made with Belgium. The Allies seeking to protect Belgian neutrality and not to antagonise Hitler – the French army moving into Belgium could have been seen as a hostile move – all meant that a plan that relied on the Allied armies establishing defensive positions before the Wehrmacht attacked, and if this objective was not met, the Allied armies would be trapped, was not rescinded. The Allied politicians and Army chiefs all knew what was at stake, but with no plan B, pressed ahead in a huge gamble, that they hoped they would win. The French army was being asked to achieve the impossible: it would take a miracle for the Breda Hypothesis to succeed. Indeed, on the morning of 10 May, Gamelin told a subordinate 'Since the Belgians have appealed to us, can you see how we can do anything else?': there simply was no other plan.[18] The French and British ignored theory and logic and based their plan on wishful thinking as their only contingency, and with few exceptions everyone accepted it without question. More than just an example of group thinking, it was a plan that appeased each Allied nation's fears. The French could move the war out of French territory with the added prestige of protecting their neighbours. For the British, it meant that they could concentrate their land forces on the Continent as close to Britain as possible and use their naval and air assets in support without compromising national security.[19] When the Germans simply focused on the weakest part of Gamelin's long-planned Allied defensive line, there was no contingency plan to meet it and due to appalling communication, the Allies had no chance to reposition their best forces in time. Months of planning around a single option had led to a predictable plan, and for the Allies, a predictable result.

Chapter 7

10 MAY 1940

At 04:30 on 10 May, eleven German gliders landed eighty paratroopers on the Belgian fort of Eben-Emael, the most powerful fortress in Europe. The French staff congratulated themselves that their event planning had been correct. Yet those eighty paratroopers succeeded in neutralising the main defences of the fortress in 15 minutes. Over 1,200 Belgian soldiers were trapped and isolated in the fort.

Half an hour later the Wehrmacht crossed the border and invaded: three million men were soon going to face each other in a campaign that was to shape the next five years. German reinforcements arrived at Eben-Emael at 10:30. The Belgians launched several counter-attacks but after 36 hours of fighting, the Germans took the fort: the Allies had anticipated it would resist for five days. The first unpleasant surprise of this war for them. The assault on the fort of Eben-Emael and at other strategic locations by paratroopers across Belgium and the Netherlands gave the illusion that the main German attack was to be in this sector. As the German high command had anticipated, the Allied General Staff congratulated themselves that they had correctly predicted where the Wehrmacht would attack and confirmed their thinking that the Netherlands was to be the primary combat zone.[1]

At 04:00 the telephone rang in the headquarters of the *12e Division Infanterie Motorisée* (DIM). The adjutant recorded that the division was to be put on readiness. Fifteen minutes later the telephone buzzed for a second time: the 12e DIM was to be put on alert and be ready to mount its transport. At 06:00 the division was ordered to move out and occupy its positions as stated in the standing order from March under the Breda Hypothesis which gave the 12e DIM 12 hours to get to their allocated place on the continuous front. The men were to be issued five days' rations. It was already obvious the phoney war had turned to real combat: since dawn the Luftwaffe had started bombing railway stations, railway junctions and front-line landing grounds.[2] An officer with the *25e Bataillon des Chars de Combat* (BCC), part of *1re Division Cuirassier Reserve* (DCR) recounts:

> Friday, 10 May, we were woken at 04:00 by the passage overhead of large numbers of German aircraft; one squadron dropped its bombs on Pethonville: I alerted the battalion and made contact with our telephone to the Chief of Staff. For the rest of the day we were to make preparations to depart.[3]

Many French airfields were bombed, but most fighter squadrons came away unscathed. The most serious loss was at Cambrai-Hiergnies, when thirteen M.S. 406s were destroyed or so damaged as to take days to make airworthy: the losses were more than the immediately available reserves for *Groupe de Chasse* (GC) III/2.[4]

At 06:00 General Billotte informed General Têtu commanding the *Force aérienne de coopération du front nord-est* that the principal objectives were:

> As a matter of urgency identify and attack enemy columns.
> Attack enemy landing grounds.
> Operate with the Army in bombing strongpoints and areas of resistance.[5]

Under intense air attack, the French air force was grounded. Late in the day *9e* and *10e Groupement* equipped with Amiot 143s took off at dusk to bomb targets at Gladbach, Bonn-Hangeliach, Witlich and at Aix la Chappelle. The RAF also bombed three German landing grounds.[6] A far from auspicious start: the Luftwaffe had local air superiority. The bomber force had, in theory, been supposed to strike as soon as a German offensive had clearly begun: bombers were to fly to pre-determined targets, which gave time for reconnaissance units to locate targets close to the front line. Air Marshal Barratt commanding Allied Advance Strike Force (AASF) was to target bombers on the Luxembourg border, whilst the French and the RAF were to attack targets of opportunity in Belgium. Both commanders were extremely reluctant to carry out their orders. Barratt and d'Astier feared heavy losses; in the latter's case he only had two Leo 45 *groupement* and was reluctant to commit them too early in the battle.[7] Despite this, forty-four sorties were flown by the *Groupe de Chasse* and two German aircraft shot down. The new Curtiss H75 of GC I/5 claimed nine bombers over their base. However, the old Moranes flown by GC III/3 were so underpowered that they could not catch the even the slow-flying Heinkels or Dorniers.[8] The French lost around fifty fighters than day.[9] The Wehrmacht surged forward, almost totally unopposed, protected by hundreds of Bf 109s and Bf 110s, the attack heralded by Stuka dive bombers.

The *1re Armée* was assigned a 150km move to Gembloux. General René Prioux's *Corps de Cavalerie* was France's only completely mechanised corps. 2e DLM (8th reconnaissance and 13th and 29th combat regiments) and 3e DLM (12th reconnaissance and 1st and 2nd combat regiments) were deployed between Cambrai and Hirson on 10 May. The 1re DLM was detached from the corps, assigned to Giraud's *7e Armée* in the move to assist Holland. At 05:30 the *Corps de Cavalerie* were at St Quentin, and received the order to move at 07:00. The corps was to advance in four columns:

1. Cambrai to Wavre via Mons
2. Le Cateau to Noirmont via Cortil
3. Landrecies to Gembloux via Charleroi
4. Le Nuvion to Namur by Avesnes and Beaumont.

The 3e DLM were to follow routes 1 and 2, the other two itineraries were reserved for the units with Hotchkiss H-39 tanks. The 2e DLM reinforced by the *2e Bataillon de mitrailleurs motorisés* (BMM). The advance into Belgium stopped when the columns came under German air attack. Prioux's adjutant noted that when the tanks rolled into Belgium, they were cheered on the streets, with civilian's climbing up the side of the tanks to give the crews cigarettes and fruit.[10]

In the Gembloux Gap, the 12e DIM, once it had called in its detached units, was ready to move off at 21:00. The hope was that, under the cover of darkness, the columns would not be easy targets for the Luftwaffe, and instead had to be in position by 11:00 at Namur on 11 May.[11] The head of column only arrived at Maubeuge at 07:00, 90km away from its destination the following day.[12]

Elsewhere that morning the *etat major* (staff) of the *9e Division d'Infanterie* (DI) received orders to advance. The *13e Regiment d'Infanterie* was to form the advance guard. The order, timed at 09:00. ordered the division to occupy its positions as outlined in the General Order of 11 April, to occupy positions at Wortel-Turnhout-Herenthal no later than 20:00.[13] The French air force was ordered to cover the division's move from the coast at Boulogne and Saint Omer. General Didelet commanding the division issued orders to colonels to reassure their men they would be safe from air attack.[14]

The division only arrived at its stated position 24 hours later. Why? The Luftwaffe continually strafed and bombed the column of trucks which lasted all day, destroying vehicles, killing and wounding men.[15]

At 16:00 a halt order was issued: orders were issued to camouflage the trucks and men, to disperse vehicles at night, and if possible, hide them under tree and shrub cover. Once it was dark, the column was to head off, and stop at first light, around 04:00.[16] The division reached Anvers by the morning of the 11th and linked with the 25e DLM, part of *7e Armée*.[17] The division was to reach Villebroek by midday on the 11th.[18]

Gamelin's neat timetable essential for the doctrine of *bataille conduite* had not lasted 24 hours. Had no one anticipated the Luftwaffe attacking the huge columns of men heading into Belgium and Netherlands? Well yes they had. The Allies were to advance under the cover of fighters. The problem was, the Allies lacked the resolve to contest the sky. The Luftwaffe deployed almost 100 per cent of available aircraft; the Allies, terrified of losses, committed 60 per cent or less of their air assets. The result was all too predictable. The French *Groupement de Bombardement* did not take to the air till the evening: just twenty-nine serviceable aircraft were available, and only twelve took off to bomb German airfields, and had almost no impact whatsoever.[19] The timidity by the RAF and French bomber force as well as reconnaissance squadrons gave the Luftwaffe and Wehrmacht *carte blanche*. This is perhaps not surprising. At local level, the Luftwaffe achieved air superiority: just 637 French fighters were put up in the immediate combat zone against 923 Bf 109s.[20] Little wonder the Stukas and other German bombers had been able to penetrate so deeply into French lines and bomb Saint Omer! The lack of 'eyes and ears' over the German army as it advanced meant that no one at French GQG had any real idea what was happening. The initiative was 'handed on a plate' to Manstein and his colleagues.

Chapter 8

11 MAY 1940

In Belgium, after the paratroopers, it was the turn of the German armoured and infantry divisions to advance. These forces began to cross the Albert Canal, a long man-made waterway that ran from Liège to Antwerp and which the Belgians had hoped to use as a bulwark against the offensive. To counter the threat, the Allied General Staff sent its best French and British troops to the aid of the Belgians and Dutch. The *9e Division d'Infanterie* was ordered to the Albert Canal at 08:00 and if that was not possible, the division was to take up positions at Bergen op Zoom, in association with the 1 DIM.[1]

The main effort for the French fighter force was to support Giraud's *7e Armée* as it moved into Belgium: Giraud could count both on French aircraft as well as Blenheims from the RAF, and also Hurricanes. All in all, Giraud had 200 fighters and 100 bombers.[2] It was only in mid-afternoon, following a fairly devastating air attack, that the GC I/4 flying Curtiss H75s was sent up. At 16:50 twenty-six Curtiss H75s began a patrol over Giraud's sector. He had earlier detrained his tanks from the 1re DIM south of Antwerp out of fear of air attack. The French fighters claimed five victories, but two were shot down, and three damaged. On landing just six serviceable aircraft were available for the following day. An entire fighter group was out of action for 48 hours. It was portent of things to come.[3] Giraud dithered: this would not be the first time in the campaign that French senior officers could not take the initiative. As Karl-Heinz Frieser states, there was no operational 'intellectual infrastructure', since there was no training in this regard, of improvising a new plan.[4] Lacking his tanks, Giraud believed he could not dislodge the Germans holding the Moerdijk bridges: because Giraud was unable to 'think on his feet' to 'adopt, adapt, improvise' operational planning to suit real world events, at no stage did he consider using his field artillery offensively as anti-tank guns. The Germans exploited Giraud's lack of armour and initiative. A bolder use of available ground and air forces could have transformed the situation.[5]

General Blanchard, the commander of the *1re Armée*, had command of this 35km-wide sector known as the Gembloux Gap. Already by day two of the campaign, the meticulous blueprint to establish a continuous front and thereby hold the Wehrmacht back for 12 to 18 months in a war of attrition similar to 14/18 had 'gone wrong'. None of his units had made their allotted positions under the Breda Hypothesis and by the morning of 11 May no continuous front had been formed and the Wehrmacht was racing forward to break through.

The 12e DIM was at Charleroi by 08:00. At 09:30, Colonel Guedeney, *Chef de la Etat Major*, received orders that the 12e DIM was to hold its position and begin its move to Namur at 17:00, the developing situation meant that the movement had to take place in daylight despite the threat of interdiction. The *1re Division Militaire* (DM) was at Gembloux and traversed the battlefield of Quatre-Bras around 19:00.[6] The 12e DIM was to block the Gembloux Gap. The French *1re Armée* was moving as fast as it could to establish a front line between the Dyle and Meuse, east of Gembloux. General Prioux on the evening of 10 May had learned that the Wehrmacht was already at the Albert Canal and were pushing east to the Meuse at d'Huy. Realising he would not make the Albert Canal, he planned to take up positions between Tirlemont and Huy. At 08:00, Colonel Leyer of the *12e Cuirassiers*, serving in the 3e DLM, reported that the bridges over the Albert Canal were in German hands and thousands of troops were crossing the river and were moving along the Maastricht-Tongres and Maastricht-Hasselt roads. Blanchard told Prioux at 09:35, that if possible, the Tirlemont-Huy line was to be was achieved during the night with the BMM being sent forward immediately.[7] History confirms Colonel Leyer's report: late on the previous day, two Panzer divisions had crossed the river Mass on pontoon bridges and were racing to capture the Veldwezet and Vroenhoeven bridges over the Albert Canal. The bridges should have been destroyed when the Belgian and French troops fell back, but they were not because they were being used by refugees to escape. The bridges were occupied by 07:30 on the morning of the 11th. News of the bridges' survival only reached d'Astier during the course of the morning: it was precisely for targets like these bridges that the hierarchy of the French air force had been demanding manoeuvrable low-level bombers and dive bombers. The Leo 45 was 'a non-starter' for this type of operation, and the Breguet 693 carried an insufficient bomb load. Yet d'Astier sent up twelve Leo 45s supported by eighteen M.S.

406s at midday. Attacking from 800m to ensure the highest degree of accuracy possible, all bar one Leo 45 was damaged by flak. The bridges remained standing, over which poured the Wehrmacht.[8] Nothing stood between the Panzer divisions and Blanchard's disorganised *1re Armée*. In haste, Blanchard told Prioux at 14:00 that the Albert Canal had been crossed at Tongres, but the Panzers had been dispersed by an air attack by the Belgian air force. Worse, Blanchard told Prioux that Eben Emael had been captured and Liège was threatened. The flood of refugees had stopped all French offensive movement.[9]

Aware of the major threat posed by the captured bridges, General Georges sometime before midday ordered 'a massive intervention by our bomber force on the crossing points and of enemy columns (of primary urgency in the region south-west of Maastricht)'.[10] At 15:00 Georges signalled Blanchard that as it was impossible to comply with the Breda Hypothesis, instead the Escaut was to be to be defensive line and not the Dyle. Blanchard ordered Prioux to fall back to Hannut.[11]

To try and slow the advanced Wehrmacht, reluctantly at 18:00 Têtu sent up the 6e *Groupement de Bombardement,* a force of twelve Leo 45s supported by fighters. Three troop concentrations were attacked near Maastricht: a German convoy of lorry-mounted infantry was bombed and strafed heading towards Tongres.[12] The RAF attacked two German columns, one at Maastricht, the other at Vesel. Bombing raids were also sent to Rotterdam, where German infantry was surprised and shot up. The Blenheims damaged twenty-seven twin-engine Luftwaffe bombers at the landing ground at Walhaven. Seven of the Luftwaffe aircraft were observed to be in flames as the Blenheims left.[13] The French air force in the interwar period had sought autonomy from the army and rejected the concept of close air support in favour of air superiority and strategic bombing. This meant when war did come senior air force officers tended to be reluctant to provide close air support.[14] Worse, the command structure was cumbersome and unable to respond quickly to interdict the Luftwaffe. It meant that French air force was unable – nor did it ever try – to win air superiority, but rather endeavoured to contest it. According to John Buckley, the French air force's reactive stance and its notion of parcelling air units out in small quantities to provide localised air cover across the front was untenable in the face of the Luftwaffe's concentrated approach.[15] As the French fighter force was dispersed between different *Groupement des Armée*, the French air force was never able to mount large multi-squadron operations, and moreover, was unable to support units on the ground to efficiently repel the Wehrmacht.

Georges was also aware of the Wehrmacht's thrust against the Ardennes. Knowing he had to give the *1re Armée* as much as help from the air as possible to establish itself in the Gembloux Gap, he ordered more bombing raids with fighter escort against Maastricht. The Ardennes sector had to wait: all available bombers and fighters were in the northern sector. The *1re Armée* had to establish itself and the front stabilised before aerial support could move to the Ardennes. A lack of fighters, a lack of modern bombers and interdiction by the Luftwaffe had between them prevented the execution of the Breda Hypothesis, meaning when more men, more tanks, and more aircraft were needed over the Ardennes, none were available. Georges had to try and stop the Wehrmacht in Belgium before he could send reserves to the Ardennes. Gamelin had been right to worry about German troop superiority. Arguably the battle was now lost. In Paris, Gamelin was coming to that conclusion. He admitted that France lost because of a lack of modern combat aircraft, and a lack of tanks: he was absolutely right. Flak and the German fighters, notably the Bf 109s, meant the Germans controlled the skies.[16] It wasn't that France lacked aircraft, it was a lack of preparedness in rear areas to support the war. The French air force was in the process of rearming when the Wehrmacht rolled into Belgium. Many squadrons had no aircraft, and no stocks of spares had been accumulated. New aircraft were in factories, but not yet operational due to a lack of personnel to get the machines to the front. The major problem facing the French was the intensity of air operations: 387 fighters flew 400 sorties on the 11th; due lack of spares and battle damage, 345 fighters were available for the following day. Thirty-six fighters were lost on 11–12 May, leaving 314 aircraft and no reserves being sent.[17] The French air force, in keeping aircraft back for the defence of Paris and other centres, robbed any hope of meeting the Luftwaffe aggressively, and having enough aircraft to cover Gembloux and the Ardennes. The Ardennes 'had to fend for itself' until the *1re Armée* was in position to hold off the Wehrmacht in the Gembloux Gap as long as possible.[18] The *51e Division d'Infanterie Francaise* (DI), part of the *3e Groupement des Armée* stationed close to the border with Luxembourg, had been ordered at 07:30 the previous day to enter Belgium. Heavy attacks by the Luftwaffe slowed the division's move. The 51e DIF was brigaded with the *70e Groupe de Reconnaissance de Division d'infanterie* (GRDI), the goal was to advance quickly, gather intelligence and hold a position until reinforcements arrived. The diary of the *248e Régiment d'Artillerie Divisionnaire* (RAD) attached to the 51e tells us the Luftwaffe kept up interdiction throughout the morning, and the Wehrmacht by the early afternoon had made contact with the leading elements from the 51e DI.[19]

At 20:00 General Billotte arrived in person at General Prioux's headquarters to order him to advance once more towards Gembloux. Prioux and Blanchard were ordered to be in Gembloux by day 5 rather than day 8 as outlined under the Breda Hypothesis timetable.[20] The speed of the German advance had caught the French by surprise: an error compounded by the failure to demolish bridges. The Wehrmacht could move where it wanted under air cover and force encounter battles on the French defenders. Because of the extended line of communications of the Breda Hypothesis, by the end of the day, the *1re Armée* was still not yet in position.

Chapter 9

12 MAY 1940

Despite being on 'the back foot', the Allies continued to engage in Belgium. Late the previous day, eighteen Bréguet 693 aircraft from the I and II/54 Groups had bombed the roads out of Tongres, losing nine machines, brought down by flak. The goal was to cut roads and prevent the advance of the Panzer divisions.[1]

During the night, the Belgian army had fallen back from Huys: nothing stood in the way of Wehrmacht. Some of the retreating Belgian armour linked up with Prioux around Tirlemont. With the front collapsing, Blanchard ordered Prioux to form a stop line at the villages of d'Hannut-Crehen-Thisnes-Merdrop-Jandrain.[2]

Heading to the line of the Albert Canal was the 4th Division of the BEF. The liaison and intelligence officer François Madert tells us the scouts of the division arrived at Merechtem on the Belgian border at midday on 11 May: during the course of the following day, the Luftwaffe forced the leading elements of the BEF to disperse. During 12 May, the Luftwaffe attacked Alost and Termonde, cutting lines of communication and destroying the Allied columns heading to Courtrai.[3]

The 12e DIM had taken up defensive positions on the evening of 11 May behind Namur. It linked with the *1re* and *2e Divisions Chasseurs Ardennais* from the Belgian army, as well as a corps of cavalry that had arrived at Tirlemont- Huy with elements of the 1re DCR. The division's diary tells is that throughout the day the Luftwaffe had kept up its attacks, but caused no losses, largely thanks to fighters from the RAF pushing back the swarms of Stukas. At break of day, the 12e DIM sent out its light troops and motor-cycle units to scout Namur: interdiction by the Luftwaffe. Coming under fire from German troops, the 12e DIM was forced back from Namur, and in conjunction with the 15e DIM to the north and south-east *5e Division d'Infanterie Nord-Africaine*

(DINA). A hasty defensive line was established along the railway line at Bonesse.[4]

With the *1re Armée* unlikely ever to get to the Dyle, and with almost nothing standing between the Wehrmacht and Prioux's armour, Georges' primary concern was to shore up the Gembloux Gap. Rightly or wrongly, the Ardennes had to wait. A serious situation was developing in the French centre, and at 08:00 Georges ordered the French bomber force to attack targets once more around Maastricht. The first wave was in the air by 09:30.

The air strike was rather 'too little, too late' as at 07:30 the 4th Panzer Division took the town of Hannut, which had been evacuated by the French. Around 09:00 the Panzers encountered the *2e Cuirassiers* at Tongres, south-east of Liège. The Germans then pushed towards Crehen, where they encountered French tanks in what was to be the first tank-on-tank action of the campaign. Supported by dive-bombers, German tanks attacked, clashing at Crehen with the *3e escadron* of the *2e Cuirassiers*. General Prioux's after-action report notes:

> After 09:00 intense aerial bombardment was accompanied by a brutal tank actions in the region of Crehen. Attacked in front by heavy tank, and harried by light tanks, the squadron of the *2e Regiment Dragon Portés* [RDP] and the Hotchkiss tanks from the *2e Cuirassiers*, who held Crehen, had to sacrifice themselves in the place to prevent the Germans from entering. The artillery fire, that of the neighbouring strongpoint (Thisnes) and of a light element of the 2e DLM at Dieu le Garde block the overflow of Crehen, causing heavy losses to the enemy. Evacuated by its last defenders, the village will remain unoccupied all day.

Following three hours of intense fighting, the *2e Cuirassiers* lost eleven of its twenty tanks. The *Cuirassiers* and Dragoons fell back to Jandrain-Jandrenouille and Merdorp.[5] *Dragon Portés* comprised a regimental headquarters, and two battalions each with a motorcycle squadron, two squadrons transported in lorries, and a machine-gun squadron with machine-gun carriers. They were the equivalent of Motorised Infantry in the German army. Created in September 1939 four regiments of *Dragons Portés* were organised in to two *brigades de dragons portés de réserve générale* or *brigades DP de RG* and attached to the 1re and 2e DLM.[6]

To try and help Prioux, Blanchard requested more air support from Têtu sometime after noon. Approaching 13:00, eighteen Breguet 693s of *18e Groupement* were in the air, again bombing targets at Tongres, Loos, and Waremme. Heavy flak was encountered: eight aircraft failed to return. Demands for air support came in thick and fast: at 15:00 Georges, at the request of Air Marshal Barratt, was to bomb German columns at Hasselt that were attacking the BEF. At the same time, General Huntzinger, commanding the *2e Armée*, demanded targets at Bertrix and Bastogne be attacked.[7]

Despite having been blooded, the 4th Panzer Division was still a major threat. Attacking again at Crehen and at Tirlemont, the thrust was repulsed, but the sector was still vulnerable.[8] General Prioux demanded air support at Tongres. At 18:30 twelve Leo 45s of *6e Groupement* took to the air and bombed a column south of Loos with 100kg bombs. British bombers flew sixty sorties that day on the Maastricht-Tongres road. Losses for the RAF were heavy: six Blenheims from a flight of nine were shot down by flak over Maastricht: in total twenty-nine Blenheims and Battles were lost that day, principally as they had no fighter escort. In two days, 150 sorties had been flown against targets around Maastricht, none of the key bridges were destroyed. Heavy Allied losses did at least down the relentless advance of the Panzers.[9] Insufficient resources meant that the German advance was not dispersed and undaunted by the bombers. At 20:00 the 4th Panzer Division rolled forward again as an officer serving under Prioux reports:

> Taking advantage of the fall of the day, the Germans launched a very violent tank attack, this time on Thisnes, preceded and accompanied by a particularly intense air action. Thisnes was taken, but our artillery's carefully prepared fire and the flank action of a SOMUA platoon slowed this attack, causing the enemy further significant losses in armoured vehicles. A platoon of SOMUA (Second Lieutenant Lositsky, of the 2nd *Cuirassiers*) carried out a huge raid into the German lines, surprising and destroying many enemy tanks. On the other hand, many Hotchkiss tanks defending the village were destroyed. The artillery . . . continued its action during the night, carrying out harassing fire . . . The Cavalry Corps did not cease, during this day, to request aviation actions (fighters and bombing). Some fighter actions took place which generally arrived too late.[10]

Despite the bravery of the two platoons of French Somua S-35 and Hotchkiss H-39 tanks, Thisnes was taken by the Germans in the evening. The Belgians abandoned Trilemont-Huy under pressure from the Wehrmacht: Maastricht was threatened and the forts at Liège were under sustained attack by 19:00.[11]

Chapter 10

13 MAY 1940

In Belgium, Giraud was ordered by Billotte to pull his forces south out of the Netherlands: the 13th and 9th Panzer Divisions rushed over the Moerdijk bridges to the outskirts of Rotterdam soon after midday.[1] Meantime the *9e Division d'Infanterie* was ordered to defend the Albert Canal in Belgium, with orders if overwhelmed to fall back to the Villebroeck canal during the 14th.[2] François Medert, embedded with the BEF, wrote that he was ordered to Vilvoorde, Louvain, Tirlemont and Liège to gather information as communications were severed. Arriving at Vilvoorde on the 13th, he

> encountered a large body of Belgian soldiers, retreating in great disorder, many having abandoned their weapons leaving the front . . . later that morning I went to our position at Liège, but was prevented in doing so because of an attack by motorised enemy formations considerably supported by an intense aerial bombardment. I passed through Tirlemont which was on fire, and Louvain was partly destroyed. The defensive line of the Albert Canal had been crossed by the enemy in several places, where we were therefore obliged to fall back to our second defensive position on the canal at Vilvoorde. In liaison with the 2e Corps of the BEF and our French troops on the left wing of our division, a line of resistance was made between Anvers and Namur.[3]

To the south, in the Gembloux Gap, things went from bad to worse. The Allied lines were crumbling. Around 07:00 the 2e DLM deployed about thirty Somua tanks to try and retake Thisnes. As the armour advanced, the French tanks were caught under fire from 88mm flak guns lying in ambush near Crehen. The French tanks suffered losses and were stopped. By midday, the 35th, 61st and 269th Infantry Divisions of the Wehrmacht virtually destroyed the 2e DLM south of the Mehaigne, leaving General Hoepner free to concentrate his two armoured divisions against the 3e DLM, west of Hannut. For the 12e DIM supported by *1re* and *2e Division de Chasseurs Ardennais* against elements of the Wehrmacht at Villiers Perwez. The Gembloux Gap was holding, but for how much longer.[4]

For René Prioux, the day had started calmly enough:

> After the hard engagement of the previous evening, there was a certain lull on both sides as day broke but, as this lull continued, the General Commandant of *Corps de Cavalerie* considered at 10am holding out until nightfall in the current positions, reserving the right to withdraw during the night of the 13th to the 14th to the anti-tank obstacle of Cointet, installed by the Belgians . . . However, around 11am, after the position had been flown over by German artillery observation planes, the battle rekindled across the entire front of the *Corps de Cavalerie* (from Tirlemont to Huy inclusive, i.e. more than 40km).[5]

Around 11:00, after an aerial bombardment of the French positions by Stukas, the two German armoured divisions went on the attack. The 3rd Panzer Division of General Stumpf rushed towards Orp-le-Grand and Marilles, whilst the 4th Panzer Division advanced south of Hannut in the direction of Merdorp and Branchon. Fighting took place at Marilles, Orp-le-Petit and Jandrain, during which the French tanks were overwhelmed by the attackers, but not without offering fierce resistance.[6] One of Prioux's officers recalls:

> a powerful attack first emerged, in the direction of Goussoncourt and threatens the rear of the S/S Northern Sector facing the 3e DLM. Soon, the S/S Southern Sector was attacked by heavy tanks. Intense fighting took place around Merdrop, Jandrain and Jauche. Finally, in the centre of the Division, at noon, a very strong column of tanks (estimated at about 200) threatened Maret-Marilles. The Artillery and the SOMUA tanks of the 3e DLM caused heavy losses to the adversary, but the latter possessed an indisputable numerical superiority.
>
> Faced with this general attack, and at the request of the divisions, the commander of the *Corps de Cavalerie* puts at their disposal groups of tanks, which constituted the reserve. The group of squadrons of the *2e* DLM engaged towards the south where German heavy tanks attack the strongpoint.
>
> At 13:45, orders are given by the general commanding the *Corps de Cavalerie* to draw back the tanks.
>
> At 15:30 the General Commanding the 3e DLM reported that, in view of the enemy pressure having become too strong, it is urgent to consider the withdrawal of his Division.

> The order for immediate withdrawal was given and passed simultaneously to the 2e DLM by liaison officers.
>
> The 4e GRDI (Colonel Arlabosse) was ordered to participate in covering this withdrawal by establishing itself in the Grand Rosiere – Mont St Andre region.
>
> The 3e DLM executed its withdrawal upon receipt of the order. The 2e DLM, less pressured than earlier in the day, did not begin its movement until after 17:00, trying to cover the right of the 3e DLM, which was particularly threatened.
>
> For this reason, at 21:00 the elements of the 3e DLM established themselves behind the obstacle of Cointent, the 2e DLM, could not be established behind the anti-tank line until the morning of the 14th.
>
> Moreover, the Machine Gun Battalions (54e and 56e BMM) and a battalion of the 1re RDP, under the orders of General Lacroix, commanding the 4e DLM offered the enemy fierce resistance at HUY and the surrounding area, from where, surrounded, they would only escape under cover of night and on foot.[7]

Unable to oppose the better-armoured French tanks, the German light tanks broke off the attack and moved rapidly to Branchon. It was to be a hollow victory: 88mm guns were brought up, opening fire. The slow-moving French armour, unable to reply, became easy targets and were forced to retreat to Jandrenouille, despite the bravery of the tank crews. Eight tanks from a squadron of twelve were destroyed one after another as if on a shooting range, one German officer noted.[8] One French officer recalled 'throughout the day we had requested as strongly as possible for support by the Allied air force: all was in vain'. Bloodied but not defeated, the French tanks then carried out a counter-attack in the direction of Jandrain from the village of Jauche. When the tanks arrived on the outskirts of the village, they came under artillery fire and, outnumbered by the Wehrmacht, the French were forced to retreat to Jauche.[9] That day, 53 French tanks were knocked out, 400 prisoners taken and four anti-tank guns captured along with five operational tanks.[10]

In two days' fighting, French had lost 105 tanks, the Wehrmacht 195: yet for the French, the tanks could not be recovered or easily replaced. Making matters worse, the outcome was as exactly as Hitler had anticipated: the best Allied troops stopped two German armoured divisions in the centre of Belgium, while in the Ardennes, seven armoured divisions prepared to cross the Meuse near Sedan with almost nothing to stop them.

For Corap, Rommel's 7th Panzer Division was rolling towards him. By midday, Rommel had created a bridgehead 3km deep. Corap ordered units either side of the gap to attack. Facing almost constant air attacks broke up the planned counter-attack and made it almost impossible for Corap to move his reserves up. At 16:45 having received no air support, ordered d'Astier to order the GC II/2 into the air. All eleven fighters were scrambled, joining those already in the air accompanying a reconnaissance mission. The M.S. 406s were not match for the Bf 109, but they could take on the Dornier bombers: two German bombers were damaged but not shot down, while three French fighters were claimed by escorting Bf 110s. A total of eighteen French fighters could make little or no impression on the massed Luftwaffe formations bombing *9e Armée*. At 16:20 Billotte, on learning of Prioux's withdrawal, informed d'Astier that as artillery was controlling the Sedan situation effectively – he believed – it was imperative that air support was given to him if the Panzers were to be stopped. Twenty-seven Bloch MB152s from GC I/1 and GC I/8 gave direct support for six LeO 45s to attack the pontoon bridges at Dinant and the troops massed waiting to cross during the early evening.[11] The attacks had almost no effect: the bridges were not damaged. By the end of the day the Wehrmacht had thrown more pontoon bridges over the Meuse.

The Allies still believed that any major action was to be in Belgium and that German troop concentrations in the Ardennes were a feint to lure troops from the centre of operations. They played into the German trap, and once sprung it was almost impossible to escape: even the best trained and equipped army in the world cannot compensate for strategic errors. The Allies were sucked inextricably into complying with German operational planning, and thus the outcome that the Germans had predicted. As in 1914, Germany in 1940 could not economically support a long-drawn-out war of static lines: desperation to prevent such a scenario meant men like Rommell were prepared to take risks to break out. Nor does it mean that the French were 'cheese eating surrender monkeys'. With the best will in the world, once the Allies had fallen into the German trap, there was no going back.[12] The bulk of the French air force was deployed over Belgium, some 200 sorties being flown in the sector, primarily escort missions. No real effort was made to stem the flood tide at Sedan. Despite the arrival of Dewoitine D.520 fighters, none were called for. The French commanders on the ground at Sedan relied heavily on the RAF as agreed months earlier: where was the RAF? Yet we also admit, the lack of aircraft meant any operation was doomed to be shot down. Better to try than do nothing?

Chapter 11

14 MAY 1940

Near Gembloux, before sun-up, General Prioux with the *Corps de Cavalerie* as well as the *1re Armée* was ordered to hold the Cointent anti-tank line as long as possible. At break of day:

> the *Corps de Cavalerie* was installed behind this obstacle (3e DLM to the north, 2e DLM to the south, linked together by the 4th GRDI responsible for holding Thorembais). To the north, the flank was completely in the air, the British having retreated in one movement behind the Dyle. To the south, the connection with the Meuse (5e CA) was made by disparate elements. Finally, the artillery, deployed, had not had time to adjust its fire, nor to establish effective communications.
>
> Before daybreak, the enemy infantry, having crossed the obstacle of Cointet, had infiltrated Perwez, following the departure of a Belgian regiment which occupied it. From 07:30 a serious threat push to the north of the 3e DLM and forced the withdrawal of part of its tanks, while in the centre, around 09:00, after a heavy bombardment by aircraft and artillery, the enemy tanks crossed the obstacle of Cointet and began to debouche. Contained initially by the 5e DLM towards Orbais, the Germans took Thorembais St Trond from the 4e GRDI, then accentuating their effort in the direction of Gembloux and emerging at 12:00 at d'Ernage. This attack was stopped by the *1re Division Marocain* and by an energetic action of the 5e BLM. The *2e* DLM, which had only a short time to establish itself was also attacked from the direction of Grand Leez; . . . at 13:00 the *Corps de Cavalerie* only has two bridgeheads remaining in front of their HQ (Corbais for the 3e DLM and St Denis Emines for the 2e DLM). General Prioux judging that these bridgeheads hindered the action of the Infantry Divisions and artillery signed at 14:00 the order to withdraw to the two DLM. At 16:30, he moved his HQ to Saint-Symphorien.[1]

South of Prioux's positions, at 15:00 Panzer I and IIs attacked the *150e Regiment d'Infanterie* at Rhisnes. The goal for the German commander was to break through between the 12e DIM and 5e DINA. The rapid deployment of 25mm anti-tank guns stopped the Panzers. With the German breakout across the Meuse threatening to fatally break the French front, the *6e Régiment de Tirailleurs Marocains* (RTM) was sent to Sedan to counter-attack during the morning of the 15th.[2] Rather than shoring up the Ardennes, it weakened the French centre at the very moment it needed to be held. That evening both Georges and Billotte made plans for the following day. In Belgium were 300 fighters available for service. With Gembloux on the point of collapse, defence of the rear area, and Paris, was uppermost in French minds following the extensive bombing of Rotterdam, foreshadowing the London Blitz. It was also important that the rear area was covered for an equally important reason. Gamelin was preparing Plan B, and he needed the skies around Paris clear of the Luftwaffe if his plan was to develop as he intended. D'Astier was instructed to give maximum fighter cover and bomber use at Sedan. Corap, realising his forces were close to collapse, ordered a retreat. His men were to fall back to the positions they had done on the morning of 10 May.[3] Prioux was ordered to move his tanks behind the Charleroi Canal and regroup. That night orders were passed for engineers to destroy the bridges over the Sambre at Chatelet and at Maubeuge.[4]

The last tanks belonging to the 1re DCR rolled into Charleroi during the early morning. After struggling to camouflage the tanks, the men were ordered to eat and rest. At 18:40 the tanks were ready to move out, and headed towards Flavion at 19:40.[5]

To the north of Prioux, at Louvain, a liaison officer with the BEF and Belgian army reported refugees and Belgian soldiers were fleeing from the Albert Canal, coming under attack from the Luftwaffe: indeed, our officers HQ at the chateau d'Everberg was bombed, but with one He 111 being shot down in flames by French anti-aircraft crews. During the night of the 14/15th the Luftwaffe stepped up its bombardment of Louvain and the canal zone.[6] The French left wing in Belgium was holding its own, whereas in the centre at Sedan and Gembloux, the situation was critical. A gap had appeared between the BEF and the *1re Armée*, which the Germans sought to ruthlessly exploit.

As we noted above, in Paris, Gamelin, realising the battle was being lost in Belgium, began drawing up a hasty 'Plan B'. He hoped to stop the Wehrmacht on the line of the river Somme. Four days into the battle, Gamelin sought to correct his error of embedding his reserves in the front line:

> We must quickly regroup all that remains of our available forces in order to deploy in the centre of our defensive front, a strategic reserve in preparation for another great tank battle.[7]

Gamelin was correct.

Chapter 12

15 MAY 1940

At 02:00 on 15 May 1940, Paul Reynaud was woken up by the telephone. On the line was the prefect of Charleville-Mézières, who was completely panic-stricken. 'The German tanks are in the streets. The front is broken, nothing stands in the way of the advance of their tanks.'[1] Not technically true: no breakout had occurred yet at Sedan, and the Gembloux Gap still held – just.[2]

At 08:30 on 15 May Reynaud called Churchill:

> Whose confidence appeared to have been considerably shaken, and who said that the battle was lost, and the road to Paris open. He pointed to the small number of British troops in France, and begged for assistance.[3]

Churchill replied 'Come, it is impossible that this could have happened so quickly!' Churchill hoped that the initiative could be regained by a counter-attack by the French reserve. Churchill flew to Paris to reassure the French government.[4] The Dutch signed an armistice with the Germans at 10:50.

Although panic had taken hold of the French General Staff, the soldiers fought valiantly on the ground. At 08:00 General Georges ordered Generals Têtu and d'Astier to bomb the region of Mezieres in support of General Toucehonn; at 10:00 General André Corap with the *9e Armée* and Huntizger with the *2e Armée* both demanded air support at Sedan. Yet, because of German air superiority at midday, General Têtu informed Georges it was impossible for any operations to occur. By this stage, 50 per cent of the French fighter force had been lost.[5]

During the course of the day, Air Vice Marshal Playfair was ordered to fly as many sorties as possible against the German bridges at Sedan. Between 06:30 and 18:20 nine operations were sent up from the RAF and two more by the French. RAF Blenheims along with the Fairey

Battle – 'the flying coffin' -conducted 123 trips with Hurricanes defending the bombers. By early afternoon, Bf 109s and anti-aircraft units had moved up to defend the bridges; making matters worse the fighter escorts had been withdrawn to attack Ju 87s which were bombing the French positions. The RAF claimed six Ju 87s shot down. Without support, the Battles and Blenheims were massacred: thirty Battles, ten Blenheims, and four Lysanders went down in flames. The fighter units were also badly hit: twenty-seven Hurricanes were shot down and fifteen pilots killed. For the Luftwaffe forty-six aircraft were lost, of which just eight were the feared Bf 109.[6]

At La Horgne, near Sedan, the village was defended by Algerian Spahis: these cavalry soldiers came straight from the nineteenth century. At 08:30, the German assault began. Faced with unexpectedly strong French resistance, the Germans brought in armoured vehicles. Despite overwhelming odds, the French anti-tank gunners destroyed sixteen German tanks. The situation was desperate for the French, but they refused all requests for surrender. After seven hours of bitter fighting, all the French had left to hand to hold back the German offensive was the cavalry. At 15:00 a squadron of Spahis charged the German tanks. The squadron was annihilated. Sabres and carbines were no match for tanks. This may have been the last recorded cavalry charge in history. The survivors fought in the village until 17:00. In 12 hours of fighting, 610 French and Algerian soldiers were killed or wounded. On the German side, a thousand men were killed or wounded and about twenty tanks destroyed.

Not far from Sedan is the village of Stonne. It was crucial the village was held: if it fell the Germans would be able to open the road to Reims and Paris. Stonne had to be held regardless of cost. The German army's elite regiment, the Großdeutschland, and 300 Panzers tried to capture the village, which was defended by 160 French tanks, including massive B1 *bis*, and the 3e DIM, a unit of active, well-trained and well-equipped soldiers.

By the end of the day, the village had already changed hands several times as attacks and counter-attacks had taken place. It was nothing but smoking ruins, some German soldiers began to call it the 'Verdun of 1940'. The coming days were to prove them right.

At Ville-au-Montois, the 51e DI had established themselves as well as they could in concrete blockhouses and other strongpoints. Shelled by German heavy artillery, the morale of the already shattered division was stretched passed breaking point. Telephone communications were severed with *3e Armée* headquarters. Three radios were loaned from the 334e RI and a temporary Observation Point (OP) established as

Morfontaine to report on German movements. The 51e DI was on its own, with no means of communication.[7]

In Belgium, the Allies were still blocking the Germans. Around Gembloux, the situation for the 12e DIM, supported by the 15e DIM and *8e Division Belge,* their position was increasingly untenable. The centre of the French position along the Gembloux Gap was, at Ernage. It was here that the 3rd and 4th Panzer Division, supported by artillery and Stukas centred their attack. The 22e Algerians and 11e Zouaves of the 2e DINA. put up strong resistance at Ottignies and Limelette, but the *110e Regiment d'Infanterie* (RI). of the 1re DIM came close to being overwhelmed. The Wehrmacht sought to press its advantage and break the front line between the 110e RI and *7e Régiment de Tirailleurs Marocains* (RTM) through the bois de l'Hermitage. The German infantry were eventually stopped by the French artillery. The *80e Groupe de Reconnaissance de Division d'Infanterie* (GRDI) armed with mortars, four 25mm anti-tank guns and forty machine guns, and the 1re Bataillon of the 7e RTM were pushed out of Ernage. To the immediate south, the 1re RTM held its ground. Although Stuka dive bombers bombarded the batteries of the *64e* and *26e Regiment d'Artillerie d'Afrique* (RAA), the African gunners fired directly on German tanks, destroying them and leaving them to burn. The 25mm guns with the 2e RTM knocked out forty tanks along the front of the regiment. Gunners of the *1re* and *201e regiment d'Artillerie* (RA). and those with 15e DIM stopped the advancing Panzers in support of the operations of the 134e RI close to Gembloux and those of the 4e and 15e RI. The 12e DIM supported by the *1re* and *2e Chasseurs Ardennais* had held. Despite losses of losses ranging from 30 to 50 per cent of the units' strength, the Gembloux Gap had held.[8] The front broke at 10:45.

For General Prioux, things were going from bad to worse. Having been unable to contact Corap for any news from the *9e Armée,* he contacted Blanchard's headquarters for instructions.[9] Unknown to Prioux, Corap had been sacked in the early hours, and was to be replaced by Giraud. Giraud told Billotte 'my impression is grave especially on my right because of the rapid advance of the Panzers': the *9e Armée* was starting to cease to exist as a cohesive fighting force.[10] From *1re Armée* headquarters came a written order at 11:30, confirming a verbal order of 06:30 which stated that what remained of the *2e* DLM was charged with guarding the exposed flank of the *1re Armée* in the place of the BEF. After five days fighting the *Corps de Cavalerie* was 'absolutely exhausted', wrote one officer. The tanks needed fuel, ammunition and repairs, the men rest:

> General Prioux, after having sent a written report of this situation, sent an officer to the general commanding the *1re Armée*, then telephoned him himself to obtain permission for withdrawal from the battlefield of all the elements of the DLM, which, after being supplied with new material over a period of 24 or 48 hours would fully regain their combat value . . . the tanks were not to be withdrawn. Meanwhile, and due to the enemy's advance on the front of the *9e Armée*, the *1re Armée* decided to withdraw towards the Charleroi Canal, asking the *Corps de Cavalerie* to establish a withdrawal echelon on this canal. The order to set up this device was sent at 22:00, enforceable the next day at 08:30. Finally, the CC was informed of the arrival in the zone of the *1re Armée* of the 1re DLM coming from Holland (*7e Armée*). This Division was not subject to the orders of the CC.[11]

Tired men do not make good soldiers. Yet what option was there?

To the north of Gembloux, along the line of the Albert Canal the situation was desperate: 'a very violent bombardment of heavy artillery and from the air carried on all night' wrote the liaison officer between Montgomery, the French and Belgian armies. He adds that at 05:00 his lodgings were rocked by a 150mm German howitzer shell. 'The whole house shook in consequence of the violent detonations': he escaped wearing his pyjamas. Aerial attacks continued all day, supported by heavy artillery. Any movement 'was incredibly risky because of the accuracy of the German shelling and air attacks . . . we had gone perhaps 500m when were obliged to drive off the road and dive into the ditch', wrote an officer who was desperately trying to establish a liaison post close to the canal. 'On arriving at the first line of houses we were stopped by British soldiers who told me that German tanks had entered the town' – alas he does not say which town. Meeting officers from the Coldstream Guards, our French officer was told of heavy losses along the canal, and it was unlikely that a counter-attack would succeed. After meeting with the Belgian Headquarters officers for the defence of the canal, a terse meeting followed with General Montgomery. Retreat seemed the only option screened by the French cavalry, i.e. tanks.[12]

In Rouen, Brigadier Archibald Bentley Beauman commented: 'The situation remainder favourable, life continued as normal in the towns and villages, children played in the streets; there was no hint that the greatest battle in history was being played out 100 miles away. The weather was good; there was no aerial activity.' On 15 May, the news 'from Sedan was especially bad', he confided to his diary.[13]

In the wake of the events of 15 May, Gamelin emerges as a far more effective commander-in-chief than he has been given credit for. He was undeniably a bureaucrat, but an accomplished bureaucrat was precisely what the French command structure required to organise a Plan B. As a peacetime commander, Gamelin had proved himself a clearsighted and effective politician. Having learned lessons from his mentor Joffre in 14/18, Gamelin knew 'all was not lost'. In 1914 Joffre, who had made virtually every mistake it was possible to make in the opening stages of the war, was able to throw back the German invaders on the Marne essentially because the Schlieffen Plan proved beyond German capabilities. Weary and footsore, having outrun both their logistics and their heavy artillery, and with Russian armies threatening them in East Prussia, the Germans were ripe for an Allied counteroffensive by September. It was exactly this scenario Gamelin believed was to be repeated in 1940. Since the early 1930s, the French high command sought to avoid the bloodletting of the First World War, and devised a military strategy aimed at repeating a long war of attrition followed by an ultimate offensive sometime in 1942 or 1943. As in 14/18, the goal for the Allies was the defence of a static front behind which, the Allies would re-arm, mass troops and then with overwhelming force, impose *bataille conduite* and defeat Germany.[14] Indeed, British Intelligence believed that Hitler was 'working to a timetable' and had to win by the end of the year. After that, they believed that the pressures of the Allied blockade and Germany's fuel shortages would become intolerable. Was it simply a matter of holding out for half a year or so? It was this scenario which drove Gamelin's next steps.[15] Therefore, for fighting in the West, the German plan relied on the speed and psychological shock of an attack. The German high command knew that they had only a few days to win a decisive victory: it was to be an all-out offensive, in essence a repeat of 1914. It was Gamelin who had won the Battle of the Marne: he had predicted the German onslaught would 'run out of steam', move faster than its supply chain could supply fuel, food, munitions and men, and importantly replace tanks and aircraft. Wehrmacht losses were severe. What Gamelin did next was to re-fight the Marne campaign. His thinking was quite correct. His plan argued for a deep withdrawal, abandoning north France if necessary, to exhaust the enemy, all the time shorting lines of communication to the reserves for the inevitable French victory.

Late on 15 May Gamelin began an audit of what forces were available, and began commandeering railway trains to move men and equipment. By the morning of 17 May, over half a million men were receiving orders to embark on hastily co-ordinated trains to travel from the south and east of France to Paris. To ensure the trains arrived unscathed in Paris, he needed air cover, and redirected the rear-area fighter squadrons centered on Paris to patrol over the thousands of men in transit on hundreds of trains. These men were to be deployed along the Somme. Note 1151-3/OP issued at 14:00 outlined the French army would fall back on the line of the River Aisne, in four successive stages. The all-important *7e Armée* was to move to the rear from Belgium, orders being issued at 13:00 the same day. However, it soon became apparent that the *7e Armée* could not disengage as Gamelin thought and, worse, the breach in the French lines at Sedan which threated to cut off the *1re Groupement des Armée* became a much more pressing issue. Gamelin ordered the formation of a new strategic reserve consisting of four divisions which was to be operational in three days' time. These were to be joined by seven more divisions which were to be reconstituted from the large units dispersed during the German breakthrough, and which still had most of their equipment and supplies. This powerful reserve of eleven divisions was to be operational by mid-June at the latest.[16] Orders issued over the next 24 hours capably demonstrate Gamelin's desire to regain the initiative, although they do not, strictly speaking, constitute a solid and well-established strategic plan. They lack an overall vision as these orders were issued without any consultation with the British and Belgians; the first order is poorly drafted, and the second is a warning order, nothing more than a statement of intent. Furthermore, these orders were not accompanied by tactical instructions (concentration of resources, use of bomber aircraft, immediate counter-attack in the event of a breakthrough, etc.) necessary to ensure the success of the strategic counter-offensive they advocated.[17] In defence of Gamelin, this was technically not his job: 'putting flesh on the bones' of outline orders was down to General Georges who commanded the front.

Chapter 13

FLAVION

On the evening of 14 May the 1re DCR had arrived in the region of Florennes-Flavion. The tanks' arrival was slowed by having to pass through the stream of refugees and soldiers who were fleeing the front. Because their refuelling convoys had been unable to keep pace with them, the French tanks had almost no petrol. They formed a triangular defensive position with the heavy tanks (B1 *bis*) of the *1re Demi-brigade* deployed between Ermeton and Flavion, while the H-39s of the *3e Demi-brigade* waited between Flavion and Corenne. Early on the 15th, two Panzer divisions appeared before the French tanks and a fierce battle began as the commander of the *25e Bataillon des Chars du Combat* (BCC) reports:

> At around 09:00 on Wednesday 15th May, the Germans approached the edge with armoured vehicles, particularly towards Larue; the tanks fired on those of the *28e bataillon* which counter-attack and after about an hour and a half the fire calmed down, the Germans did not push back, but our machine-gun fire continued on the German motorised columns which were marching from the east to the west at about 1,200 metres. Using my tank, I went to the line to assess the situation, which I found to be good. At this time, although some tanks had consumed a fairly large amount of ammunition . . . during a movement of the tanks of section Coulon, one tank fell into a marsh and could not be taken out despite the meritorious efforts made to rescue it.
>
> A little later, accompanied by Walschots I went to Larue and had the tanks change some positions and I told Walschots to push my HQ towards the clearing. I then went to Commander Pinot who asked me to hold the position with everything I had to ensure the protection of his rear. Around 13:00 or 14:00 after my return to HQ a very violent fire of 105mm fell on our lines, starting with Laure then Robergeaud while quite a few shells also fell on Potut and around my HQ: a tank of Robergeaud's section was

> hit and burst into flames . . . the big brothers [the B1 *bis* companies] with whom we were in contact made various movements to escape the fire and moved away from us. Around 15:00 a violent fight began on my left between the B tanks and the German tanks that were attacking, it seemed to last a good hour, but I couldn't see anything. I had confidence in the B and I only thought about my mission, to hold out to prevent the position from being out flanked. Around 17:00. the fight seemed to be calming down, I sent a non-commissioned officer to see Major Pinot to ask him for information and tell him my situation. The non-commissioned officer came back a few moments later, telling me that he had found no one else, but that, on the other hand, he had seen a tank that he did not know about 200 meters from Laon. Alarmed by this report, I took a tank and decided to verify the fact myself. Arriving near Pinot's old HQ, I was greeted by shots from anti-tank weapons or tanks; six shells hit my turret in a few minutes without my being able to discern their origin. Realising that the battalion was isolated and surrounded, I retreated.[1]

An officer with the 28e BCC adds more detail:

> Houses in Flavion are in flames. The anxiety is growing. For two hours a considerable noise of caterpillars was heard, which seemed to stop in the vicinity of Anthée. Then a disturbing silence follows these noises. Another cause for concern was that the refuelling did not arrive and the tanks only had to walk in the tanks for an hour: this changed the battalion's mission. 'Hold out at all costs, prevent the enemy from crossing the general line Ermeton on Biert – Flavion' . . . 8:10 a.m. The silence is broken by a few bursts of automatic weapons.
>
> 8:30 a.m. The German attack is launched from Anthée on Flavion. The 5th Panzer Division descended, deployed, the slopes of Anthée and swept over Flavion in the direction of Philippeville. The 3rd Company opened fire, many enemy tanks were hit. The PzKW III and IV went into action. The fight became intense on the entire front of the Battalion.
>
> The fire of the Bs was terribly effective, however, without stopping the waves of German armour followed one another, the breaches that were made were immediately filled. The 3rd Company was attacked head-on by numerous machines. Others headed for Flavion to go around it from the south and the 3rd Company was launched on the counter-attack on Flavion and its western edges . . . In this baptism of fire, the crews showed remarkable composure, reasoned bravery combined with precise reflexes. The radios pass and receive calmly and without error. However, the fight was hard, the crates resounded under the shells that slammed on the armour.
>
> At 10:30 a.m., after two hours of fighting, the exhaust pipes were pierced; the antennae torn off or sheared. Already the ground is strewn

> with the corpses of enemy tanks. The Bs are constantly firing from all sides, forwards, backwards, right and left.
>
> In front of the 3rd Company, seven PzKW IVs are inert. Six other tanks were on fire in front of the tank PHILIPPEVILLE. In an instant, the tanks TAMATAVE and the SOUSSE each destroyed three. The 1st Company will have more than 3 enemy aircraft on its hunting list.
>
> The tank QUINCY, attacked by about fifteen PzKW III and PzKW IV, had its radiator pierced. Its engine stops. And it is only thanks to the slope of the pitch, by 'coasting', that he can escape the fire of his opponents. Its crew was picked up by the TUNIS.
>
> The TIMBUKTU, as a result of an oil leak immobilised in the wood where it has arrived. Its steering brakes no longer work. The Commander wanted to enter the fight, asked his crew to make a supreme effort, and tried to get out of the cover. Eight enemy tanks opened fire on him. A fire was started, and the assistant pilot managed to extinguish the fire. The struggle resumes. On the tank TIMBUKTU caterpillar was hit . . . Immobilised, the crew exited, pistol in hand, through the emergency door of the hull, but were picked up by the German infantry which surrounded the tank; the crew were to be shot by the attackers but thanks to the intervention of a German Colonel who was touched by their bravery, their lives were spared. (This Colonel is none other than Rommel).
>
> The tank BRAZZAVILLE was hit by a direct 150 round. Its front was not pierced but a shower of shrapnel gushed out inside. Under fire, the crew evacuated the tank and brought back three wounded that the tanks TUNIS and CASABLANCA picked up.
>
> One by one, out of gas, the tanks came to a standstill. The ammunition ran out, the fire slowed down while the German attack was still as violent as when it began. Under fire, rage in their hearts, the tanks were abandoned and set on fire by their crews who, crawling, tried to escape. Some were taken prisoner, many were those who, at the cost of a thousand dangers, risking their lives, joined the division several days later.

The 1re DCR had met the 5th Panzer Division, which took heavy initial losses against the 1re Demi-brigade. Throughout the day the French B1 *bis* fought to their last drop of fuel. But in the end, targeted on all sides by German artillery, Panzers and Stukas, the 1re DCR had to fall back, scattered 'to the four winds.'[2]

Before dawn, 16 May 1940, obeying orders issued earlier that morning by the commanding officer of the *1re Armée*, at 03:00 General Prioux began moving the *Corps de Cavalerie* behind the Charleroi canal with the 54e and 56e DMM being deployed along the canal, with the 32e DI forming the left of the line with the chateau de Seneffe forming a strongpoint. The right of the line ended at Charleroi. A rearguard was formed from the 3e DLM and the *Division Marocaine,* fighting actions across the battlefields of 1815: Quatre-Bras and Wagnelee once again resounded to the thunder of guns, this time not heralding a French victory, but a far worse defeat that Waterloo.[3]

For the 1re DCR, following the total failure in communications in enabling tanks to be refuelled and co-ordinate the tank action at Flavion:

> At dawn, I found Postel-Viney and his tank in Mettet, but not Pradat, who had gone for fuel. Despite about fifty shells, including 18 in the right-hand undercarriage, which caused two road wheels and a roller to break off Postal-Vinays tank, the tank was repaired and refuelled, and back in working order. I also found Captain Guillou of the 6th Infantry Regiment of the 28th Infantry Regiment. I then reported to Colonel Preaux, commanding a Reconnaissance Group, who asked me to participate with his forces in the delaying campaign he was going to wage:
>
> 1. to clear the elements in contact.
> 2. to protect the southern flank of the retreating army.
>
> Despite my desire to return to the division, I accepted his reasons and we went on from place to place accompanied by 105s which were falling in the surrounding area, until we arrived at Gerpinnes (south of Charleroi)... At Gerpinnes, I met tank commanders Aumont of the 2nd, Coulon of the 3rd, as well as Warrant Officer Laurent, Sergeant Pech of the 3rd, and another tank of the 3rd mounted by a non-commissioned officer (Vandembroucke and other tanks). I had the tanks positioned facing south-east and east to block the German motorised vehicles. They made no serious attempt. I was informed that the Reconnaissance Group was being directed in another direction and that the latter was being replaced in its mission by the 8th Dragoons. I went to Major Kuntz, commander of this regiment, to ask for instructions and to inform him that a large German motorised column was marching from east to west about 2.5km away. This officer asked me to stay to cooperate in the defence of Gerpinnes because he no longer had any armoured vehicles at his disposal and also to allow him, at night, to unhook it and ensure the protection of his rearguard during the flank march that he had to execute to get behind the fortified line of Maubeuge 'at Quatre-Bras'.[4]

The 1re DCR had been scattered after its initial contact with the Wehrmacht. The French had only 351 tanks to oppose the Germans, including 126 Renault FT-17s from the First World War of the *33e Bataillon de Chars de Combat* (BCC). Pierre Cazenave, a French soldier, recalls:

> We were taken away from our modern Renault R-40s, which were to be used for training, to equip us with old Renault FT-17s, slow, poorly armed and poorly armoured. Our battalion was engaged in a real suicide mission against Guderian's Panzers. The German tankers were firing at us as if they were on exercise, their shells piercing the turrets of our tanks from one side to the other. Our speed limit of 8km/h made us ideal targets.

Predictably, this battalion was totally annihilated. What did the French high command expect the outcome would be other than this? Out of sixty-three tanks engaged, from the 33e BCC fifty-five were destroyed. Out of 132 crewmen, only 22 survived. The last tanks were buried, leaving the turrets uncovered in an attempt to better resist the Germans. The French air force had, reluctantly, sent up nine Breguet 693s from *18e Groupement*, and six LeO 451s to support the attack. Due to battle damage no other aircraft were available. The Breguet were deployed as dive bombers: they dived at 45 degrees down to 1,500m before dropping their bombs: the French were desperately trying to copy the tactics of the Luftwaffe, in aircraft that were not 'up to the job'.[5]

As a cohesive armour group, the 1re DCR's effectiveness was now nullified as the tanks were scattered and broken up, acting as mobile artillery as the infantry pulled back. Any idea of regrouping the 1re DCR and acting offensively was not considered: the inability for tanks to communicate with each other due to lack of two-way radios, and with other French units around them, made co-ordination and re-grouping impossible. The worst fears that Inspector Keller had raised six months earlier had come true. Our battalion commander from the 1re DCR continues on arriving at Gerpinnes:

> We were attacked by planes; an officer of Char B who had left his turret was wounded by a bullet next to me. The column set off around 21:00., via Flashes, Malinnes, Thuillies, etc. in order: cavalrymen from the company of Guilliou, Postel-Vinay who had taken back his tank, myself, Coulon, Aumont, Coulon, Pech, Laurent. The Char Bs and our tanks had little fuel. The road we took was in a disastrous state, as along it we found many villages that were left as burning ruins and blocked by the smoking debris of a bombed convoy. As we passed Malinnes, we were able to refuel, except for the Char Bs which had no pump, thanks to the fuel contained in an abandoned truck. Where re refuelled was grim: we

> were in the middle of the square where all the houses were burning. We continued to Thuilles . . . the road was very cluttered by another demolished convoy which we passed with difficulty, losing contact with the elements that preceded us. Having found an abandoned tank, Sergeant Pech set it back on the road, but we had to destroy it a few kilometres further on . . . I took the risk of heading directly to Maubeuge.[6]

Maubeuge became a key strongpoint for the French to try and stem the flood tide of Panzers. No air cover was provided: no fighter cover to keep the Stukas at bay. Rather than operating around Charleroi, at 07:00 General Têtu demanded that General d'Astier assign more fighters to him to cover his bombers on a raid to Montcornet. At 08:30 twelve LeO 451s from *6e Groupement* were in the air, with fighter protection, heading to Montcornet. The fighters were ordered to machine-gun anything that moved.[7] The lack of French fighters and modern bombers to cover the French army was now being keenly felt. Barratt was proving to be an unreliable ally with his overcaution, and the Allied air Strike Force was busy bombing targets in Germany and not over the battlefields of France and Belgium.

The adjutant of the 12e DIM noted that the Division still held the position it had done the previous day at 04:30 on the morning of the 16th. He noted 'due to a lack of precise information of what was happening in the south, the commandant made contact with a liaison officer who said we were to counter-attack and with a division of cuirassiers'. With the centre seriously weakened, the 12e and 15e DIM and 5e DNA were ordered to draw back to strengthen the centre. The division was to retreat due west and traverse the battlefield of Ligny and of Gilly from those momentous days of 1815. Headquarters were to be established at Frasnés les Gosselies, with infantry plugging the gap between Mazy and Jemappes. The left wing of the retreat was to be covered by 38 B1 tanks when the movement began at 07:00, but at 09:00 the movement order was rescinded and new orders issued at 10:00. At 10:00 news arrived that the *9e Armée* had been defeated at Dinant-sur-Meuse by the 39th Panzer Corps: the risk of becoming surrounded from the south-east forced the right flank of the *1e Armée* to abandon the ground it had so fiercely defended. They were to fall back behind the Brussels-Charleroi canal. He comments that on hearing news about Sedan the soldiers cried 'Treason, Fifth columnists!' The movement to Fleurs and the line of the canal began at 16:00. The B1 tanks, supported by 25mm anti-tank guns from the 25e RA commanded by Colonel Parent, held off tentative strikes by panzers. Heavy artillery and aerial bombardment slowed the move to the canal line by the 12e and 15e DIM.[8]

At 11:00m six Bloch 152s from 6e *Groupement* were heading to Montcornet, the objective was to shoot up the German troops heading to Montcornet. At 13:30 nine Breguet 639s flew to attack the same columns this time at Rethel. The Breguets were followed by a third wave of twenty-six aircraft, only four of which returned.[9]

Around Namur, fighting was also raging. Sensing that the Gembloux Gap would fall, the Luftwaffe stepped up its operation. Maubeuge, a French garrison town surrounded by forts, was bombed by the Luftwaffe at the end of the morning. Civilians took refuge in cellars and shelters, bombs and fires ravaged 90 per cent of the historic centre of the city. André Boutoille remembers: 'There was fire in the city, a barracks and a hospital were burning. The German planes were having fun over our heads, but they didn't strafe us, they spared us there. It was after that that we understood why we were in Maubeuge and the Germans were already in Avesnes-sur-Helpe.'[10]

The German were able to advance as rapidly as they did due to air superiority. The Panzer Divisions operated under an airborne shield of fighters as well as light and medium bombers. As well as communication, long-range reconnaissance and short-range proving operations were flown by HS 126s, with HS 123s and Ju 87 Stukas acting as airborne artillery. The lighter aircraft would have been easy pickings for the Allies, had it not been for the dominance of the Bf 109. Despite the RAF sending more Hurricanes to France, the Allies were to pay a high price for failing to develop effective systems and the right aircraft for infantry support, as well as training and tactics to make them effective. The Allied air forces could do little more than mount standing patrols and send like 'lambs to the slaughter' more of the obsolescent Blenheims up in suicidal missions to bomb German lines of communication and troop movements.[11] Tactically and equipment wise, the Allies were unable to respond to the Germans. None of the RAF aircraft had any armament that could damage anything more than a soft-skinned vehicle: the .303 machine gun was almost totally useless against ground targets, and none of the pilots were trained for ground attack.[12]

Maubeuge was a key location to capture if the road to Paris was to be open. The Germans were now set on invading the north of France. It was at Clairfayts, in Sambre-Avesnois, that the German general Erwin Rommel crossed the border. Disregarding his orders to wait until German infantry caught up, Rommel pushed on alone, with just his Panzers and motorised infantry. The border was presented by blockhouses as an extension of the Maginot Line. A German tank commander testified: 'The fortified position breathes fire. Anti-tank guns also fired and hit the command tank, the radio operator had his leg torn off. Heavy fire of medium-calibre artillery from the enemy.'[13]

The Trieu-du-Chêneau blockhouse was the first to be attacked. Entrenched inside, the twelve men under the command of Lieutenant Marconnet destroyed two Panzers with their anti-tank gun. During a second assault, a shell hit the gun mantlet and put it out of action. Unable to resist, German infantrymen invested the blockhouse. The lieutenant and a soldier were wounded in the assault. The 101e Fortress Infantry Division (of which the 84e and 87e Fortress Infantry Regiments were part) occupied the border blockhouses around Clairfayts and defended vigorously, but at nightfall German motorised infantry destroyed the French defences with flamethrowers and hollow charges in a repeat performance of similar actions in Belgium. Having broken through, Rommel's tanks rushed towards the nearby village of Solre-le-Château where they again came up against a line of blockhouses around 23:00. At midnight, the Germans entered Avesnes-sur-Helpe but the French did not surrender. The night would be very long for the soldiers on both sides.

Throughout the day, the Belgians, French and BEF had clung to the Albert Canal line. That night, Brussels was 'blitzed'. So too was Louvain as an eyewitness writes: 'Louvain was in flames. In the direction of Brussels, immense fires illuminated the night sky.' Driving all night without food, the liaison HQ arrived at Egem-Erpe-mere and escaped 'being massacred' by the Luftwaffe.[14] Another witness to these events, François Madert with the 14th Division of the BEF explains following a landing by Fallschirmjäger behind the Albert Canal and had trapped a portion of the BEF and French forces retreat was the only option, and on:

> 16 May . . . we received the order to return to the French frontier. Throughout the day we were bombarded and replied till we were behind the l'Escualt at Oudenaars and Avelgem.
>
> Attacks north of Avelgem were sustained by the 10th and 12th brigade which allowed the 1st Corps of the British Army to retreat. At the last moment, the Germans opened fire with their machine guns, we then detonated the two bridges over the Escaut north of Avelgem. During our retreat as we entered the village two German machine gunners blocked our way . . . after a short combat we rejoined our division and followed it on its movement to the line of the river Lys to the north of Courtrai . . . the gravity of our situation was not lost on us . . . at a little after two o'clock in the afternoon, the Germans gained Tourcoing, and I received the order to go the 12th brigade of Infantry to the heights of Mont Kemmel. The relations between the British Officers and the

> French personnel attached to them was very bad from this time, it was impossible to obtain any direct information on the development of the battle, and where we were to go.
>
> Throughout that day, during our series of operations were harassed by the Germans, who were proceeded by and accompanied with air attacks in great number and artillery fire.[15]

At Rouen, an urgent conference was organised amongst the senior officers of the BEF. The conclusion was, the French would be unable to close the breach in the continuous front at Sedan with sufficient speed to prevent a German breakout. General Headquarters (GHQ) passed orders to improvise a flank guard at Cambrai, where it seemed the German armour and infantry would head next.[16]

To the south, around Sedan, the French lines started to bulge as the Germans advanced. With most of the armour in Belgium, the sector relied on tanks from 14/18 and very few modern designs. That being said, the few modern tanks available to the French performed remarkably well. A solitary B1 destroyed a column of thirteen German tanks, despite the 140 projectiles that hit it. The French dug in, knowing the Germans would attack again. Based behind where the *9e Armée* had been based were the 1re and 2e DCR. These tanks were to be the last-ditch gamble to cut off the Panzers. By the end of the day the 1re DCR virtually ceased to exist, the 3e DCR was heavily engaged at Stonne against the 10th Panzers.[17] The 2e DCR was so hopelessly dispersed that three of the four French heavy armoured divisions had been effectively neutralised. No sizeable French units existed between the Wehrmacht and Paris or the Channel coast. With no reserves closer than 72 hours away, the breakthrough by the Wehrmacht was complete as 16 May 1940 came to an end.[18]

The situation was about to get worse, a LOT worse. Captain Bruneau of the 1re DCR reported:

> On the night of May 16, around 23:00., he got out of his tank, which was about a hundred meters away, and found himself facing a column of German tanks advancing toward Avesnes, constantly firing incendiary bullets and launching flares. Trapped on the ground, he was only able to reach his tank later, after seeing, he said, an entire Panzer division advancing a few meters away from him.[19]

Only one B1 *bis*, out of seventy, made it back into France. As the relentless advance of the 7th Panzer Division had not been thwarted, the sacrifice of the 1re DCR had been totally futile.

Chapter 14

17 MAY 1940

After a week's fighting, it was still possible for the Battle of France to slow the advance of the Wehrmacht and buy time for reserves to be brought up from the west and south of France. The front may have been broken, but French soldiers were putting up obstinate resistance. In response to the German advance, Paris was declared a military zone and martial law was declared, with police being armed with rifles. With the military situation rapidly deteriorating, Édouard Daladier as the French Minister of National Defence and War was held to blame, and to assuage the political right Reynaud sacked him and replaced him with Marshal Philippe Pétain who was added to the Cabinet as deputy premier.

In the Gembloux Gap, the first line of defence may have been shattered, but contingency planning allowed for the creation of stop lines as the French pulled back to the Somme. The 12e DIM had reached the Charleroi canal by break of day, leaving a rearguard. They reached the canal and were in their new defensive positions by 21:00 the previous evening, the 15e DIM to their left and 5e DINA to the right. 'In the first hours of the day the enemy attacked', wrote the adjutant of the 12e DIM.[1] Heading directly for the 15e DIM was Erwin Rommel.

Shortly before 01:00 the streets of Avesnes-sur-Helpe rang to the rattle-clack-squeak of tanks. Disobeying orders, Rommel had crossed into France, and now his armour drove through the town, writing enthusiastically in his diary:

> The way to the West is now open. We had crossed the Maginot Line! It was hard to believe. 22 years ago, we stood in front of the same enemy for 4 and a half years, won victory after victory and still lost the war. And now we were deep into enemy territory. It wasn't just a beautiful dream. It was reality![2]

As the Panzers emerged from the town, they stumbled upon a French motorised division bivouacking for the night along the road between Solre-le-Château and Avesnes. These French soldiers, who had withdrawn from Belgium, must have felt safe behind the border, happy to be able to take a little rest before facing the Germans again. With little infantry, Rommel ordered his tanks to charge. This was no simple advance. Driving at full throttle with the tanks' guns and machine guns firing as they went, an officer of the 7th Panzer Division remembers: 'Hundreds and hundreds of soldiers and civilians are woken up with a start by the armoured regiment rushing at full speed . . . Their faces are distorted by fear.'[3]

Leaving his infantry to mop up the terrified French, Rommel drove on with his Panzers. He drove headlong into a squadron of sixteen French tanks that had survived the Battle of Flavion in Belgium and had retreated until then, among them the formidable B1 *bis*. Rommel had no choice; he had to turn back and fight until 04:00 in the streets of Avesnes. German losses were significant but finally the French tanks ended up retreating.

Once again, General Rommel decided to continue towards Landrecies to take the bridge of the town before it was destroyed by the French. Rommel's tanks charging forward without trying to consolidate their positions, and in doing so created total chaos among the French units. The French nicknamed Rommel's division 'the phantom division', because it always appeared where it was not expected. During this extraordinary night, 10,000 French soldiers were taken prisoner while Rommel lost only 105 men. At 06:00, his Panzers were at Landrecies, and half-an-hour later they were at Cateau-Cambrésis. Not everything went to plan for Rommel: two French B1 *bis* tanks destroyed 100 German armoured cars and light tanks parked in the streets of Landrecies. The B1 *bis* was the most powerful tank of the time, but very heavy: it consumed a lot of fuel. The German tanks, lighter and faster, sped away and destroyed the supply lines, forcing the French to constantly retreat to regroup. The French armour was totally reliant on constant supplies of petrol being delivered in lorries. French tanks did not carry 'Jerry cans' of petrol like the Germans. Worse, the petrol bowsers were not tracked, and were unable to adequately keep pace with the tanks across country.

On halting outside Cateau-Cambrésis, the German general realised that he had covered 50km in one night. This offensive conclusively opened the road to the English Channel for the Germans.[4]

The French intelligence service informed Gamelin that it was their understanding that the Wehrmacht was not heading to Paris: its objective was to cut off the Allied army in Belgium and north France, and head to Calais.[5] Because of heavy loss of fighter aircraft, Air Marshal Barratt was requested by Georges to co-operate with the French more; the fighters were needed to provide bomber escorts and to intercept and destroy Luftwaffe bombers. Reinforcement from the RAF was 'absolutely vital. The Allied fighter force had not been reinforced and had been greatly reduced by enemy bombers and interdiction, so that it was too weak to offer anything but the weakest support.' Dowding and Whitehall refused. Without reinforcements, the French had to do what they could with dwindling resources to support ground troops and interdiction of the Luftwaffe bombers. At 11:15 and at 12:45 General Têtu received desperate pleas for assistance in the Gembloux Gap: due to lack of aircraft he could do nothing.[6]

The 1re DCR had arrived at Quatre-Bras around 06:00:

> In position, I was asked to assist the defence of this point before the rails blocking the road were put in place, as many units were retreating every moment.
>
> Around 9:00 a German armoured vehicle appeared, emerging from the Cousolre ravine signalled by the panic of a herd of cows. It was saluted by two shells and disappeared. Around 12:00 the officer commanding the operation had my crews and I eat and take a little rest. I was ordered to telephone Commander Lacroix of the 1st Battalion of the 85th Infantry Regiment to try to obtain information on the situation. Commander Lacroix asked me to come to Cerfontaine with my tanks. He had me assigned assistance to avoid the roadblocks of the arrest line. Upon arriving at Cerfontaine, I was almost shot by the occupants who had mistaken us for German tanks. After providing explanations, I was told by Captain Rolly of the 8th Infantry Regiment the Germans had passed Avesnes and were marching on Maubeuge. They could arrive at any moment. He then asked me to participate in the defence of Cerfontaine, facing south towards Ferriere-la-Petit and Ferriere-la-Grande. I had my remaining tanks positioned quickly in ambush, believing that combat was imminent: Hautmont facing Ferriere-la-Grand, Coulon facing Ferriere-la-Petite and myself on the main road facing a level crossing, having no illusions of what would befall us. I then burned all my papers. My mechanic was very smart after a few moments, seeing nothing to cause fear, and who then said that I could withdraw to Maubeuge where the presence of tanks had been reported. At that moment, Commander De Lacroix was advised that the troops would have to withdraw to the north bank of the Sambre.[7]

As a consequence of Rommel's audacity, and the disintegration of the 1re DCR and the *9e Armée*, the 12e DIM now had Panzers between its southern flank and the *2e Armée*: the Gembloux Gap had been smashed open. Charleroi became the scene of bitter fighting: under intense aerial bombardment, like the *9e Armée* as a whole, the 12e DIM slowly but surely began 'to come apart'. The 12e DIM at 13:00 was ordered to hold and stand and organise a counter-attack to thrust south to close the gap Rommel had smashed through at Avesnes. At 19:00 orders came through that there would be no counter-attack, and instead the 12e DIM and 5e DINA were to retreat to the Forest of Mormal, and take up positions west of Maubeuge. The perfect opportunity to cut off Rommel before his infantry could catch up had been lost. The adjutant of the 12e DIM noted 'the men were totally exhausted' and found it almost impossible to execute the movement order. The Division did not move off till midnight, first having set fire to all stores in Charleroi. Due to lack of petrol most of the vehicles were left behind, the retreat being covered by the *3e Cuirassiers*.[8]

For General Prioux the future seemed to be uncertain. The previous day, he had been told to ready his tanks for a counter-attack at Cambrai. General Georges telephoned him at 09:00, Prioux was told to join Georges' HQ as soon as possible:

> Leaving most of his General Staff at St Symphorien, alert and ready to move, General Prioux left with his Chief of Staff and two officers. Arriving in Valenciennes during an air raid, there reigned at the GQ of the *1re Armée*, which is preparing to move on Douai, a certain nervousness coming in particular from the information received from the *9e Armée*, indicating that the enemy, moving from Vervins, had reached the Oise in the region of Guise. General Blanchard planned to entrust General Prioux with the command of a group of forces responsible for covering the very south-eastern flank of the army.
>
> General Prioux asked that in order to accomplish this mission, that he be given the three DLM (including of course, their tank brigades) with which he would take charge of a counter-attack on both sides of the Mormal forest. He himself saw the Army dispatcher to obtain trains to transport the tanks of the 2e and 3e DLM; but the Belgian railway workers already did not want to work anymore. Moreover, the 1re DLM found itself at that moment engaged in isolation by the *9e Armée* south of the Mormal forest. Seeking to provoke orders, General Prioux telephoned General Georges, then went to General Billotte's HQ (Douai) and then returned to the *1re Armée*.
>
> Faced with the impossibility of gathering the necessary resources in time, it was decided that the *1re Armée*, abandoning the Charleroi Canal, would continue its withdrawal, supported by all the armoured elements of the CC with the exception of a discovery regiment which would go to Bavai, to support the troops of the 4e DI and the Bejard Group (3e DLM), tasked with covering the army towards the east by holding the Sambre

> from Charleroi to Berlaimont. The rest of the *Corps de Cavalerie* (artillery and machine gunners) would establish itself in withdrawal echelon on the Dendre.[9]

That afternoon, Prioux telephoned orders that the 2e DLM was to be stationed between Ath and Mons, and the 3e DLM between Lens and Mons. The infantry, machine gunners and artillery to be in echelon as reserves.[10]

Further east, in Stonne in the Ardennes, fighting still continued. The French armour continued to resist: a B1 *bis* tank crushed a group of German infantrymen under its tracks and allowed the French to recapture the village in the early afternoon. The village changed hands seventeen times in three days. At 17:45 the Germans retook it, this time definitively. General Wagner, a senior German officer, said after the war: 'There are three battles that I will never forget: Stonne, Stalingrad and Monte Cassino.' The armour available to the French was crippled by the collapse of logistical support. Air support was also very, very limited. At 13:55 eleven Farman 221s from *15e Groupement* and four Amiot 143s from *10e Groupement* bombed targets at Hirson and Mezieres.[11]

Hoping to at least slow the German advance, the RAF and allied air forces still vainly hoped to destroy the bridges over the Meuse: fifty-three bombers of RAF Bomber Command were ordered to attack the bridges in a nighttime bombing raid, ostensibly hoping the cover of darkness would protect the bombers from the Luftwaffe. Struggling to find their targets, as navigation aids and training were inadequate, a quarter of the bombers returned with their bomb loads. Most of the bombs missed the target area by miles. With poor information about troop locations, RAF Blenheims bombed French troops around Cambrai. Aware that air power was a significant factor in stopping the Germans, Paris asked Churchill for fighters to act as airborne artillery against Panzer divisions. Churchill refused: he was already aware that the Battle for France would inevitably become the Battle for Britain.[12] That evening an ad hoc formation of four Amiot 143s and twelve Breguet 639s attacked targets at Rethel: without fighter protection, all bar four machines were destroyed before they reached the target.[13] The Wehrmacht had smashed through the Ardennes; despite Stonne still being held, the Panzers turned to the Channel coast. De Gaulle attempted to stop the flood tide of armour at Montcornet. His tactical defeat meant nothing stood in the way of the Allied armies in Belgium being surrounded. The events at Stonne and the Ardennes are described in our companion volume *Hitler's Blitzkrieg in the West*.

Chapter 15

18 MAY 1940

On Saturday 18 May, the new government was in a state of flux. Pétain regarded Gamelin, along with politicians like Edouard Daladier and Paul Reynaud, as 'gravediggers' of France, responsible for the unfolding military catastrophe. Without Daladier to protect him, Gamelin was now 'target number 1' for Pétain. By the close of the day, he had invited Weygand to take command: both Pétain and Weygand understood the military to be above civil authorities and its obedience was not to be absolute to the state. Both men had almost complete disdain for the Third Republic's parliamentary system. Both represented a traditionalist, right-wing faction of the army that was sceptical of democratic processes, favoured authoritarian solutions to national decline, and championed anti-communist and anti-parliamentary ideologies. Indeed, the fear was of the war unleashing a wave of communism destroying the social order, which could only be prevented by ending the war and in essence a military coup, meaning that the Third Republic was on 'borrowed time'. Pétain and Weygand's political stance in the 1930s directly predicted their behaviour in 1940. Reynaud chose to overlook Weygand's unstable personality and both his and Pétain's well-known political views in favour of some form of national unity.[1] By the close of the day, Reynaud was both Premier and Minister for National Defence. Pétain was already convinced that the military situation was hopeless, laying the groundwork for his request for an armistice a month later as our companion volume *The Fall of France* explores.[2]

The new government had barely been formed when it had to deal with tragic news from the front. The Maginot Line had been breached by the Germans. The fort of La Ferté, 15km from Sedan, had been targeted the day before. The Germans concentrated 250 artillery pieces at this location, thousands of shells were fired at the fort and its surroundings: La Ferté resisted the bombardments.

Therefore, during 18 May a commando of German engineers infiltrated the blockhouse and placed a charge of 40kg of explosives on one of the steel turrets. The explosion created a small opening through which German soldiers threw explosives and smoke bombs. A fire spread, causing the ammunition to explode, which tore off the fire doors. Trapped underground, the 107 men of the garrison of the fort died from asphyxiation. After having experienced so much difficulty in reducing a single small fort, the Germans avoided attacking the strongpoints of the Maginot Line. Le Quesnoy had held out for three days before surrendering. In the evening, the Wehrmacht moved into the Mormal forest where fighting raged for two days led by the 1re DLM.

The previous day, fifty Panzers had arrived on the edges of Cateau-Cambrésis and orders had been given to blow up the bridges at Marcoing. Giraud was told at 19:00 that German infantry was on the outskirts of Cambrai, and that after almost three hours of stubborn fighting, Cateau had fallen, the French troops falling back to Valenciennes. One eyewitness to the fighting around Cambrai, Captain Bruneau of the 1re DCR, comments:

> A Panzer 1 tank appeared, which we greet with cannon fire and which disappeared immediately. The German commanders attempt a frontal attack which we stop and then try to outflank us, but each time we succeed in stopping them. It is during one of these attacks that I see for the first time distinctly an enemy tank armed with a cannon (probably 105) firing in the axis of the tank. It seems to us to have destroyed two of them successively with bursting shells. After a while, the Germans seem to have given up on an attack based solely on tanks and after a lull we see the infantry emerging. The guns fire on sight, at point blank range. We defend ourselves with rifle fire but we are not numerous enough.[3]

Alarmingly, two German tanks had forced a passage across the bridge at Eswars, 4km north of Cambrai, and threatened the French rear.[4]

Hampering French and Allied offensive movements, by 18 May almost two million Belgian and Dutch civilians had left their homes since 12 May. In their headlong rush to safety which they believed could be found in France, they created congestion on the roads and also meant that key bridges which were to have been destroyed across rivers and canals remained standing so civilians could flee. The timeline of Gamelin's plan had never considered a mass of refugees blocking roads and bridges. Gamelin, so careful and calculating, had failed to understand human nature and the flight of civilians.

In the midst of this chaos, fighting continued. Maubeuge held out. At Cerfontaine, the remains of the 1re DCR were caught up in a rearguard struggle:

> Around 10:00 a cavalry officer (Lieutenant Calvuat) came to report to Colonel Mariage that the Germans had crossed the Sambre at Maubeuge, that they were trying to break out of the Mons gate and that the cavalry tanks were having difficulty containing them. The Colonel asked me to intervene. I immediately sent Pradat from the section, which alone had 37/38 tanks, with orders to oppose the German tank raid for as long as possible. His departure was very moving, I still see him. This section engaged very brilliantly and fulfilled its mission from 11:00 to 18:00, destroying five German tanks, including two large ones, one of them under the Mons gate, blocking it for quite a long time. During this engagement, Lieutenant Postel-Vinay received a shell fired by a large tank in his turret and was killed: the tank caught fire.
>
> Arriving near Fort Sars, due to a mistake, the two remaining tanks were fired upon by a gun from the 75th Infantry Regiment of the 12th Artillery Regiment, which fired a shell into Pradat's turret, killing him instantly. Only Aumont's tank was not riddled with bullets. Meanwhile, Colonel Mariage, having a battalion of the 6th RTM occupy the anti-tank trench facing Maubeuge, asked me to support him with a tank company. I designated Guillou's company, which took up a waiting position on the outskirts of Elsemes. Recent's company remained in reserve at Boussois, where I had moved my headquarters alongside Colonel Mariage's. Two more or less able tanks, an R-35 and an H-39 equipped with 37/38 cannons, were used to hold respectively: the R the Boussois bridge, the H, the Assevent bridge.[5]

As night fell, the bridges were still in French hands. The German columns around Maubeuge went untroubled by the French air force.

Rommel's Panzers were caught by the French air force leaving the Landrecies area. At 16:15 twelve Leo 45s bombed the tanks: because Rommel had dispersed his armour across a wide tract of land, the French bombers were unable to knock out a single tank. Undeterred at 19:15 eight Breguet 693s were sent to attack Rommel's Panzers. Heavy flak and machine-gun fire from the tanks brought down four machines.[6] The aircraft allocated for army co-operation had lost 30 per cent of their effective strength.[7] At Ville-au-Montois, the 51e DI, comprising the 48e RAD, 248e RAD and 139e RIF were held up south of the town. With no communication to superior command groups, they were on their own.[8]

In Rouen, chaos reigned supreme. Lord Gort had ordered all available troops north to Doullens: they had been attacked and routed by German armour: 'the situation' reported Brigadier Beauman, 'was chaotic and confused – Amiens and Abbeville were bombarded'. Four battalions of the 46th Division, which included the Duke of Wellington's Regiment and the East Surreys, were forced back to Dieppe.[9]

During the course of the day, Blanchard continued to plan a counter-attack at Cambrai outlined two days earlier. At 14:00 Prioux received an order from Blanchard timed at midday to move the *Corps de Cavalerie,* the armoured units included to area of Douai-Denain-Aubigny-Bouchain. Orders were given at 15:30 to prepare to move, with headquarters moving out at 17:00 to Blaton sur Erchin, the *Corps de Cavalerie* follow at 18:00. The farcical nature of the French communication system now comes into play. At 18:35, Prioux received an order – sent by a motorcycle courier – from *1re Armée* timed at 12:35 cancelling the 12:00 order and instead ordering Prioux to regroup in the order of Marquion-Arleux and Cambrai. Prioux gave orders to move the *Corps de Cavalerie* to Cambrai. At 20:00:

> General Prioux returning from the *1re Armée* where he had been informed of the situation (enemy motorised elements coming from the South-west in the direction of Cambrai), decided to execute the first order given to him directly by General Blachard . . . officers were sent during the night to meet the columns to direct them to the first planned destination (2nd DLM HQ at Mastaing, 3rd DLM HQ at Fressain)[10]

For Prioux, a whole day had been lost. That morning, Georges had received orders from Gamelin for a counter-attack to cut off the Panzers from the accompanying infantry and support vehicles: with no Petrol the Panzers could not operate: to that end Gort met General Billotte that evening. Billotte outlined the French GQG plan that Billotte's *1re Groupement des Armée* would attack southward, and was to covered to the east by the Belgian army, which would gradually withdraw to the Yser River. Simultaneously to Billotte's attack south, *3e Groupement des Armée* would advance northward from the Somme.[11] Billotte, apparently, had no faith in the plan; moreover, Gort was unable to confirm or deny that the French had sufficient forces to attack. Gort had two choices: support the French thrust to the Somme with all his available forces after leaving a small rearguard, or do nothing. Gort reasoned that if the attack south to the Somme failed, then he would not be able to evacuate the BEF out of Dunkirk. Gort informed the British War Office that a withdrawal to the coast would shortly become the only chance for survival and he had no other course open. From this point on Gort only offered token support to the French: in essence his fear of losing the port facilities at Dunkirk meant he was torn between his desire to aid his Allies and being cut off from his line of retreat. He was convinced the French attack would fail.[12] Gort's timidity – cowardice? – and inability to take calculated risks meant that the Allied armies became fatally sucked towards Dunkirk rather than the Somme. The overriding desire to be able to save the BEF compromised its battlefield effectiveness, and undermined combined operations with the Belgian and French armies. The French press reports that from 22:00 to 03:00 fifteen waves of German bombers dropped more than 3,000 bombs on Dunkirk and the port. The oil refinery would burn until the beginning of June.

Chapter 16

WEYGAND TAKES CHARGE

May 19th 1940 was a Sunday. In Paris the faithful headed to Notre Dame to pray for deliverance, just as they had done in 1870: the entire French government attended Mass that morning. The relics of St Louis and St Genevieve were paraded as hearts and minds clamoured for divine intervention. Maurice Gamelin was at his headquarters by 08:00. Having spoken with Georges, Billotte and others, at 09:45 he issued the following order:

> I consider at the present time:
> There are grounds for continuing the [illegible] of prolonging to the west the front of our armies east & close covering of Paris and of maintaining union with No. 1 Army group.
> That as regards No. 1 Army group – rather than let it be encircled, we must act with utmost boldness; first by forcing, if necessary, the road to the Somme, and secondly, by throwing in especially mobile forces against the rear of the German Panzer divisions and motorised infantry divisions which are following them. There would seem, at present time a vacuum behind the first echelon.
> An offensive with all available means should be directed against the bridges at Mezieres.
>
> The complete strength of the French and British aviation must now devote itself to joining in the battle:
> - For the fighters to keep mastery of the air on the G A 1 front as a matter of priority, and as far as possible to protect our side-stepping movements.
> - For the bombers to operate against German columns on the march towards the west, take them in the rear and follow up on their westward route. [illegible] action should make itself felt especially on the southern groups of Panzer divisions.

- Subsequently, at the requisite moment, to hold themselves in readiness to support the movement of the Second Army.
- During the intervals to operate by bombing and mining the Meuse bridges.
- The whole is a question of hours.[1]

Gamelin was correct: the Panzers were outpacing the infantry behind: he was planning a counter-attack to separate the Panzers and nullify the threat. He left Vincennes at 10:00 and went to meet Georges at his headquarters. At 15:00 he met with General Sir John Dill, Chief of the Imperial General Staff. Dill informed Gamelin that the Wehrmacht were heading to the river Aisne and Seine, but had not yet crossed; the goal, Dill believed, was to use the two rivers to protect the Wehrmacht's flank whilst men and tanks were moved up, no doubt aware of the gap opening up between the armour and infantry, and the risk it posed. Gamelin made Dill aware that he believed the next phase of the Wehrmacht's operations would be a thrust towards the Channel ports, on the Calais axis, to encircle the BEF and French *1re Groupement des Armée.* Gamelin further told Dill that a strong Wehrmacht column was heading to Amiens where recently-disembarked elements of the BEF were then in the process of organisation.

During his interview with Georges Gamelin had learned he faced an immediate issue: *9e Armée* had disintegrated, thus no formed bodies stood opposing the Wehrmacht. To bolster his position, Gamelin had authorised Georges to move all his reserves from the eastern sector along the Maginot line, to screen the Aisne. Dill noted 'both General Gamelin and General Georges are clearly very tired . . . General Georges is quite calm . . . one gets the impression . . . that all that is possible has been done and that there is nothing much left for the High Command to do but to wait and see how the battle turns.'

Dill added 'it is clear, that at the moment, the main enemy is the tank, and that all resources including air should be devoted to its destruction, and, with this end in view, the light bomber forces of Air Marshal Barratt might be increased'. He closed his letter to Whitehall by noting that General Georges had told him in confidence:

> Lord Gort was contemplating taking action independent of the French northern group of armies under Billotte and withdrawing on Boulogne. This, if it was true, would at this moment be psychologically disastrous. The French will certainly have difficulty stabilising the front, and we must help them by land and in the air. At this critical

moment, we can't leave the French unsupported and they should be so reassured.[2]

So Gort was already thinking of evacuation for the BEF! Gamelin, aware that the *1re Groupement des Armée* could be cut off by the Wehrmacht heading to the coast, telegrammed Admiral Darlan, commanding the French navy, about planning the evacuation of the French army from Dunkirk and landing them behind the Somme. The telegram read in part:

> Although the situation does not justify the immediate taking of this step, it would be prudent to provide for it from this moment by assembling transports to evacuate certain units, without it being possible to establish in advance the number of ships necessary and the ports of embarkation.

Darlan thought the idea ridiculous:

> Summing up, such an operation carried out in that area against enemy opposition from ground and air forces appears to me doomed to disaster. On the contrary it seems to me less of a risk to supply the units resisting enemy pressure.

Darlan preferred holding onto Dunkirk as a fortified beachhead and trying to supply the isolated forces which could counter-attack from there, with a new defensive line on the Aisne with a second line along the Somme.[3]

Gamelin returned to Paris at 15:45. At 16:45, having understood the issues at hand from Dill and Georges and realising that holding existing positions was foolhardly, if not impossible, he issued orders for the various French army groups under his command to retreat behind the Somme in all haste. Commanders were ordered to identify units to fight a rearguard action to allow the bulk of the Army to pull back, and regroup.[4]

At 19:00 Gamelin received a telegram to report back to Vincennes. He arrived at 19:45:

> When I arrived, I found Gen. Weygand in conversation with officers of my staff, who were explaining the situation. I took him into my private office. He told me that that the President of the Council, M. Paul Reynaud had told him to make himself acquainted with the events . . . we remained together for nearly an hour. Before my arrival my officers had shown him my instructions of the morning which I had sent to them

> without delay. He declared he was in agreement with my conception. We envisioned together the general development of the battle . . . As he left he said to me ' you know that Paul Reynaud does not like you?' I replied simply 'I know' . . . at 8:15 pm without any previous notice from anyone, I received a letter from M. Paul Reynaud acting in the capacity of President of the Council, Minister of National Defence and War.

This told Gamelin he had been sacked. The letter was countersigned by Pétain. Weygand, Pétain and Reynaud had met in secret between 18:15 and 19:00 when the order to sack Gamelin had been agreed and issued. It read:

> First Decree.
> Article 1.
> General Weygand has been named as Chief of Staff of National Defence in replacement of General Gamelin and as commander in chief of all forces in the theatres of operations.
> Article 2.
> The President of the Council charges the Minister of National Defence to execute this order and to publish this in the Official Journal of the French Republic.
> Second Decree.
> Article 1.
> The post of commander in chief of land forces is suppressed.
> Article 2.
> The President of the Council charges the Minister of National Defence to execute this order and to publish this in the Official Journal of the French Republic.

At 21:45 Gamelin telephoned Weygand's aide-des-camp, *Commandant* Gasser, telling him, he would hand over command at 09:00 the following day.[5]

Gamelin's thinking was theoretically sound: regroup remaining armour as a strategic reserve, proposing a plan to pinch off the German armoured spearhead with simultaneous British and French attacks from both north and south, and if that failed to fall back on a new defensive line along the Somme. Gamelin, an enemy of Weygand, Reynaud and others was sacrified as, to quote W. S. Gilbert, ' A victim had to be found.' Gamelin became the scapegoat for Allied failure. Vichy, German and British propaganda has made much of Gamelin being an abject failure: yet the facts of the matter don't support this judgment. Be that as it may, Gamelin's career was over, he was disgraced, and is blamed for the defeat of France. As with Emmanuel

Comte de Grouchy in 1815, despite all the available facts, both men are 'damned' for the defeat of France. Both men are more sinned against than sinners.

Away from the politics in Paris, having broken through at Sedan and the Gembloux Gap, Guderian and Rommel were heading for the English Channel with all speed. Gamelin's objective, during what would be his last day in command, was to get the BEF, the Belgian and the French armies to the Somme before the Wehrmacht closed its trap, encircling and cutting off the Allied armies from France. His goal was to thrust a force south and link up with divisions being sent north from the south of France along with additional armour and aircraft. He hoped to cut off the panzers from their lines of communication and, importantly, the German infantry. After a short meeting, Georges ordered Air Marshal Barratt and General Têtu to employ every possible means to destroy the German lines of communication.[6]

To lead the thrust north in support of *3e Groupement des Armée,* as planned by Gamelin in *Instruction Personelle no. 12.* the Queen's Bays and other units from the BEF were ordered to the Somme.[7] Time was of the essence to spring the trap and cut off the Panzers, but time was one luxury the Allies did not have. The plan relied heavily on inter-Allied co-operation which was in desperately short supply. Lord Gort's objective was to evacuate the BEF from Dunkirk before it became encircled. For Georges, the priority was the counter-attack and creating the second line of defence along the Somme. Without the French army to cover the BEF, the evacuation would be impossible: likewise, the French needed the BEF as rearguard. It was an impossible situation.

Montgomery ordered his troops to fall back on Lille. 'Immense columns of refugees in lamentable condition,' wrote Montgomery's liaison officer, blocked the roads: 'the spectacle of little children, abandoned and on their own was appalling', having been separated from their parents. He continues: 'these vast columns blocked all the roads, the disorder was indescribable'.[8]

To buy time to prepare a counter-attack, the French GQG hoped to use the river Escaut as a new anti-tank barrier and stop the Germans there. Prioux with the *Corps de Cavalerie* at 05:00 received an order from Blanchard timed at 23:50 from the previous night, in response to an order from Georges at 20:56, outlining he was to engage the Wehrmacht in the direction of Cambrai and St Quentin:

> At this moment, the 2e and 3e DLM were still moving towards the Mastaing-Fressain area. Neither of the two tank brigades had been

able to be recovered; they were fighting . . . The 1re DLM was engaged near the Mormal forest. All these units had been moving and fighting without rest for 9 days. General Prioux, therefore considering that this mission was impossible to accomplish, at least immediately, went personally to General Billotte, then to General Blanchard. He returned at 07:45 carrying an order from the *1re Armée* ordering the Cavalry Corps to regroup (1re, 2e and 3e DLM) between Douai and Arras, with cover on the Scarpe, with a view to a counter-attack later in the direction of St Quentin. Movement orders are issued immediately:

- the 1re DLM to go to the Villers au Tertre region, covered to the south by the 1re GRDI (Colonel Preaud) established on the Sensee and the Escaut from Aubigny to Bouchain.
- the 2e DLM, which will establish a cover of *Dragons* and Artillery from Biache to Arleux.
- the 3e DLM which will establish an identical cover on the Scarpe, Arras to Biache.
- the *12e Cuirassiers* to reconnoitre and ensure Bapaume-Ecoust St Mein-Haucort and if possible Marquion are held . . . The *12e Cuirassiers* after having patrolled in the prescribed region, does not find the enemy until around 17:00 and in the Cambrai region north of Cauroir and Sains. During this time, the divisions carry out the prescribed device, but the troops are exhausted and fall asleep at the small posts: the energy alone of the cadres keeps them still in a fighting state.[9]

By the time the order was issued, it was impossible for the 1re DLM to withdraw. The unit was still in action at Mormal.

Elsewhere, the 1re DIM (comprising the 43e *Régiment d'Infanterie de Forteresse* [RIF] from Lille, the 110e RIF from Dunkirk, the 1re RIF from Cambrai and the 15e and 215e from Douai: hence the Northern Division) had been given the mission of preventing the Germans from crossing the Escaut between Bruay sur l'Escaut and Saint-Amand-les-Eaux, alongside the local soldiers from the *54e* RIF which were to occupy the blockhouses along the river. At Fresnes-sur-Escaut, at 17:00, the Engineers blew up the Sarteau bridge. Giraud noted that the attack by the Northern Division at 09:00 had failed, and encirclement by the enemy continued. Panzers were spotted at 10:00 north of Cambrai with other motorised elements of the Wehrmacht. Other elements of the Wehrmacht encircled Havrintcourt, 10km south of Cambrai where they crossed the canal at Crevecoeur and Bantouzelle, surrounding Cambrai from the north and south. By 16:00 German forces were observed heading to Arras and an hour later Cambrai was invested.[10]

At Cerfontaine, the 1re DCR faced an attack from the direction of Assevent, which was being defended by the *31e Dragon Portés*, the 34e RIF and 158e RI. The French armour came under artillery fire from German 105mm guns as well as air attack. Rifle shots and machine-gun fire continued all night along the banks of the Sambre in a desperate bid to hold back the German steam roller.[11]

Close by in the Forest of Mormal to help the French infantry, the French General Staff ordered an air attack be launched from the airfield at Berck. This is where a naval aviation squadron was located with its brand-new Loire-Nieuport bombers. The Loire-Nieuport LN 411 was an equivalent of the Stuka, a light bomber capable of dive-bombing with up to 500kg of bombs. Built from 1938, France had only about eighty aircraft of this type, while in May 1940 Germany had 316 operational Stukas. At 18:15, twenty aircraft took off for Berlaimont, south of Maubeuge. Flying in low so as not to be spotted by enemy aircraft, without escort from fighters as protection the dive bombers were incredibly vulnerable from air attack. Over their target by 19:30, the planes bombed the area of the Berlaimont bridge where Panzers were concentrated. Baudouin d'Edesse, an officer at the Berck base, saw the survivors of the raid return:

> The aircraft filled with holes like common sieves, spitting oil, oozing gasoline, smoking engines, shredded tail planes . . . On the ground we understood, silently we count those who land . . . With a heavy heart, we hope that the others have only been delayed, that they have lost their way, that they will soon arrive. Twenty left, only ten came back.

German anti-aircraft guns shot down ten French aircraft either over Berlaimont during the attack or on the way back. Three pilots were killed and six taken prisoner. The ten remaining aircraft were repaired and the squadron moved to Marck-en-Calais.[12]

Away from the Escaut, having regrouped during the 18th, the 4e DCR, with 150 tanks, made a second offensive thrust against the Germans. Moving from Laon, crossing the river Serre at Crécy-sur-Serre and Mortiers. The bridges were taken by 09:00. The goal was to hold the bridges then thrust north to Cambrai. Lacking infantry and anti-tank guns, the objective was unattainable, as de Gaulle's adjutant notes:

> The bulk of the enemy forces, instead of directing towards Paris, marched from East to West, following the Marles-La Fère axis. The 4e DCR. was given the mission to attack it in its flank, following the general direction LAON – CRECY-sur-SERRE – PARGNY les BOIS.

The operation was carried out by three groups, made up respectively from West to East by the SOMUA tanks of the 3e *Cuirassiers*, the 6e and 8e Demi-brigades whose objectives were:

1. Ruisseau de CHERY les POUILLY – Moulin de BARENTON,
2. Ponts de la Serre de CRECY à MORTTIERS,
3. Possibly, the line MONTIGNY sur CRECY – PARGNY les BOIS, southern edge of the wood of PARGNY.

Coverage is provided by the 10e *Cuirassiers* Reconnaissance Regiment (under the orders of Lieutenant Colonel HAM) and by two companies of the 4e BCP. who occupied CHAMBRY and guarded the bridges over the BARENTON stream, the other companies in reserve.

The tanks reached the SERRE line, but could not pass it. They were subjected to very well-aimed and lethal fire from anti-tank weapons. The bridges over the river are mined. In the early morning, an enemy reconnaissance plane flew over the tanks. From then on, the bombings by plane, which operated in a dive, followed one another without interruption. The tanks suffered little from this, but the result was a dispersion that made it difficult to command the units.

Colonel de Gaulle decided to regroup the Division south-east of Laon in the region of Laval, Montchalons, Vorges and Chamouille.

Throughout the day, light enemy elements, flank-guards of the columns which, on the edge of the SERRE, marched towards the West, attacked the flank and rear of the Division. The 4e BCP, surrounded in CHAMBRY, disengaged with great difficulty with the help of the 10e *Cuirassiers*. During the night of the 19 to the 20 enemy pressure increased in the north and east.

Colonel de Gaulle decided to transfer the Division to the south of the Aisne in the area: JONCHERY, MURVILLE, ARCIE le PONSART, FAVEROLLES, using the corridors of URCEL – CHAVIGNON, VAILLY – BRAISNE and that of BRUYERE – VANDRESSE – FISMES. On 10e *Cuirassiers* reinforced by a battalion of R-35 tanks covered the movement. Due to the many enemy infiltrations, each unit had to cover itself on its own account and sustain a series of skirmishes. It is a veritable guerrilla war in which the spirit of initiative and thoughtful courage prevails. The units of the Train were attacked on the Craonne plateau and tested important doors in terms of personnel and equipment. The troops crossed the Aisne in good conditions during the morning. The disengagement of the rearguard, surrounded at Festieux, was extremely painful. The Colonel ordered the doctors to remain at the bedside of the many wounded and, under the protection of the tanks, he tried to make a sortie, succeeded in jostling the enemy and joining the AISNE in the afternoon of 20 May. On May 19 at 12:00., on May 10e *Cuirassiers* still had 35 AMD. He had only 11 left on the evening of May 20.

The fighting in the region of Laon on 17 and 18 May caused the Division great losses in equipment. But the 4e DCR. also inflicted very heavy damage on the enemy, it stopped its advance in the direction of the S.W., slowed down its march towards the west and allowed the French troops to establish themselves firmly on the line of the AISNE.[13]

An officer from the 24e BCC adds that in the aftermath of the attack:

On 20 May, it is not the same. Quartered in the wood of Lavergny, on the 24e BCC was bombed: two killed and two wounded.

Around 10:00, the battalion disengaged from the wood and encountered a column of German cavalry which was repulsed with heavy losses. At 11:00., it received the order to withdraw, while forming three delay jams at Aubigny, Corbeny and Ville-au-Bois. Shortly after, the 3rd company was ordered to clear the Hurtebise farm where a column of cars was blocked by the enemy. Two tanks of the 3rd company, then the 1st company as a whole, attacked the German anti-tank defences and cleared a large part of the column. A tank was destroyed during this operation, its crew missing. The withdrawal was carried out in difficult conditions, with the equipment, which had been badly tested, being destroyed or scuttled. According to reports, ten to eleven tanks were destroyed or abandoned, four of which were able to be repaired.

D'Astier had sent up some air cover for de Gaulle: the focus was, however, on the Forest of Mormal, rather than where de Gaulle was. So parlous was the state of French communications, d'Astier only learned of de Gaulle's difficulties around 16:00, and at 17:00, eight hours after his advance had been stopped by the Luftwaffe, GC III/1 and II/2 were ordered to put up fighter cover. Expert handling of the situation by the Luftwaffe prevented the French fighters interdicting the Stukas.

Air superiority was starting to take a heavy toll on the French army's ability to move during daylight hours and take the offensive. Arras was blitzed by eighteen Dornier bombers. Two trains crowded with civilians were destroyed. This raid caused 217 casualties. At Cambrai, the railway station was targeted: this raid was to 'soften up' the area before Rommel's Panzers arrived. Guderian's mission was to rush to the English Channel to cut the Allied system in two and isolate 1.1 million French, Belgian and British soldiers north of the Somme. His armoured division was the tip of the 'coup de faux', the strategy devised by von Manstein to destroy the main Allied armies in northern France before turning on France. Driving across the Somme battlefield of 14/18, and met no resistance. Cambrai fell with almost no resistance. Blanchard and Billotte still hoped to mount some form of counter-attack. At 22:00

Prioux received orders that he was continue his move to Arras and he was to support the BEF which was preparing to attack at Arras during the course of 20 May.[14]

Yet it was undeniable that as the day closed, the *1re Armée* had been pushed out of the Mormal forest, but a hopefully secure stop line had been created along the banks of the Escaut Canal and the river Sensee to Arras, which was held by the BEF and also the line of the river Scarpe. The best of the French army were trapped in the north of France and Belgium. Whitehall had ordered the RAF to leave France, the fighters operating from the south coast. Four hundred aircraft, mostly airframes on the ground, had been lost. The air war was now decisively lost as Dowding marshalled his forces for home defence, believing that France had fallen, and soon Hitler would be turning his attention to the invasion of England. Over 18–20 May, the French fighter force had flown around 300 sorties a day, with just 250 aircraft on average in service. By the morning of 20 May just 200 fighters were operational.[15]

Chapter 17

20 MAY 1940

On Monday morning, 20 May in Whitehall at 07:00, Churchill chaired the War Cabinet. Gamelin's withdrawal to the Somme had met with agreement in Whitehall, and would take seven to ten days to achieve. It was hoped to occupy Arras and that the Belgian Army would follow the BEF behind the Somme along with the French. Lord Gort and General Billotte had agreed to Gamelin's thinking the previous night, Gort agreeing the BEF would make a stand.[1]

Across the Channel, Weygand returned to Vincennes at 08:30, and after a terse meeting with Gamelin, assumed command. Charles Huntziger, Commander of the Second Army, wrote, 'Weygand has replaced Gamelin. A wave of relief passes through the whole army.'[2] Huntizger, like many senior army officers, viewed leftist parties with profound mistrust, fearing that the Popular Front's reforms might undermine discipline or lead to revolutionary chaos. While not inherently fascist during the 1930s, Huntziger's actions as part of the Vichy regime – such as signing anti-Semitic statutes – suggest a mindset that valued obedience to authority, stability and hierarchical order above democratic ideology. Writing as he did, Huntziger reflected the French Army's mistrust of Gamelin because of support for and by the left-leaning government, and for his loyalty to the Republic: Huntziger was among the professional elite who were more associated with the traditional, conservative officer corps, which became increasingly detached from the ideals of the Third Republic. For Huntizger, and most of his contemporaries, Gamelin could do nothing right.

Gamelin before he left Vincennes informed Weygand of his plan to attack the Panzer columns from the north and south simultaneously as outlined in his *Instruction Personelle no. 12* and to prepare a second defensive line along the Somme. Weygand cancelled the order and in his order of the day announced that morning: 'the coming battle will have us at a numerical inferiority of two against five. The remains of our army will be further weakened by the loss of an enormous amount of irreplaceable material due to the complete absence of reserves.'[3]

Despite having being handed a comprehensive dossier by Gamelin on the current situation, Weygand disregarded everything his predecessor had prepared, and embarked on a personal tour of the front line before issuing orders: Weygand, in failing to 'pick up' where Gamelin left off, handed the Wehrmacht the initiative as our companion volume *The Fall of France* explores in depth.

Away from Paris, in Maubeuge, at dawn German 105mm and 210mm howitzers began a massive bombardment. Along the barricades facing Assevent, the 158e RI was mown down. Air attacks increased and at 16:00 German infantry were on the outskirts of the town. The remaining French tanks fought on as best they could:

> The situation was totally desperate. Lieutenant Bailby of the 39e and Lieutenant Goupil of the same battalion are killed. Commander Boullier is seriously wounded. Lieutenant Gontrand of the 6e battalion is seriously wounded. The tanks that we had left were more or less disabled: guns had been dismounted, the periscopes broken, turrets were perforated: the running gear of many was more or less in ruins, yet other tanks had received a hundred 37mm shells without any shots piercing the armour. The crews are exhausted, wounded or killed. Ammunition and gasoline are running out. It is obvious that we can no longer make any effort.[4]

The few remaining tanks and men from the 158e RI stubbornly clung on. At 21:00 the order to retreat was given. What remained of the 1re DCR fell back to Maubeuge.[5]

Amiens had fallen around 09:00 to the 1st Panzer Division: it covered 110km in a single day, starting to move north and towards the port of Boulogne-sur-mer. The 2nd Panzer Division in the wake of successive air raids took Abbeville at 08:30. In the raids 2,500 civilians were killed, and 850 Abbeville residents and French, Belgian and Dutch refugees were trapped in the streets of the city. At the time it was believed that 75 per cent of the city was destroyed.

That morning, every bomber that could be gotten into the air, was. At 11:00 ten Leo 45s and fourteen Breguet 693s were ordered to attack the panzer columns supported by *6e Groupement*: in the first wave six Leo 45s were lost, and the remaining forty aircraft were all so badly damaged as to be unusable. Of the Breguets, none returned. That evening *9e Groupement* dropped 30 tonnes of bombs on the halted German columns. Fourteen Amiot 143s delivered 10 tonnes of bombs in like manner. Forty-eight sorties had been flown that day.[6]

To the south and west of Arras, German panzers operated freely. As they headed north to Boulogne, they could cut off the Arras garrison. To the west of the strongpoint, nothing was in place to even slow the Panzers. Gort and Billotte had met on night of the 18th and again on 19 May to discuss the attack planned by Gamelin – and supported by Weygand – to thrust south, cut off the German Panzers from its infantry, and having done so, withdraw to the Somme, thus escaping from the German trap. One observer recorded 'the intention of Gort was to attack in the environs of Arras in the direction of Bapaume' using the 5th and 51st Division and armour. The plan agreed between the BEF and the French GQG was for a combined force under Major General Harold Franklyn, consisting of the British 5th and 50th Divisions, supported by the 1st Army Tank Brigade and the *Corps de Cavalerie,* to attack southward from the old First World War battlefields of Vimy Ridge and Arras. General Prioux received:

> At 09:30 am, intelligence arrives one after another from the DLM discovery and observatories, all reporting enemy movements from Cambrai to Arras (landings at Tilloy and Monchy-le-Preux, threats to Athies) and even artillery fire presenting itself as preparations for an attack on the right of the Cavalry Corps, which is at this moment completely in the air.
>
> In order to escape this threat, General Prioux then decides to reach the enemy's wing and attack it in turn on its western flank. He therefore orders the DLM to disengage under the protection of the few tanks in the 3e DLM which have just arrived (the tanks of the *2e* DLM have still not joined) and to move to the West and South of Arras while maintaining the link, in this town, with the British Battalion which occupies it.
>
> HQ moves to Vimy, but at 10:50 a liaison officer of the *1re Armée* brought the order to suspend this movement, the DLM were to remain in place to maintain the line of the Scarpe in liaison with the British who were due to arrive in the Arras region. The counter-order reached the divisions before the start of the execution of the previous order.
>
> The search for intelligence is however actively continued in liaison with the 12th British Lancers. It results in the day's intelligence given by the 8th and 12th *Cuirassiers,* that German light tanks and other troops held Cambrai, that others troops were at the Dury crossroads, and that movements have taken place on the Cambrai-Arras road, movements that the DLM artillery had violently bombarded. It seems that the enemy is guarding itself with small elements facing north to protect its SE-NW movement . . . Aviation activities, null.

At 21:00 the order was given to the 3rd DLM to relieve the British Franklin Group.[7]

Blanchard, and inter alia Georges and Billotte, was informed at 20:00hrs 'the counter-attack of the British has rolled up' at Arras, meaning it had failed.[8]

Chapter 18

21 MAY 1940

At 02:00 on 21 May, the Wehrmacht was standing on the Channel coast. Manstein's goal to cut off the Allied armies from France had been achieved. If Weygand was to save the situation he had to attack, and attack soon, before the breach in the Allied lines could be flooded with infantry to sure up the narrow corridor created by the Panzers and motorised infantry. The arrival of the Wehrmacht on the coast placed the Allied armies in a serious, but not yet hopeless position. Everything rested on Weygand and as history would show he was the wrong man at the wrong time as the new commander-in-chief. The Panzers had advanced so rapidly that they could be encircled and neutralised if the Allies took the initiative. A distance of perhaps 30km separated Arras from the French forces along Somme.[1]

An officer with Montgomery's staff noted 'the news is very bad. The Germans are at Amiens and also Arras. General Weygand has replaced General Gamelin. Mandel, the interior minister, says the situation is very grave but not yet desperate.'[2] In Paris, Weygand was still pressing ahead with getting the encircled French and Allied armies out of Flanders: he still hoped to withdraw to the coast, and evacuate the army by sea and land the forces behind the Somme. On discussing the plans with the navy, Admiral Darlan told Weygand at 12:15 that: 'I have already informed the general-in-chief that evacuation by sea would be doomed to disaster and that it is surely less risky to try to resupply their units resisting the enemy than to evacuate them.'

Why Darlan refused to even discuss this is lost to history, but the British Admiralty had told Gamelin the same 48 hours earlier: it was impossible to evacuate the BEF and French *1re Groupement des Armée* by sea and then land them back in France on the Somme. History tells us they were wrong: for Darlan what mattered was fortifying the Channel ports, enabling the French army to be resupplied. Weygand agreed with the admiral, the goal was to make Boulogne, Calais, Dieppe and Dunkirk into defended perimeters. When pressed on the issue, Darlan argued that the French navy could, however, re-supply the BEF, French and Belgian forces. Weygand was between a rock and a hard place. Aware that the Wehrmacht would not stop at occupying Belgium and the Netherlands and that France would be the next target, just over 24 hours after he had canceled Gamelin's orders to fall back and form a new defensive line, Weygand announced he to hold the Wehrmacht on the Somme, just as Gamelin had.[3] To do so, Weygand rescinded Gamelin's orders for reserves to move up from the south and east of France to link with what could be saved from Belgium in a move to the Somme and more intensive air cover from the RAF and French. In canceling and then rescinding his cancellation order, Weygand had cascaded chaos into Gamelin's timetable to get the reserves to the front. Trains moving soldiers had been stopped and the men were back on trains heading away from Paris. Weygand's dithering had delayed the arrived of hundreds of thousands of reinforcements, munitions, tanks and aircraft at the front by 48 to 72 hours. Yet history says Gamelin was incompetent![4] Howard Vyse, acting as liaison between Weygand and Lord Gort, detailed his own discussions over the previous two days since Gamelin had proposed the ambitious amphibious lifting of the Allied forces to the Somme. The War Office in Whitehall said that yes it was possible to re-supply the Allied forces: they would need to requisition ships sufficient to transport 250,000 rations, and would be directed by Vice-Admiral Dover. Whitehall agreed in principle and left the detail to the Admirals of Dover and Dunkirk.[5]

This was a brief moment of Allied co-operation on future strategy: defend the coastal ports whilst French reserves came north. A translated cypher – a telegram – from the BEF GHQ arrived with General Georges at 14:25, two hours after it had arrived with the French GQG. The Belgians were holding the Terneuzen canal at Gand and the line of the Escaut, supported by the BEF. The *1re Armée* had been pushed back by the Germans along the line of the Escaut, at Cambrai, Sensee, Scarpe and Arras – the entire front in the northern sector under Georges was collapsing. The Wehrmacht was headed in the direction of Abbeville, Hesdin and St-Pol. Georges was still hoping to send his armour forward at Cambrai as planned with the BEF.[6]

In the suburbs of Maubeuge, the shattered 1re DCR came under German artillery fire around 10:00, of an intensity that was reminiscent of 14/18 according to one officer who survived it:

> A violent barrage began and the Germans launch an assault. They arrive from all sides preceded by a hail of bullets . . . the Germans arrived in front of the HQ, Colonel Mariage and I are captured. He asks for an officer to recommend his soldiers tend to the wounded who are in the cellars . . . we are grouped together, we are taken to Maubeuge, everything there was burnt or demolished, our house seemed intact to me.[7]

With Maubeuge falling, the *9e Armée* fell back. The 1re DCR, the pride of the French army, ceased to exist.

Rommel was hoping to cross the river Scarpe at Aubigny-en-Artois with his 7th Panzer Division. So rapid had been his advance, his armour had pulled away from the SS Totenkopf motorised division and his infantry. It was precisely for this reason the British and French decided to counter-attack in the early afternoon. Georges ordered Air Marshal Barratt and General Têtu that the principal effort of the French bomber force for the day was to knock out Rommel's Panzers. At midday, twelve Breguet 693s from *10e Groupement* were in the air: none returned to base. French air operations were increasingly suicide missions.[8] The bombers achieved almost nothing impactful on the battlefield which was increasingly dominated by the Luftwaffe, as an officer serving under General René Prioux recounts:

> The relief of the 3e DLM by British elements along the line Biache to Arras only took place from 06:00 instead of 01:00. The 3e DLM regrouped to the west of Arras, holding the Scarpe, from Duisans to Arras, where it detaches itself from the British who were placed outside the western suburbs of the city.
>
> At 08:30 the commander of the *Corps de Cavalerie* requested the 1re DLM to bring a group of SOMUA tanks in reserve of CC in the West wood of Viny.
>
> The British having decided to mount during the afternoon of the 21st an operation supported by tanks in the direction of Bapaume, the General Commanding the CC ordered the 3e DLM (operations order No. 17) to cover the flank of the British army on the Warlus-Hindecourt-Boiry-Hamelincout axis. It will be reinforced by the tanks of Group 515. The *76e regiment d'artillerie* and 2 Groups of the *329e regiment d'artillerie* deployed in the Farbus-Vollerval-Ecurie-Roclincourt region will support this attack.
>
> From 15:00 the British advanced to the outskirts of Arras; the 3e DLM on the contrary encountered serious resistance. Despite this they seized a battery of German 105mm at the Agnez cemetery and cleared the south-west outskirts of Arras. The enemy reacted with heavy tanks and artillery fire at Berneville; it's very numerous air

> force bombarded, without stopping Etrun, Anzin, Vimy and the western outskirts of Arras. At the end of the day, the line reached by the Franco-British forces passes through Agenx-Warlus-Dainville-Beaurains-Tilloy. The English tanks have suffered many losses and are retreating. Liaison activities are carried out with the headquarters of the Franklyn group in Viny to organise the resumption of the attack on the morning of 22 May.[9]

At Arras, the German infantry found themselves face to face with an offensive of eighty-eight British tanks in the vicinity of Achicourt. General Franklyn had assembled the force at Vimy Ridge during the course of the 20th to attack the following morning. The British armour comprised sixteen Matilda Mk IIs, fifty-eight Mk Is armed with only machine guns, and twelve other light armoured vehicles. As the French officer notes, seventy SOMUA from the 2e and 3e DLM joined the attack further west towards Dainville. The British armour was massed to the right of the French and debouched at 14:00 on the Saint-Pol to Arras Road. At 16:00 Rommel turned his Panzer division around to support his beleaguered infantry. Encountering strong German resistance, 88mm flak used as anti-tank guns, and supported by Stukas, the action stalled by 17:45. At nightfall the British armour retreated to its starting position under considerable attack by the Luftwaffe at Beaurains and Duisans.[10] Our French officer again:

> The 1re DLM which sent a new detachment towards Valenciennes and Bernerain in order to supply the Group of Colonel Cansons, assumed at Quesnoy, could not establish liaison with him. Its Somua tanks arrived at Vimy around 16:00.
>
> The *2e* DLM was attacked at the end of the day towards Arieux and Tortequenne; in the face of its resistance the enemy did not continue its pressure.
>
> The British and French reconnaissance patrols were very active throughout the day, and the rear HQ of the CC stationed at Berincout, reported:
>
> 09:45: Willunan, Linzeux, Flers occupied by the enemy.
> 11:00: Motorised column of about 3 squadrons, tanks, 8 pieces of 77mm at Vielhesdin.
> 12:20: German column at Montreuil
> 13:50L Avesnes le Comte occupied by the enemy.
> 15:55: large motorised column between Doullens and Auxy-le-Chateau.
> 18:25: Aubenecheul and Paillencourt abandoned by the enemy.

This information is all passed on to the 1re DLM; the enemy clearly continues to seek envelopment from the West.

The night of May 21-22 marks the end of all hope of an immediate breakthrough in the direction of Arras-Cambrai for the CC. In fact, General Franklyn made it known at 03:00 in the morning that by order of the GHQ all English offensive action south of the Scarpe was to be stopped. The CC was ordered to contain the enemy: facing south, from Arleux to Arras with the 2e and 3e DLM and cover the flank of the *1re Armée* facing west with the 1re DLM.[11]

As the French officer notes, early on the following morning, a combined British-French armour thrust was to be made to Scarpe and Mont St-Eloi. However, Franklyn felt he was about to be outflanked and the BEF cut off, and ordered his armour to fall back to Lens.[12] Only twenty-eight British tanks out of the eighty-eight engaged managed to leave the battlefield: the Mk 1s were hopelessly outclassed. The French lost twenty tanks in comparison. Without air support, and with insufficient infantry and artillery, the offensive was a failure.[13] Faced with the unprecedented harshness of the fighting, particularly around Arras, some German units gave in to the temptation of reprisals: they took revenge on civilians in the villages of the Arrageois. In Mercatel, six civilians were shot dead by the SS. In Simencourt, five civilians were killed and their homes burned to the ground. In Habarcq, a Belgian refugee and his 17-year-old daughter were shot. These were only the beginnings of the reprisals in the region.[14]

Around midday, Weygand left Paris by plane to inspect the front. Landing in Calais, he headed to meet the King of Belgium who was waiting to see him at the burgomaster's office at Ypres at 15:30. Here he met General Billotte, Admiral Abrial, and Admiral of the Fleet Sir Roger Keyes, Chief of the British Mission to the King of the Belgians. Unfortunately, Lord Gort was not present. By the time Gort arrived at 20:00, Weygand had left. Billotte explained his commander's thinking:

to counter-attack from the north and south in order to cut the enemy forces;

to withdraw the Belgian Army back of the Yser in order to maintain contact with British-French forces; and

to hold on to the northern ports at all costs because, if evacuation became necessary, they would be needed to salvage the heavy equipment. And, at any rate, the longer the German forces were held in Flanders, the longer they would be delayed in starting the offensive against the Somme front, which it was now evident the Germans were preparing to launch.[15]

Fate was decidedly not on the side of the French: when General Billotte left this meeting by car, he was the victim of a road accident in Locre, near Bailleul. He died two days later. 'It was really too many misfortunes at once,' Weygand commented, 20 years later in a televised testimony.[16]

Chapter 19

THE BATTLE OF ARRAS

The German army had successfully broken through the Ardennes and was driving towards the French ports, creating a corridor across northern France. This split the Allied forces, with a large portion of the French army and some British forces trapped in a pocket in Artois and Flanders.

In the Rouen area, the rear-area troops of the BEF were preparing to move north: the idea was to close off the German armour before the infantry could arrive. The Queen's Bays had already been sent to support the French on the Somme. The Queen's Royal Lancers, as well as the 4th Battalion of the Borders Regiment and 10th Anti-Tank Artillery Regiment were to move up to the Somme from Saint Pol. Brigaded with the 10th Hussars, lacking auxiliary support elements from the Royal Logistics Corps and Royal Engineers, the tanks had to travel 60km. They linked up with the Queen's Bays on the morning of 23 May; it took 20 hours to move the distance because of the narrow roads, encumbered with fleeing refugees and abandoned cars and carts.[1]

Further north, at Mont-Saint-Eloi, French armour was preparing to attack Cambrai; this time with air support. Despite the attack being checked, the French were not prepared to lose heart and fall back. During a lull in the fighting, the French organised themselves to block the German advance at Mont-Saint-Eloi, and General Prioux deployed his forces as follows:

> Facing South.
> The 2nd DLM, which was attacked on the 21st at nightfall, in the Tortequenne region, held its ground without major losses on the Biaches-Arleux line. It was to be relieved during the night of the 22nd or 23rd May by the 5ᵉ DINA.

The 3e DLM withdrew at daybreak to the Dainville-Maroeuik line, then relieved by an English brigade; it was placed in reserve. HQ Mericourt. The Dragon Portés were at the Bois-Bernard at the end of the day under the orders of Colonel Pimon (1re DLM). Its artillery remained in the Reclincourt-Ecurie region to support the 40th British Division.

Facing West.
The General Commandant of the CC has been worried since the day before about enemy movements to the West since the day before about enemy movements to the West of Arras towards Saint Pol and Bethune. On the 21st, he brought Colonel Puinon of the 1re DLM to Vimy, with a group of SOMUA tanks from the *18e Dragons* which were deployed from the morning of the 22nd to the South and North of Neuville St Waast, facing the West – a group of *329e Regiment d'Artillerie* was attached. The 1re DLM which occupies the Sensee receives around 07:00 the order to move to the ACQ region. This movement will be very slowed down by violent long-term bombardments by German aircraft and by the congestion of the roads. From 09:00, information indicates that the enemy is advancing to the West of Arras. Tanks at Aubigny at 09:00 – armoured patrols at Lilliers at 10:45 – Tanks at Duisnas, Avesnes, Agnez, Montennescourt, Infantry at Etrun, Acq, Bray.[2]

As the morning of 22 May drew on, General Prioux became increasingly concerned about the operations of the Wehrmacht:

the *1re Armée* was informed of all these movements; unable to reinforce the CC with reserve troops, it placed the British forces to the West of Arleux, Corbemen and Noyelles under the orders of General Prioux at 14:00 . . . At 14:00 an enemy attack is reported from Avesnes towards Mont St Eloi. Colonel Pinon receives the order to execute a tank counter-attack . . . the action seems difficult; it will be brilliantly carried out around 17:00, thanks to the arrival of the *4e Dragon Portés* under the orders of Commander Amarnich, preceded by the tanks, supported by the Group of the 329e RA and by the 74e RA which without waiting for orders puts itself in battery, Mont St Eloi was taken the by the *4e Dragon Portés* destroying several enemy tanks and taking 150 prisoners, including 4 officers and 1 Colonel. At 19:00 the 1re DLM occupied Bray-Mont St Eloy-Garency-Souchez . . . we learned that enemy tanks had passed through Gou-en-Gohelle. To face this threat, Colonel Leyer – *12e Cuirassiers* – and the 3e DLM received the order to block the enemy movement in direction of Lens the next day by establishing themselves on the Souhcez-Noeux les Mines – Bethine road (Special Order No. 76, at 22:00).[3]

The German divisions were halted by Prioux's audacious attack and suffered heavy losses: 700 men killed or wounded in one afternoon and about 20 tanks destroyed. In Berlin the General Staff, shocked by the French counter-attack, became feverish and imagined that another counter-attack was possible. Hitler ordered the advance of the Panzers to be halted.

Unbelievably Georges knew nothing of what Billotte had agreed: Weygand had learned of the success of the BEF at Arras at 21:15, and that the battle was developing favourably, from a cypher sent six hours earlier. Georges only learned this on 22 May at 17:40: that it had taken over 20 hours to send Georges' vital information speaks of the colossally slow and cumbersome French system of communication.[4]

Be that as it may, the French forces in the Ardennes were now separated from the main force in Belgium and north France. Weygand never seems to have thought of how to react to the events in the Ardennes, his concern being Belgium, leaving the French armies at Sedan to cope they best they could with little instruction from Paris.

The Allied counter-attack at Arras was intended to relieve pressure on the forces trapped in the Flanders pocket and disrupt the German advance. The attack was a tactical success for the Allies, but it ultimately failed to achieve its strategic objectives. The Allied forces were forced to withdraw to avoid being encircled. The counter-attacks at Arras and Cambrai were failures, but their moral impact on the German high-command was significant. It caused the Wehrmacht to pause the advance: the fear was the Allies could attack again, and cut off the Panzers from their lines of communication. The Panzers were again ordered to stop. The attack at Cambrai, although failing, gained a few hours of respite which allowed the British to send troops from England to the ports of Boulogne, Calais and Dunkirk to reinforce the defences. The first troops from England arrived on the evening of 22 May and began to entrench themselves for the coming battle. That evening, thirty-two sorties were flown dropping 19 tonnes of bombs onto the German troops by *9e Groupement* in the immediate vicinity of Prioux's men. *10e Groupement* flew thirteen sorties dropping 11 tonnes of bombs. The French had intercepted Luftwaffe communications. The Stukas who had arrived as reinforcements in the skies over Cambrai were awaited by eighteen French Dewoitine fighter planes, and eleven German planes were shot down.[5]

The German columns at Peronne and Bapaume were bombed that night to prevent or at least slow an envelopment at Saint-Pol. Twelve Glenn-Martin 167 bombers, operating for the first time since delivery from the USA as replacements for *6e Groupement*, supported by eight

Breguet 693s attacked and halted German armour. Amiot 143 groups were also in action, 24 tonnes of bombs being dropped on German targets.[6]

During the course of the day, the Wehrmacht began killing civilians and prisoners. The most notorious incident was at Saint-Venant. In the fighting around the town over the course of the previous 48 hours, the SS Totenkopf division lost 248 men. As the SS advanced towards Saint-Pol-sur-Ternoise, they began to terrorise the inhabitants and the refugees they met, on the pretext of looking for fleeing British or French soldiers. In Berles-Monchel, SS men threw grenades at a convoy of refugees and shot at the fleeing civilians. Forty-five people were killed. At Aubigny-en-Artois, the SS arrived about 09:00. Searching houses, a teenager was hanged and sixty-four men aged between 16 and 73 were taken hostage. In the afternoon, they were shot in a quarry on the outskirts of the town.[7] The war was taking a sinister turn: no one was safe.

Chapter 20

23 MAY 1940

By the early hours of 23 May the German tanks were moving again: the Allied forces around Arras were in an increasingly untenable position. The French units identified to support Weygand's counter-attack were increasingly sucked into defensive operations along the line of the Somme. If Gamelin's strategic vision of holding the Wehrmacht on the Somme was to be enacted, Arras had to be recaptured: with a toehold across the Somme, the Wehrmacht had already compromised Gamelin's plan. Unless ejected back across the river, Weygand would have to formulate a Plan C; something he was probably incapable of. In sticking doggedly with Gamelin's plan, Weygand knew that the BEF would be unable to help in any further operations; the British were retreating to Dunkirk. He had to decide if the best course of action was to allow the *1re Armée* to fall back to France or head to Dunkirk. He seemed incapable of making this judgement. Indeed, the fighting at the Channel ports by the 23rd had already reached a critical stage: Boulogne and Calais were surrounded. The French army now found itself fighting a rearguard action as it was sucked not to the Somme, but to Dunkirk by the retreating BEF.

Along the line of the Escaut the Germans crossed the Hergnies bridge but were unable to go any further due to strong resistance from the French. At Aire-sur-la-Lys, French units held out until 28 May, forcing the Germans to fight hard to cross the canals. At Arras, the British thought they could resist and entrenched themselves to block the Germans. But the Scarpe was crossed by the German 12th Infantry Division not far from Athies. At Maroeuil and Anzin-Saint-Aubin, the British defences also gave way. At Mont-Saint-Eloi, Stukas multiplied their attacks on the positions of the French, who were forced to retreat. Further north in Belgium, along the Lys, the Belgian army was still fighting and trying to block the German advance to Ghent.

The situation in Dunkirk was desperate: repeated attacks by the Luftwaffe were slowly destroying the town and making the port area increasingly untenable. The mayor of Dunkirk asked the military authorities for permission to evacuate the civilian population, but the governor refused. The land around Dunkirk was drained by a system of canals, locks and pumps: the wateringues. The day before, the locks had been opened to ensure a defensive flooding of the city: 25,000 hectares would be covered with brackish water. Dunkirk was transformed into a kind of lagoon with a depth of up to 2.4m. The flooded landscape, it was hoped, would impede the Panzers. The French Admiralty and their counterpart at Dover had given up on the plan of re-supplying the Allied armies. Whitehall told Gamelin to create a defensive perimeter around Dunkirk and to destroy bridges and hinder the approach of the Wehrmacht.[1] In an undated memo from General Ironside, he told Georges that he had full confidence in General Blanchard and that two Canadian brigades were to be sent to Calais, where they would link up the remaining armour and infantry of the BEF and head to St-Omer and Hazebrouck.[2] This was wishful thinking.

Calais was already under attack. At Cape Gris-Nez, French sailors blocked the Germans for a few hours on the road to Calais thanks to their artillery. The 10th Panzer Division mustered perhaps 14,000 men and 140 tanks. Opposing them were 3,000 British and 1,000 French soldiers and about sixty tanks. Attempting to slow down the German advance, twenty-four mostly British Mk 1 tanks were destroyed by German tanks on the outskirts of the city.

In Boulogne, the 2nd Panzer Division attacked. The defences had been bolstered by the French navy: two large destroyers, eight light ones, two subchasers, and two motor torpedo boats, all under the command of Captain Yves Urvoy de Porzamparc aboard the destroyer *Cyclone*. The previous day a Guards' brigade as well as anti-tank and anti-aircraft guns had come ashore, some of these units being engaged on the night of 22/23 May on the southern outskirts of the city, but re-embarked the following morning during the course of the battle. By late afternoon there was no longer any chance of holding Boulogne, but the efficacy of the French naval gunfire was recorded by General Guderian. At 18:00 some thirty German bombers hurled themselves at the French destroyers, seriously damaging the *Frondeur* and setting fire to the *Orage*. Yet the port held out for two more days, as did the small French fleet. Further north, elements of the BEF headed to Poperinge. They were ordered to destroy all vehicles and dispose of all belongings except a gas mask, weapon and helmet.[3]

Weygand and Georges still hoped to thrust south at Amiens. The re-formed *7e Armée* was to spearhead this attack and link with the *1re Armée*. Bombing raids were carried at Arras and Cambrai: a systematic barrage was to be dropped from the air and by artillery to cover advancing infantry and armour.[4]

Prioux was covering the southern flank of the *1re Armée*. Before dawn the *12e Cuirassiers*:

> Several hundred German infantrymen arrived in Bruay and a large detachment of medium and heavy tanks headed from Bruay-sur-Bethune. At noon with the Beaufort squadron (1 Hotchkiss platoon, 2 Somua platoons of the 3e DLM) he counter-attacked the enemy from the flank in the direction of Petit Sayns (south of Noeux-mes-Mines) – Mouchin (south of Bethune). This brilliantly conducted counter-attack surprised two infantry companies and then engaged with a line of enemy tanks; these only owed their salvation to the intervention of multiple anti-tank guns, whose infiltration to the centre and on the flanks of our own tanks forced the latter to withdraw, inflicting losses on them. The enemy, however, did not pursue. Contained by the 1re DLM, and held in check by the Meyer Group, the Germans did not worry us, until the night and the flank of the *1re Armée*, could then re-organise itself in complete safety, at least from land attacks.
>
> The 329e RA took advantage of this to regroup and carry out reconnaissance for the defence of the Canal from Pont Vendin to Meurchin. The activity of the enemy aviation was particularly intense throughout the day . . . in the evening the British seemed determined to stay in Arras, yet the *1re Armée* learns by telephone at 03:00, that the 2nd Division of General Franklyn abandons Arras and withdraws in an unknown direction. General Franklyn asked the 1re DLM not to leave its positions before 04:00 in order to cover the withdrawal of the English infantry. At 03:30 General Prioux signed an operations order re-establishing the Army's line along the Haute Deule channel and the Bassee Canal.[5]

Chapter 21

24 MAY 1940

By midnight on 23 May 1940, the Wehrmacht had effectively cut off Allied forces north of the Somme, isolating the BEF from its supply lines. As 24 May dawned Weygand was obsessed with re-taking the Amiens bridgehead and committing ever more forces to the action at Arras. Georges ordered that the bombardment by the bomber force was to be reminiscent of the bombardment of the Somme in 14/18. At the same time, *6e Groupement* was withdrawn from the front lines: 30 per cent of its pilots were dead, and 75 per cent of aircraft were lost or damaged beyond repair. Prior to the attack scheduled for the earl hours of 24 May, forty-four Amiot 143s bombed targets in the Arras, Amiens and Cambrai sector.[1] Rather than moving under cover of the bombing, at 02:00 the British armour was ordered to leave Gisors and arrived at 07:00 at Hornoy-Selincourt. At 13:15 they linked up the Borders regiment, then holding the wood d'Ailly. The mission objective was to secure Amiens.[2] Liaison officer Jacques Chenu, attached to the 5th Anti-Aircraft Brigade of the BEF reports that rather than being sent north in Belgium, he was ordered south to defend the landing ground at Glisy on the Somme and to establish their HQ at Blangy-Tronville. They were to organise anti-aircraft defences. Ordered to Blaringhem on 22 May with orders to defend the Canal de Neufosse as far as Saint Omer. The position was shored up with the arrival of two 25mm anti-tank guns and three B1 *bis* tanks from the *7e Groupement des Armees*, as well as twenty-three light tanks. The Wehrmacht attacked at 16:30, led by motorcycle units. The picket outside of Blaringhem was forced back through heavy and accurate machine-gun fire. The Wehrmacht units were reinforced by a 37mm anti-tank gun which knocked out two of the B1 *bis*.[3] One tank officer noted:

> The German infantry, heavily supported by anti-tank weapons, demonstrated a tenacity and a will to resist that deserved to serve as an example. The elements pushed back on the 24th by the columns of Girier, reformed despite their losses in the first cover they found, constantly received reinforcements probably committed at the initiative of their leaders, counter-attacked without stopping.[4]

German armour arrived at 18:30. Without engineers to blow the bridge, the canal was crossed and the French troops made POW.[5]

The previous evening Commandant Fauvelle on the staff of General Blanchard met British Major Archale. He was told that the British armour that had been defeated at Arras were to be evacuated by the Royal Navy, and would begin destroying bridges along the Deûle between Lens and Lille as they headed north. Fauvelle, in the company of Colonel Humbert, on learning that the BEF were retreating and were no longer wanting to co-operate with their French and Belgian allies, went to speak to their commanding officer, General Blanchard. Arriving at Attiches in the early morning of 24 May, Fauvell found Blanchard and his staff:

> crushed with fatigue. Most of them had not had a moment of rest for days. However, a pathetic discussion had just broken out, raised by the commander of the 3rd Army Corps, General de La Laurencie, haunted by the tragic situation of his army corps, which he was trying to free from the encirclement of Flanders.
>
> The news that we brought made us strengthen the theory that the BEF was going to re-embark at Dunkirk.
>
> It was absolutely necessary to inform General Weygand of the situation, to make contact with General Gort, to know his true intentions.
>
> If the head of the BEF no longer wanted to fight under the orders of the French, it did not matter, he only had to fight under his own. General Blanchard went without delay to General Gort's HQ. He could only speak with his chief of staff, General Pownell. The latter seemed surprised. There was, however, a certain reticence in his attitude. Blanchard hesitated no more. It was necessary to inform General Weygand of the ambiguous attitude of the British command.[6]

After meeting with Pownell, Blanchard telegrammed Weygand about the intentions of the BEF. Blanchard received news from Weygand at Vincennes with GQG at 11:15, that the BEF during the night of 23/24 May had evacuated Arras and were heading back behind the line of the Haute-Deûle canal, destroying bridges at Bethune and Pont-a-Vendin. The attack had failed.[7] On the second matter, whether the BEF was planning to 'run away', Blanchard had no reassurances. In Arras, around 02:00, the British left the city. They headed for Douai but at Saint-Laurent-Blangy bombardment by German artillery blocked their progress. By 09:00 the British had fought past the Germans. Along the line of Aube, the French *5e Corps d'Armée* supported by the 3e DLM, was due to attack along the Douai-Cambrai front in the direction of Bapaume and Péronne. At 21:00:

> Captain Marquet, liaison officer of the *1re Armée*, communicated to General Prioux an order from General Blanchard, foreseeing an offensive of the 5e CA in the direction of Douai-Cambrai, an offensive that the CC would be responsible for covering on its western flank.[8]

Prioux's tanks were to be supported by 43e DI, supported by a British brigade, which was to stand alongside the 131e RIF and elements of the 5e DINA. The concentration of forces was to be carried out overnight for an attack a dawn on the 25th.[9]

Aware of the Allied counter-thrust being assembled to cut the German line of communications, in confident mood, Weygand met with Paul Reynaud and with General Spears. Weygand pressed the BEF on their intentions about retreating from Dunkirk and future co-operation. At this point it is important to consider the exact command of the BEF with the French army. Initially deployed as we said earlier, the BEF was placed between the *7e Armée* and *1re Armée* in the sector of operations of General Gaston Billotte, commanding the *1re Groupement des Armée*. However, the British forces were not under his orders. In spite of the lessons of 14/18, an over-all command did not exist – at least not at Billotte's level. Making matters worse, Gort came under the orders of General Alphonse Georges, Commander-in-chief of the North-east Front, with this reservation, expressly written in Gort's instructions, that: '. . . If any order given by him [Georges] appears to you to imperil the British Field Force, it is agreed between the British and French governments that you should be at liberty to appeal to the British Government before executing that order.' It was only after hostilities commenced that General Billotte was personally delegated the authority to coordinate Allied operations. With little co-operation between Gort and Georges, it is hardly surprising that Gort sought to withdraw the BEF from the largest port available, Dunkirk.

In spring 1940, Dunkirk was the command post of the Commander-in-chief of the French Naval Forces of the North – in short Admiral, North – whose command extended from the Belgian frontier to and including the Cotentin Peninsula in the west. Appointed on 21 December 1939, Admiral Jean Abrial commanded the sector.

The importance of his command rested on the fact that Dunkirk constituted at the same time the southern support of the Allied Pas-de-Calais sea barrier and the interface between French naval and land frontiers. Abrial had two essential liaisons to maintain: the naval one with his British opposite number, Vice Admiral Sir Bertram H. Ramsay, Flag Officer Commanding, Dover; the other, on land, with General Henri Giraud, commanding the French *7e Armée*. With Gort falling back onto Dunkirk he became commander-in-chief of ground forces at Dunkirk. Abrial was present at key meetings and disagreements between the BEF and the French army. An eyewitness to that meeting noted that:

> The evacuation and the withdrawal of BEF raised more or less embarrassed denials from Spears, who insinuated that it is probably only a hypothesis. I remain formal, however, adding that Admiral Abrial spoke to me of the embarkation of English material already reported from the port of Dunkirk, and, adding a significant detail, the governor of Lille reported to me twenty-four hours earlier that the British soldiers were crossing the city shouting 'the war is lost.' . . . In the situation in which the 1st French Army finds itself, surrounded in Flanders, if it fights alone, without British help, the battle in the North is lost before it is begun and its inevitable capitulation in the more or less short term. I can only see two hypotheses: either try to evacuate by sea all that can be saved of the 1st French Army; or fight on the spot, provided that the BEF continues the fight on our flanks. As General Blanchard explained to me, a powerful Allied counter-offensive is still possible in the direction of Bapaume and Peronne. The German Army has suffered considerable losses.[10]

General Spears writing after the war – and this fact is important – remembers that Blanchard told Weygand and Reynaud the *1re Armée* was too weak to counter-attack, it was impossible to mount a counter-attack, and added that Blanchard felt it was appropriate to surrender as the war was lost.[11] Spears added that Blanchard sent orders cancelling the counter-attack.[12] Weygand's own order is rather ambiguous:

> The means at our disposal to hold the front of the Somme, the Ailette and the Aisne are out of proportion to those that the enemy can launch in the attack. It is not certain that we can save anything from the armies of the north.
>
> The German losses are however heavy.

German soldiers pictured by the memorial to Georges Guynemer on the promenade at Malo-les-Bains after the end of Operation Dynamo. Guynemer was a top French fighter ace with fifty-four victories at the time of his death on 11 September 1917.

A street sign on the old D16 running into Dunkirk during or just after Operation Dynamo. Note the destroyed vehicle in the background. (Historic Military Press)

A German despatch rider liaises with other troops amongst abandoned British and French vehicles and equipment near Dunkirk during Operation Dynamo. (Historic Military Press)

British troops making their way into Dunkirk as the evacuation gathers pace. According to the original caption, as 'the stream of soldiers and trucks must not be held up', a 'French marine fills in a crater caused by a German aerial bomb'. (Historic Military Press)

British troops entering Dunkirk pass the smouldering wreckage of a lorry, a small part of the debris of war that came to increasingly litter the streets of the port. (Historic Military Press)

A French soldier passes the same burning lorry that can be seen in the previous image. (Historic Military Press)

A French Army Renault UE Chenillette light tracked armoured carrier is pictured having been abandoned in one of Dunkirk's side streets. (Historic Military Press)

Assorted French and British military vehicles, including at least two Universal Carriers and a Morris Quad, block a road into Dunkirk and its environs. (Historic Military Press)

Apart from the East Mole in Dunkirk itself, there were just the soft, sandy beaches, stretching for 16 miles eastwards from Dunkirk to Nieuport, from which to rescue the men – beaches at places such as Malo-les-Bains, Bray-Dunes and La Panne. This image shows Allied troops on one of these beaches forming into long winding queues ready to take their turn to board small boats which took them to larger vessels. (Historic Military Press)

A remarkable shot of the beach at La Panne during a German air raid on 29 May 1940. It was taken from the decks of HMS *Oriole* by Sub-Lieutenant Crosby; he had turned and captured the very moment that a pair of German bombs fell on the sands and exploded. (Historic Military Press)

The graves of French and British troops, possibly killed during the loss of the paddle steamer *Crested Eagle,* are examined by German troops after the evacuation. This is the stretch of beach where *Crested Eagle* was beached and wrecked, the paddlesteamer being immediately out of view to the right. (Historic Military Press)

Abandoned Allied vehicles, including at least two Universal Carriers, at the top of the beach at Malo-les-Bains, to the east of Dunkirk, towards the end of Operation Dynamo. Note the harbour arm or jetty that can be seen in the background. (Historic Military Press)

An abandoned British or French gun on the promenade at Malo-les-Bains. In the background is the wreck of the French destroyer *L'Adroit*, which was bombed and sunk by Heinkel He 111 bombers in shallow water off Malo-les-Bains at 12:00 hours on 21 May 1940. (Historic Military Press)

French and British troops on board ships berthing at Dover, 31 May 1940. (Historic Military Press)

Abandoned vehicles and equipment litter the seafront at Dunkirk in the immediate aftermath of Operation Dynamo. The abandoned Thames sailing barge in the centre background is believed to be *Ethel Everard*, which had been towed across the Channel by the tug *Sun XII* in company with another barge, *Tollesbury*. The building in the distance with the round tower is the Malo Terminus Casino. (Historic Military Press)

Taken by a German soldier in the immediate aftermath of Operation Dynamo, this picture shows abandoned British and French vehicles on the quayside in the harbour at Dunkirk, with, in the background, the East Mole or jetty that proved so important during the evacuation. (Historic Military Press)

> It is therefore decided to make a stand at all costs. If our lines are broken, we will form resistance zones and we will hold wherever possible, for as long as possible to inflict the maximum losses on the enemy.[13]

Was the attack on or off? In the same document, Weygand spoke of a strike force to attack in the west: formed from what units? Lead by whom? Was he still thinking of attacking at Arras? Weygand's policy was not purely centred on shoring up the line of the Somme and Aisne. His strategic thinking was that if the French could re-take the bridgeheads at Abbeville, Amiens and Péronne, not only would it boost flagging French morale, it would also cause major operational difficulties for the Wehrmacht. With Dunkirk becoming an almost myopic obsession, now was the time to strike. Weygand demanded a more vigorous integration of air support, especially bombers, to the ground offensive. Moreover, Weygand ordered that the French were to hang on as long as possible at Dunkirk for reinforcements to come up and the Weygand Line completed. The more distracted the Germans became about taking Dunkirk, the more time it bought Weygand to move reserves up. Weygand was altogether a more active commander than Gamelin had ever been.

Weygand ordered Georges and Têtu to plan to attack Péronne. After agreeing to Weygand's orders, Têtu ordered that afternoon that the region of Péronne and Bapaume was to be the target for the French bomber forces. After suffering huge losses, American Glenn-Martin 147 and Douglas DB 7m types were coming online. At 15:00 thirty Glenn-Martin bombers, each carrying 800kg of bombs, attacked columns of motorised infantry in the environs of St Quentin. An hour later, six Breguet 693s, coming in fast at treetop level, machine-gunned German troops in the area of Peronne. The same targets were bombed by Amiot 143s from *9e* and *10e Groupement* and Farman 221s.[14]

In Flanders, the 4th Division of the BEF was 'scattered' during its retreat to Dunkirk. One officer took two days to rejoin the headquarters:

> At Dunkirk . . . under an intense bombardment I arrived with my section . . . we now took up refuge behind the fortifications of the port until the ships arrived. After waiting for about ten hours . . . I discovered that the officers commanding our detachment were missing or dead . . . I took an abandoned car from the port and with two agents who worked for French liaison went in search of where we were to embark at Malo-les-Bains and Bray-Dunes. During the course of the journey we encountered at Furnes, the staff of the 2nd Corps . . . I found the 4th Division after two days . . . this formation along with the 3rd Corps organised the

> defence of the perimeter and had a large body of soldiers at La Panne and Bray-Dunes . . . the situation was extremely difficult because of the continuous bombardment of artillery and the treason of certain sections of the Belgian army which attacked us with machine guns.[15]

This was an unfortunate friendly-fire incident. In Belgium, near Kortrijk, four Belgian divisions were pushed back and then outflanked by eight German divisions. Despite being outnumbered, the Belgian army managed to plug the gaps with reinforcements. The fighting was very violent, especially in Kuurne. Calais was being attacked, so too Boulogne. The French defended Calais from the sea. Darlan ordered the guns of the destroyers *Léopard* and *Le Frondeur* to bombard the road to Wimereux and the fort of La Crèche occupied by the Germans. Attacked by Stukas, *Le Frondeur* had to return to Cherbourg. In Boulogne, Panzers were attacking from the north, south and east. A large number of officers and men were killed on the barricades along the roads leading to the port. At 12:00 the 13e RI counter-attacked to buy time. That evening dozens of Stukas and He 111s bombed the town, reducing it to rubble.[16]

In Dunkirk, during the course of the day 2,000 incendiary bombs fell on Malo-les-Bains and across the town. The docks of the port were machine-gunned and bastion 32, the headquarters of the Allied forces in Dunkirk, was bombed by Stukas. Under the falling bombs, French General Fagalde was placed in command of setting up the defence of the port of Dunkirk and a camp to receive and reorganise the French troops who were taking refuge on the coast in increasing numbers. The first area chosen for this transit camp was the border dune area at Bray-Dunes, where in 2025 the Perroquet campsite is now located. Realising that the French could not fight to the Somme, what remained of the Allied armies were trapped: two choices existed, 1. Evacuate all land forces, 2. Hold on as long possible and re-supply by the sea.

Weygand and the French GQG wanted to make Dunkirk an entrenched camp to resist the Germans for as long as possible and prevent them from turning south to invade the rest of France. In London, Eden wanted to evacuate the BEF as quickly as possible.

And yet fate handed the Allies a golden moment to counter-attack. So concerned by the threat of a counter-attack to cut the Panzers off from the main body of the German army, on the evening of 24 May, despite the Germans being barely 15km from Dunkirk, yet Hitler ordered his Panzers to stop. By this stage, some Panzer divisions had lost 50 per cent of their tanks. Crews were exhausted: the Allies had fought the Wehrmacht to stalemate.

Chapter 22

ON THE JOB TRAINING

The first ten days of combat had shown all too starkly the failings in French training and doctrine, as well as in the senior officers. Mythos implies the Maginot Mentality prevent the French army from learning: Two officers who did 'look and learn' were Generals Georges and Keller.

Keller realised that if the French had any chance of succeeded against the Wehrmacht, they had to learn how to 'play the same game' as their opponents. The Wehrmacht's tactics played to their strengths: the faster-moving Panzer IIs would mass around the slower French armour, harrying a tank like a wolf pack, which bought time to move up anti-tank guns or a Panzer III or IV to knock out the heavier armoured French tanks. By concentrating fire at tracks, engines or the turrets the SOMUA or B1 *bis* could be immobilised.[1] This exploited the slower rate of movement and fire of the French armour. That is not to say French tanks were 'sitting ducks'. On 17 May it was reported by the 6th Panzer Division that it took twenty-six direct hits from an anti-tank gun to knock out a B1 *bis*, but only by destroying the tracks. A single B1 had knocked out thirteen Panzer IIs and two anti-tank guns the previous day, despite sustaining 140 hits from German guns, none of which penetrated the armour.[2] Clearly French tanks were a formidable battlefield threat.

During the course of 25 May, Keller published a long memorandum about tank actions, and how to combat the apparent German superiority:

> The enemy armoured units were able to advance rapidly without encountering suitable resistance.
>
> These elements must be stopped at all costs: a matter of common sense, will and command.

> The notion of line must be replaced by that of control of all communications.
>
> Experience has just proven that any strongpoint barricaded in all directions, bristling with fire in all directions and commanded by a leader determined not to surrender was impenetrable to tanks.
>
> Any commander of a Large Unit must therefore seize all communications in his zone by establishing a complete grid of strongpoints, equipped with anti-tank weapons or 75s, without hesitating to give this zone even exaggerated depth.
>
> Every small unit commander must realise that the location he has been given the mission of defending is a strongpoint or cover, and by solidly barricading all access routes.

Keller added, correctly, that:

> Our anti-tank weapons, serviced by resolute teams, overcome all tanks. the losses admitted by the enemy prove it.
>
> The Artillery must always be included in the strongpoints. Apart from these missions of protecting the approaches to neighbouring strongpoints and harassing enemy paths, it contributes to the anti-tank defence of the strongpoint in which it is installed. Enemy tank attacks have been stopped dead by the fire of a well-ordered artillery.

The French had the weaponry to stop the Wehrmacht advance, and were very quickly learning how to use it effectively: the Wehrmacht had learned these lessons in Poland, which gave it a marked advantage over the French who were learning to combat the Panzerwaffe in the defence of their nation. About Panzers, Keller noted that if the communications and logistical support could be cut, the advance would stop due to lack of ammunition and fuel: the key was to cut off the Panzers from the bulk of the Wehrmacht. He added that an attack by German Panzers was rendered all the more successful because of close air support, which had a larger impact on morale than on killing or wounding soldiers. Keller continued that:

> All portable weapons must fire against attacks by low-flying aircraft . . . Defence against aircraft is an integral part of the organisation of a strongpoint and the conduct of fire is an obligation of the leaders. Our airmen most often return their aircraft riddled with bullets from the enemy's ground defence. This is the best proof of the effectiveness of this defence. It is therefore necessary to demand it from our troops, and to look at the more impressive than deadly effect of the bombardment.

Soldiers were not to flee to cover but to open fire, he stressed. Furthermore:

> Defence must be complimented by offensive actions of our tanks and armoured cars:
> - local actions of clearing away elements of low importance.
> - or counter-attacks led by Large Mechanical Units under the orders of their leader who, not only directs the combat, but ensures the establishment and the guard of their base of supply.

Keller's report landed on Weygand's desk sometime on the morning of 25 May. Weygand agreed with Keller's assessment, and issued orders to that effect. So much for the myth of a French army that had ossified behind the Maginot Line![3]

At the end of the day Weygand and Keller issued the following memorandum to tank crews:

> During recent operations, the Tank Units engaged have faced an enemy vastly superior in number with a bravery and a spirit of sacrifice worthy of the Army's past. The task to be accomplished remains immense. The German tank is our most relentless adversary. The French tank must be the most ardent defender of the country. I count on all to adapt immediately to a new form of warfare that demands maximum drive, initiative, sustained effort and courage.[4]

By issuing new instructions, Keller and Weygand hoped French armour could respond better to the situation it faced.

Chapter 23

25 MAY 1940

On the front lines, at just after two in the morning, Blanchard's HQ received word that the 25e DIM was to join the combat along the Escaut and the objects were to capture and hold the bridge at Sensee and to send out a strong force towards Marchienne-Peronne.[1] It was Blanchard and Prioux's 'last throw of the dice'. Gort had refused to come to the aide of his ally. The French bomber force was ordered once more in support of the attack on the following day.

An hour later at 03:15 GQG received news from Admiral Nord based at Dunkirk, communicating the situation as of 23 May. Better late than never! German motorcycle troops had arrived in the southern suburbs of Boulogne, and had engaged with the BEF. The coast defence artillery batteries had opened fire to cover the British. At Saint-Omer the Germans were advancing along the Hesdin and Lumbres roads, with the advanced motorcycle units already in the town. The French infantry division that had embarked on a destroyer to be evacuated disembarked to begin the defence of the town, engaging pockets of German infantry at Samer, Desvres and Neufchatel.[2] At Ville-au-Montois, at long last came orders to retreat. The 51e DI and 71 GRDI were ordered to prepare to retreat to the south-east towards Boulogne on the 24th where they arrived the following day. The mass of troops had been cut off from their immediate command group due to a total failure of communications.[3]

The order had been sent at 12:57, but did not arrive with GQG till 16:00. By the time Blanchard, Georges or Weygand could respond, the situation on the ground would have changed again. The French could not respond at the necessary pace to react in a timely fashion to the Wehrmacht. It is also obvious that by 25 May any degree of co-ordination between the various Allied units in the field had collapsed. The lack of radios was beginning to be keenly felt. The cumbersome French cypher system built in security but also huge delays. All dispatches from the front line went to GQG before being parcelled back out to Georges or other commanders. This delay in some cases was considerable. Worse, the Germans knew this. Senior Wehrmacht officers had correctly concluded from radio intercepts before the campaign that the French response to their offensive would be slow because of the cumbersome communications security systems. The Wehrmacht was also well aware that the French had fewer radios or other means of receiving urgent orders. Thus, before the campaign began the Wehrmacht had a huge advantage.[4]

At 15:00, Blanchard and Weygand learned that the Belgian army had crossed the river Lys between Walcheren and Beveren, smashing open the front for a width of 5km. The BEF was ordered to Hazebrouck to try and fill the gap, but did not do so.[5] A dangerous gap was opening up on the Allied left flank that threatened to cut the Belgian Army off from the BEF.

At 16:50 news arrived at GQG that the leading elements of the Wehrmacht were advancing on the region of Capelle-Brouck and the Watten area. The 48e DI were engaging them. In Calais the 21e DI were engaged with the German advance guard. However, it was not till 19:10 that a 'decryption' appeared on Georges' desk.[6] Five hours or more had been lost between receiving news from the front and the information being available. As we said earlier, the French simply could not respond in a timely manner to situations as they arose at the front due to the constraints place on communication by reliance on telegrams. Nor was this just a French issue. The BEF's communications with Weyand and other senior officers was tenuous at best. It was not until almost midnight that the French learned that over the course of previous day, General Nicholson with elements of the BEF had renounced their intention to defend the perimeter around Calais: they fell back to Bastion 11, destroying their tanks as they fell back. Absence of armour would be keenly felt. By 17:00 on the 25th, the Wehrmacht occupied the positions vacated by the BEF. An hour later Bastion 11 was attacked by German armour. Why it had taken so long for the BEF to tell the French and call for reinforcements we will never know. By the early morning of the 26th, the French sent reinforcements to reinforce the Bastion.[7]

Calais was not the only port under attack from the Wehrmacht. The British had sent the 20th Guards Brigade to reinforce Boulogne to prevent the Germans from accessing the harbour and blocking the evacuation route to Dunkirk. Believing the port to be lost, the Guards were finally evacuated by late on the 24th. With the garrison running low of ammunition, and without British support, at 08:30 Boulogne fell:

> German tanks had approached the barricades during the night, all our soldiers opened fire. A group of attackers was defeated but rendered useless due to lack of munitions were all our automatic weapons, we had not food and water.
>
> The enemy breached the defensive line in the Northern sector (gate of the Dunes) and the sector North-east (gate of Calais) supported by large bodies of men: severe losses were sustained on both sides. The South-east sector (gate of Gayole) was violently contested.[8]

Around Valenciennes, fighting was still raging. On the Escaut the Germans had obtained reinforcements. They concentrated their attacks on a front of barely 1km at Bruille-Saint-Amand, but the soldiers of the 43e RI still held. At Bouchain, Moroccan Infantry from the 5e DINA supported by 45e RI, they received the order 'the instruction is the same as yesterday: HOLD!'[9]

At Lille General Alan Brooke, on being told that the Germans were close to taking Boulogne, ordered the 2nd Corps of the BEF to move. The HQ at Armentières had been under heavy aerial bombardment since the day before, one officer noting 'great fires could be seen burning in the direction of Lille and Roubaix – the aircraft that passed over head were beyond counting. The sound of the ack ack was never ceasing. The sky was illuminated by the fire . . . it was impossible to obtain information from our British colleagues.' Our writer adds 'we hoped that a counter-attack would save us'. No attack came.[10] But one was being planned.

During the day, the French had attacked a German thrust in the Belgian section, and were to deploy two divisions of infantry and whatever armour they could gather attack the German line between Mouevres and Cambrai.[11] The counter-attack 'was of great importance' and that preliminary operations were to begin imminently for a major offensive on the following day. After having blocked French plans, both Gort and Blanchard were in agreement about the operation, to which the 1st British Armoured Division would be committed. Whitehall was fully in support of the attack and had full confidence in Blanchard.[12] Gort assigned the 51st Division to the attack.[13] In the late afternoon, Colonel Jacques Humbert a staff officer serving with the *Conseil supérieur de la guerre, groupe d'armées du Nord* telegraphed French GQG: 'For immediate effect, with the highest authority we must co-ordinate our forces . . . it is absolutely essential.'[14]

It was an appeal in vain to make the BEF support the attack. Weygand could not change Gort's mind: when 'push came to shove' Gort dithered, as an officer with General Prioux remarked:

> At 08:00, the *Corps de Cavalerie* received a written order from the *1re Armée* concerning the planned offensive operation which confirmed the verbal directives already given to General Prioux: a group under the orders of General Altmayer, Commander of the 5th Army, is tasked with leading the operation in the general direction of Marchienne-Peronne with the 2nd British Division and 3rd French Army Corps (their objective: Cambrai – Bois de Bourlon – Marquion bridgehead south of the Sensee upstream of Arleux). The CC acting in the direction of Flets-Monst st Eloi must clear the north bank of the Scarpe to oppose any threat north of the Douai. . . . At 18:00 the army was told that the projected operation was to be delayed by 24 hours.[15]

Blanchard was committed to 'going it alone': the operation became a 'what-if moment'.

Blanchard's priority was to create a stop line on Somme and Aisne rivers to resist the Germans when they had finished with the Allied forces stuck in the Nord and Pas-de-Calais: the problem was the line of the Somme was already compromised. Between Péronne and Ham, the French wanted to retake four bridges over the Somme, which had fallen into the hands of the Germans a few days earlier.[16]

For once in May 1940, the French army was to innovate, having learned valuable lessons from the Wehrmacht. At 18:00 in preparation for the attack, fourteen Breguet 693s were ordered to attack the German troops defending the combat zone. None returned. At 20:00 six Glenn-Martin bombers came in at 800m, dropping their bombs onto German troops along the line of the river. That night thirteen Amiot 143s bombed the same targets, two aircraft did not return.[17] Using armour and infantry at night immediately in the wake of the bombers, the bridges were taken by 03:00.[18]

Yet there was to be no exploitation. At the moment of success, General Prioux reported: 'At 23:15 a special order from the 1st Army made it known that the British Commander-in-Chief having suspended the participation of the two English divisions in the planned operation, the latter was to be postponed.'[19] What had caused this breach?

General Dill earlier in the day had informed General Swayne that he had spoken with Lord Gort. The situation in the North was becoming desperate: the BEF held a line 140km long with seven divisions, with three territorial divisions defending bridges. The BEF's front passed from Dunkirk to St Omer, Aire, Bethune, Carvin and Raches where it linked with the French *1re Armée*. The French lines extended to Denain, St Amand and Bourghelles; the Belgians were behind the line of the river Lys at Gand. Gort believed he had no choice but to retreat and shrink the front line.[20]

Weygand, after speaking with Gort, Blanchard and Georges, now realised that he could not strike south and fight the French Army out of the encirclement. He had little choice but to accept the inevitable of withdrawing the French forces towards Dunkirk. At 19:10 he entrusted this mission to General Blanchard, who immediately ordered the army to retreat to the Lys north of Lille:

> The 1re French Army, the British Army and the Belgian Army will gradually regroup behind the water line marked by the Aa Canal, the Lys and the Diversion Canal so as to form a bridgehead covering Dunkirk for a large part. This bridgehead will be defended without a spirit of retreat.[21]

For some French soldiers, exhausted by the fighting on the Escaut, this represented a march of more than 60km. At 21:45:

> General Prioux learns by telephone from Colonel Vignol, Deputy Chief of Staff of the 1st Army, that he is receiving command of the army in replacement of General Blanchard, who is called to take over the army group. General Langlois, commanding the 3rd DLM, takes command of the CC. He is replaced at the head of the 3rd DLM by General Lafont.
>
> General Prioux summoned General Langlois and then, amidst the visible emotion of the officers present, embraces his Chief of Staff and leaves the army during the night.[22]

Blanchard had taken command of the *1re Armée* on Billotte's death on the 23rd.

Despite the almost totally negative news, some positives did occur that day. The first load of supplies landed. The Dunkirk perimeter was holding as night fell. Whitehall reported that due to German artillery it was impossible to land troops at Calais, and the Royal Navy had sent two torpedo boats to bolster local defences. The French admiral commanding Dunkirk stated: 'It is extremely urgent and extremely necessary that as many fighter aircraft are deployed on the coast between Gris Nez to be able to secured the western approach to Dunkirk.'

The Luftwaffe was slowly pounding the Allied armies into dust.[23] The French air force had been eviscerated and with the RAF covering the coast from bases in England, the Luftwaffe had local air superiority. The Germans were now confident of total victory. General Jodl, one of Hitler's closest aides-de-camp, declared 'The war is won, all that remains is to end it.' With any hope of the French army escaping south gone, Weygand abandoned the troops trapped in the Dunkirk pocket: his priority was to strengthen the new defensive positions along the Aisne and Somme. The French air force was detailed to protect the troops on the Somme and also the rail heads behind: the Luftwaffe concentrated its attacks on Dunkirk, giving Weygand some breathing space.

The French used this respite to rebuild their depleted air force: brand new Curtiss H75s were coming online along with the Dewoitine D.523: these aircraft gave French, Czech and Polish pilots fighters comparable to the Bf 109. France did not lack pilots; it lacked modern aircraft.[24]

Chapter 24

26 MAY 1940

May 26th 1940 was a Sunday. The faithful would be preparing to attend Mass and beseech God and the Virgin to intervene to save their country. Before the angelus would toll its mournful appeal, as day broke Weygand issued orders from Paris:

> The battle on which the fate of the country depends will be fought without a spirit of retreat, on the position that we currently occupy.
>
> All leaders, from the Army Commander to the section commander must be animated by the fierce desire to fight on the spot until death. If the chiefs give the example their troops will hold, and they will be obliged, if necessary, to force their obedience.
>
> To be certain of stopping the enemy, it is necessary to demonstrate constant aggressiveness.
>
> If the enemy manifests offensive intentions in a sector, it is necessary to respond with brutal, harsh counter-preparations.
>
> If the enemy succeeds in making these bridgeheads on our front, which he uses to push tanks into and then move on to an armoured attack, however small this bridgehead may be, we will immediately throw the enemy back to his lines by crushing him under artillery and aircraft fire and by counter-attacking.

Weygand continued, building on the thinking outlined in his order of two days earlier:

> Infiltration must be answered with infiltration. If a unit finds that it is no longer in contact on one of its wings because the neighbouring unit has been shaken, it must not fall back at any cost; it must try to reestablish the situation, and, if it cannot, form a defensive redoubt and make any resistance possible. This is as true for the division as for the regiment, the battalion, the company.

> All the rear areas of the main line and on the greatest possible depth must be divided into a grid of resistance centres, in particular on the main access routes by which, until now, the Germans have always advanced . . . activity, solidarity, resolve.[1]

More a rallying cry than a strategical masterpiece, Weygand was adapting as best he could to Blitzkrieg, with a French army that was staring defeat in the face.

Soon after break of day, Generals Blanchard, Prioux and Gort met in conference: the meeting was held to try and co-ordinate a joint retreat between the French and BEF.[2] Following the meeting, Blanchard accepted that no elements of the BEF were able to mount an offensive on the Lys at Courtrai, thus the Belgians, BEF and French were to withdraw behind the line of the Lys canal. The French *1re Armée*, it was hoped, could be able to respond on the night of the 26/27th. The Belgian army was now cut primarily cut off from the Allies, and held a tiny defensive pocket at Courtrai.[3]

René Prioux, commanding the *1re Armée*, issued orders at 03:30. The army was to fall back to assist the BEF, the *2e* DLM was to help the Belgians at Courtrai. By the morning of 27 May the 1re and 3e DLM were to have established themselves behind the Lys positioned between Armentières and Estaires. At 09:00 the Wehrmacht rolled over the Deûle canal, debouching towards Carvin and the wood of Epinoy. They were met by the 2e DINA, the 3e DLM and a brigade from the BEF, supported by a group of SOMUA tanks from the 1re DLM. By 11:25, the French positions were being outflanked by German armour: relentlessly attacked from the air, by dusk the *1re Armée* had no choice but to fall back.[4]

Prioux had requested air support, but the ludicrous situation was that General Têtu, commanding the GAO, was allowed to choose his targets at will and was able to disregard field commanders. D'Astier was also operating at will, with little thought as to the needs of the Army. General Georges by now had realised that not having the air force under army command was a colossal error.

Nothing exemplifies the error made in allowing the air force to choose its targets than the fact Têtu ignored Prioux's request and at 15:00 he ordered seven Breguet 693s into the skies with no escort. The bombers strafed a column of German motorised infantry in the Bapaume area. None returned. At 19:00, repeating the same error, he ordered twelve brand-new Glenn-Martin bombers into the fray. The aircraft bombed and strafed a German column in the Albert-Amiens axis: two aircraft failed to return.[5] Yet co-operation was possible. Four

Breguet 693 groups and two fighter groups were made available for the first time, and allocated to General Frere's *7e Armée* to support attempts to eliminate German bridgeheads at Amiens and Abbeville. On the ground de Gaulle was at his cavalier best leading the 4e DCR. He was able to put 120 to 130 tanks into the field as a single large mass, although General Delestraint, commanding what was left of the 2e DCR, complained he had one battalion of tanks, as the bulk of his unit had been parcelled out piecemeal to the infantry which 'without tanks would not hold' adding that 'the High Command was constantly torn between the real knowledge that it possesses of the necessity of using tanks en masse and its concern to give moral support to the infantry.'[6] Thus, any hope of a strong, co-ordinated attack was nullified.

Perhaps with Georges' words ringing in their ears, the commanders of the new groups kept their aircraft on standby, with aircrew on alert, allowing them to intervene almost immediately when needed. Ironically, this is the first recorded instance of such thinking! Be that as it may, despite poor weather, forty sorties were flown that day on targets around Abbeville.[7]

About 13:30 Hitler allowed his tanks to move for the first time in three days: Rommel was the first to resume the offensive, he attacked near La Bassée, in Violaines. The objective was to cross the canal with sunken barges but the attempt failed. During the night, the Engineer troops succeeded in building a bridge of boats at Givenchy-lès-La-Bassée. The French defended the canal zone with the 7e GRDI. By the evening, a pontoon bridge was in operation, allowing Rommel's panzers to advance.

Elsewhere, the Belgian army threw its last reserves into the battle to plug the gaps opened near Ghent. The Belgian counter-attacks pushed the Germans back everywhere, but the end was near for these exhausted troops. At 20:20 Blanchard learned the Belgian Army had been pushed back towards the Ypres canal, the BEF and 2e DLM were heading to the canal to shore up the position. Blanchard with Weygand and Whitehall's blessing, was still planning for the counter-attack with the 1st Armoured Division on the following day.[8] Gort was concerned that the French troops sent to hold the Lys and evacuate the Belgians would in turn be surrounded. He felt the BEF should pull back lest they get trapped and were unable to embark at Dunkirk. Increasingly the BEF took little part in the fighting, leaving the French and Belgians to shoulder the burden of conflict. To that end, the French were to occupy the line from St-Omer-Hazbrouck-Armentières, Lille and face east; a second line would be from Lille-Comines-Ypres.[9]

Along the Escaut, between Saint-Amand-les-Eaux and Fresnes-sur-Escaut, the Germans attacked in force. At 10:30, the French were outflanked but managed to retreat towards the Raismes forest. The French suffered huge losses: the 43e RI lost nearly two-thirds of its men killed or wounded. A commemorative monument pays tribute to them near the blockhouse of the Tour-du-Moulin in Bruille-Saint-Amand. At Bouchain, the Germans attacked in force, in the morning, along the railway line. The French positions fell one after the other after their ammunition had been exhausted by 14:00 with the 45e RI retreating on Lille.

At 09:30 German artillery began pounding Calais. Facing artillery bombardment and running low on ammunition Bastion 12 surrendered at 10:15. Sensing victory, a huge aerial armada bombed Calais in support of an all-out assault by German forces. The defence expended the last of the French ammunition. Bastion 11 surrendered at 14:30. An hour later the Germans were in Calais heading towards the citadel. At 16:00 the garrison of Calais, out of ammunition, surrendered. Isolated groups of Allied soldiers fought until the next day near the ferry terminal. The French and British lost 2,000 men (300 killed and 1,700 wounded) defending Calais. The Germans in comparison lost 800 soldiers killed and 2,400 wounded. It was a bloody encounter.[10]

Learning of the setbacks of the French, Lord Gort received a telegram from the Secretary of State for War, Anthony Eden, containing the formal permission to go ahead with the evacuation of the BEF. The British established a perimeter around Dunkirk using the canals that surrounded the city. From that moment on, the British soldiers filtered the flow of soldiers and equipment that entered this perimeter. Only men and small arms are allowed to cross the canals. At 18:57, in Dover, England, British Vice Admiral Bertram Ramsay officially launched Operation Dynamo, the green light for the re-embarkation of the BEF from all the beaches east of Gravelines and the port of Dunkirk. Gort by midnight had completed his defensive positions on what he called the 'Canal Line'. Admiral Abrial and General Fagalde organised the western defences of Dunkirk.

Chapter 25

DUNKIRK

On Monday, 27 May 1940, the Luftwaffe unleashed 'hell on earth' at Dunkirk. According to Dunkirk historian Patrick Odonne, from 08:00 to 20:00 waves of 30 to 40 German bombers followed one after another every 20 minutes: 15,000 incendiary bombs and 30,000 explosive bombs were dropped on the city, causing more than a thousand deaths, mostly civilians. Despite the bombing, on that day, 18,000 soldiers managed to embark for England. Weygand at this stage had not been formally notified officially of Gort's preparations for the evacuation, but the indications were unmistakable, and General Georges Blanchard sent one of his staff officers to Paris late on the 25th to inform Weygand. On being told the news, Admiral Darlan decided immediately to send Captain Paul Auphan, the chief of his operations division, to England to seek clarification. On arrival at Dover the during the morning of the 27th, Auphan could not fail to notice that Operation Dynamo was in full swing. Knowing that Darlan and Weygand had both realised that the French sooner or later would have to evacuate Dunkirk he met with Admiral Ramsay to discuss the best way to co-ordinate the French evacuation.

Being convinced of the need to evacuate, 48 hours earlier Darlan had ordered the requisitioning of all small ships in the Channel and in Brittany. He now issued instructions to speed up their sailings. Rear Admiral Marcel Landriau was designated to take command of the flotilla that was to be assembled from the Pas-de-Calais and received orders to proceed to Dover on board the sloop *Savorgnan de Brazza*. On returning to La Havre, Auphan contacted Weygand, informing him that yes, the BEF was evacuating; a British liaison officer would be sent to Admiral Abrial commanding Dunkirk to co-ordinate the evacuation, whilst on the ground Gort and Blanchard were to co-operate. Darlan was hoping to lift the French troops off from Dunkirk, rest and resupply them in England, and then embark the soldiers back in France to continue the fight: which is what history shows happened.

The bulk of the *1re Armée* and what remained of the *9e Armée* were 110km from the coast. Six divisions sacrificed themselves in defending Lille, an action delaying the general attack on Dunkirk. For the other divisions it was to became a hard retreat.[1]

Early that morning in Cassel and somewhat unwisely given the proximity to the front line, the British and French High Command held a high-level meeting at the Hotel du Sauvage. Lieutenant General Sir Ronald Adam represented the BEF and General Bertrand Fagalade the French. In attendance were Generals Blanchard, Prioux and Koeltz (representing Weygand). At the meeting the British for the first time informed their French allies, in coded terms, of their intention to evacuate the entire BEF. It must have been obvious what was happening, yet the British only felt once things were in motion to tell their ally. No date was set, but the goal was for the total evacuation of the BEF. It meant the French had to fight on alone: the British were defeated, were increasingly worried about 'what next' from Hitler and were therefore unwilling to continue the fight for Europe on the soil of France. Anthony Eden in London believed France had already fallen, and there was no need to send British soldiers to their deaths fighting a lost battle. No Canadian divisions or any supplies were to be sent to bolster the beleaguered French. He felt moreover in a memorandum to Gort that the counter-attack to the Somme was doomed to fail, and suggested in the worst-case scenario, Gort could surrender. The only thing left Whitehall could do in France was to save the BEF, and let France fall. No consideration about evacuating troops from Dunkirk to Cherbourg to get behind the Somme line was considered. Since 18 May evacuation of the BEF had 'been on the cards' and planning for it began on the following day. How much of the event planning to escape from Flanders shaped Gort's strategic thinking we will never know. He had a line of escape – he and the BEF could run away and fight another day – an option the French did not have. It was here in Flanders that the fate of Europe was played out: it was a battle the British increasingly did not want to be part of.[2]

Understandably, the French weren't happy with the British plan. The BEF would leave a token rearguard and were unwilling to continue the fight. Weygand was firmly of the opinion that everything had to be done to try and hold territory in the north to 'bleed the Wehrmacht dry'. Secondly, Weygand need to continue the fighting in the north as long as possible to ensure that the new defensive line was completed. The 'Weygand Line' on the Somme needed time to be prepared, and moreover, time was needed for reserves to be brought up from southern and eastern France. Should hostilities in Belgium cease before the Weygand Line plan was completed, it would enable the Germans to concentrate their troops for a decisive attack on the rest of France and face little to no opposition. Despite the reluctance of Weygand, it was agreed that Dunkirk would be defended: the French would be responsible for the sector west of Dunkirk and the British, everything east of the town. Referred to as the outer perimeter, it was 25 miles long and approximately eight miles deep and made the best use of the canal and waterways around Dunkirk to aid defence. In addition, low-lying areas such as Les Moeres on the eastern side of the perimeter were deliberately flooded to impede the Wehrmacht's operations. The French-held sector ran from Mardyck – Spycker – Bergues. The British sector ran through the axis Bergues – Bulscamp – Furnes – Nieuport.

Learning lessons

As our earlier chapter commented, the French army were not unable to adapt to the tactics deployed by the Wehrmacht. Before the Polish campaign had ended, on 21 September 1939, Gamelin wrote to General Georges, warning him of the importance of German air support of ground operations and advised him moreover that counter-attacks headed by armour should be prioritised as the preferred method of contesting any breakthroughs in the French line of defence by German armour. This was new, as it meant risking an encounter battle, which went against French thinking. Georges was told to train his men to make them acclimatised to the noise and shock of air raids, so that the shock did not send the mean reeling away, breaking morale and unit cohesion, and to ensure that he used his air assets as best he could.[3] Gamelin reprimanded Georges, with whom relations were notoriously difficult, in December 1939 for not concentrating on training his men, beginning a letter to him with 'I am very annoyed, and I know that they are very annoyed in high places too' about the lack of training recent inspections had revealed. Gamelin demanded that artillery be pushed further forward and tactical training improved. Moreover, he urged his subordinate against static defence and recommending 'varied reconnaissances and active patrols' – Gamelin's stance reflecting the fact that he had more front-line experience of the Great War than any other senior general in the French army. Georges, who had spent only a few days at the front before being seriously wounded, prioritised central control. He ordered commanders were to submit plans for raids to him for prior approval, a requirement that many saw as stifling initiative. Prételat, commanding a sector on the Maginot Line, asked permission for local commanders to submit several scenarios in advance so that they could respond before the Germans took counter-measures.[4] Perhaps too little too late, French senior officers were showing the initiative Gamelin had asked of them months earlier in attempting to effectively hold back the seemingly unstoppable Wehrmacht, particularly the panzer divisions. In a memo dated 27 May, in reply to Weygand and Keller's memorandum, which we mentioned earlier, General Georges acknowledged that:

> the close cooperation of the enemy aviation and the armoured elements of the panzer divisions, themselves supported by elements of infantry, is at the base of the successes of our adversary . . . this cooperation is found, with different modalities of application as well in the phase of rupture of our initial defensive device as in the phase of brutal exploitation which follows. It is essential to examine these modalities in order to be able to ward it off in the shortest possible time.[5]

Georges and his staff also noted:

> Airpower and its preponderant role – it assumed the mission of preparation.
>
> Its action was massive, almost continuously over the entire attacked zone . . . continuous in time during the entire duration of the day.
>
> With a mastery of the air that was only contested at rare moments of the day, it was able to act with impunity, choosing its targets.
>
> The effect produced is above all moral, in the sense that despite relatively minimal losses in men, the troops subjected to the bombardment are suffering from nervous breakdown, as if struck dumb.
>
> This effect is also the same among the enemy under the action of our bombardment.[6]

The failure by the French air force to interdict the Germans was due to the lack of fighter aircraft, as much as the lack of an early warning system like Chain Home. A lack of aircraft had gifted air superiority to the Luftwaffe. Inferiority of aircraft type had further compounded this. However, by the end of May, more and more aircraft were coming online. French, Czech and Polish aircrew were also taking to the skies in increasing numbers. The first of the Douglas DB7s flew their first operations on 27 May. Sixteen aircraft bombed the area around Cambrai. New, and better aircraft were coming on line: what was needed was time to get them to the front line.[7] If Dunkirk and Lille could hold out like Verdun to bleed the Wehrmacht dry of men and equipment, to buy time for the Weygand Line to be completed on the Somme, then just maybe the Wehrmacht could be held back.

Learning lessons also dealt with doctrine and training failings. Georges acknowledged that a lack of training of NCOs and junior officers in anti-aircraft defence, meant that despite machine guns being available to open fire against incoming aircraft, the men fled for cover. On Georges' recommendation, Weygand ordered that changed immediately. Weygand demanded that rather than running for cover, the soldiers were to stand their ground and fire back. Better communication was also essential, Georges noted. Little could be done about the lack of radios; field telephones were to be used. Georges does not explain who would lay the cables as no signals sections existed to do so, but it was a case of 'needs must'. Georges was desperately seeking solutions to appalling communications problems, which had no 'quick fix'. His recommendation, which was ordered by Weygand to be put into standard operation procedure, was that in case of an attack by armour being prevented, or slowed down by enemy by anti-tank gun fire, the local commander had to telephone for a detachment of aircraft to intervene and bomb the enemy positions. The armour would then continue its attack. Anti-tank guns had to accompany armour at all times,

George was also scathing of how the French army, the infantry in particularly, reacted when attacked. Moreover, rather than running for cover when attacked, the French soldiers had to be taught to react. When German armour attacked a town or village, the defenders should occupy the houses, throw grenades at the tanks and soldiers, and defend the ground. When defence was impossible, the houses and buildings should be fire bombed. Georges concluded his memorandum to all field commanders that:

> The general principles of our defensive tactics, continuity, depth, counter-attack, remain.
>
> The notion of strongpoints, of circled resistance centres, must be extended to the entire zone where the troops are stationed.
>
> Active defence against air attack must be pushed to the extreme.
>
> But it is above all the energy and character of the leaders at all levels of the hierarchy that must be called upon so that my defence measures are effectively and efficiently applied.
>
> It is only on this condition that the enemy's attacks can be broken.

Georges noted: 'In short, it was by controlling a road network that was largely left free, and by energetically applying a tactic of close cooperation between tanks, aircraft and infantry, that the enemy was able to rapidly develop its position.'

Georges was attempting to implement this in the French army, months after he had been ordered to bring about these changes: how history may have been different if he had obeyed his superior officer! IF he had time, a very rare commodity in May 1940, then maybe the French army had the potential to 'adopt, adapt, improvise.' It relied on Dunkirk and Lille being held as defended bastions. Eden in Whitehall, as we said, understood France had lost, and that Dunkirk was not to be a defended bastion from which to launch a counter-attack. This disagreement on 'what happens next' arguably lost France the campaign.[8]

Chapter 26

FIGHTING CONTINUES

Gort's order for the day was that the BEF would hold part of the line Lys–Armentières. During the course of the day, German pressure resulted in the Belgian army collapsing at Ypres–Yser. To 'plug the gap', Gort ordered the 3rd Division of the BEF and the 50th Division into the Ypres sector. On learning of the Belgian surrender, Eden in Whitehall gave orders to evacuate the BEF. To that end, during the night, Gort issued orders for a general retreat to the area of Dunkirk–Furnes-Nieuport, covered by the French *3e Corps* and the *1re Armée* at Lille.[1] This left the French flank at Lille exposed. With Gort falling back, Weygand and his staff were coming to realise that evacuation of the French army might be necessary.

Gort was informed of this by General René Prioux. Gort insisted he was retreating and would not be swayed by Prioux's appeals. Trying to make the best of a bad situation, Prioux hoped to defend the line of the river Lys with what remained of *1re Armée* along with the wrecks of the *5e* and *6e Corps d'Armée* which would allow the *Corps de Cavalerie* and the *3e Corps d'Armée* to retreat to the north. He feared – correctly – that the retreat of the BEF would expose his flank, allowing his body of troops to be surrounded by the Germans.[2]

Thoughts of stemming the flood tide of Panzers had not been totally given up. The Allies were still capable of offensive operations, even if doomed to failure: rather than *bataille conduite,* they were forced to act reactively in an encounter battle. Without adequate preparation of munitions what happened next was all too predictable. Between Gravelines and Watten, 8,000 French, 1,000 British and a dozen tanks faced the 1st Panzer Division, the Großdeutschland regiment and the SS division Adolf Hitler, around 50,000 soldiers and 130 tanks. Facing overwhelming odds, following a short but bitter standoff, the French had to retreat behind the banks of the Mardyck Canal. In Saint-Venant, the psychiatric hospital and its 2,300 patients and caregivers were shot by the SS. Only 80 of the 700 British who had defended it made it to Dunkirk: the SS killed those soldiers too weak or badly wounded to save themselves.[3] A few kilometres away, in Le Paradis, a hamlet of Lestrem, a battalion of British soldiers from the Royal Norfolks was not able to retreat rapidly enough and were taken prisoner by men from SS Totenkopf division commanded by Hauptsturmführer Fritz Knöchlein. Obeying his orders, the SS took the English out of the farm and lined them up along the wall. A machine gun was set up in battery and the prisoners were shot in cold blood. Knöchlein gave the order to finish off the wounded with bayonets.[4]

In the south, at Abbeville, the British attempted an armoured attack to relieve German pressure on their troops who were retreating towards Dunkirk. To do so, the 9th Lancers and 10th Hussars had arrived at Ailly-sur-Somme late on 25 May. The following day they were ordered to regroup at Villers-Campsart with orders from General Altmayer. The two British tank regiments were to go into action at Fresnoy-Oisemont-Maisniere in support of the 2e DLC, the 3rd Brigade of the 1st Armoured Division was to support the 5e DLC. An eyewitness writes:

> 27 May, the 2nd Brigade was ordered to attack at 5 o'clock in the morning. We left our positions at 6 o'clock without artillery support and across terrain we did not know. – the Queen's' Bays were to our right, the 10th Hussars to the left, 9th Lancers in reserve.
>
> The Bays, on the right were stopped by anti-tank guns, the 10th Hussars made a tentative attack, the 9th Lancers were not engaged.[5]

The 1st Armoured Division had suffered 50 per cent losses; sixty-nine Cruisers and fifty-one Matildas had been knocked out.[6] General Ewans had launched 180 British tanks into the battle, supported by about 20 French light tanks. Thanks to the German anti-tank gunners, it was a massacre. In a few hours, 120 British tanks were destroyed. French liaison officer Lieutenant Julotte was present at the fighting:

> The shells penetrated on one side, and came out on the other. The tanks were on fire and the crew was killed. The moral qualities of the English during the battle were unparalleled. Almost all of them were facing fire for the first time. There were many deaths, but this failure did not lower the morale of the survivors.[7]

Poorly conceived and without air support, this offensive had no chance of success. In the evening, General de Gaulle and his heavy tanks prepared to replace the British and attack the next day at the same place.

The Belgian collapse

Fighting along the river Lys at the Belgian town of Kortrijk had begun three days earlier. With no air cover, what remained of the Belgian army was fighting a desperate rearguard action. Lacking food and shelter, and shattered moral resulted in contingents of two regiments surrendering without putting up any resistance at Meigem in total defiance of their orders. In another incident, the soldiers shot their officers, because they believed any further resistance to the Wehrmacht was pointless. The Belgian army finally began to collapse during the course of 27 May: the rail network had been almost completely destroyed and in excess of 1.5 million civilians were on the move, clogging up the roads. Ammunition stocks were almost exhausted and the focus moved away from defence and to the denial of assets to the soon-to-be conquerors; equipment and weaponry was destroyed and stores were burned. Belgium had capitulated on 17 May. That the army kept fighting was remarkable, more so considering losses were a staggering 40,000 in the previous few days alone. The Belgian resistance had been vital to the Allies: the Belgian Army absorbed the weight of the German frontal attack from the north, and allowed the elements of the BEF in Belgium to retreat to Dunkirk, protected by Belgian and French soldiers. Condemned ever since by Churchill and the British, the Belgian sacrifice was vital in the evacuation of the BEF. For five or six days prior to the collapse of the Belgian army, the French and Belgians had been asking for support and air cover from the BEF which Gort did his best to ignore: his mission was to evacuate the BEF, not defend Dunkirk as an armed bastion, as doing so would suck in more men from the BEF who he reasoned should be evacuated not condemned to a grave. Gort ordering the withdrawal left the Belgian army exposed and almost completely surrounded by the Wehrmacht. Lacking ammunition and feeling betrayed, the Belgians looked to an armistice. It seems Gort had failed to inform the Belgians of his retreat and to order them to fall back in consort with the BEF.[8] As night fell, the Belgian army was in a state of collapse during the Battle of the Lys. Facing relentless German attacks and lacking resources, the Belgian forces began to crumble, with the line breaking in several areas. The Belgian army was rapidly losing ground. They were facing breaches in their defensive lines, particularly north of Maldegem, near Ursel, and towards Thielt and Roeselare. Near Ghent in Belgium, in the vicinity of the village of Vinkt, German soldiers looted houses, supposedly looking for snipers. The day before, they had lost several hundred men during a counter-attack by the *Chasseurs Ardennais*. This time the Wehrmacht attacked in strength and the *Chasseurs* were forced to abandon Vinkt by 16:00, having lost thirty-nine men. The attacking Germans murdered eighty-six civilians in retribution for the Belgian resistance. As well as lack of food and munitions, the Belgian army was increasingly unable to co-ordinate its operations: roads were clogged due to the large number of refugees (both those already living in the area and those fleeing the fighting). The collapse of the Belgian army contributed to the vulnerability of the British escape corridor to Dunkirk and ultimately led to the Belgian surrender. On the evening of 27 May, the message sent by the Belgian Army Headquarters to Vincennes was not very reassuring 'The Belgian army is very discouraged . . . the time is rapidly approaching when it will be in no condition to fight. The King will find himself forced to capitulate to avoid the debacle.'[9]

Yet not everything was going favourably for the Germans during the course of 27 May. Late that evening Göring was told that the Luftwaffe had already lost 1,005 aircraft, 810 of which were destroyed. The losses in aircraft, pilots and navigators was not sustainable. Slowly but surely the Luftwaffe was being exhausted. The RAF were flying from bases in southern England to cover Operation Dynamo. That day, 18,000 soldiers managed to embark for England.

Chapter 27

28 MAY 1940

After eighteen days of fighting, King Leopold III, as commander-in-chief of the Belgian army, ordered the surrender. At 04:00 the Belgian army laid down its arms. King Leopold III had considered allowing his army to fall back with the Allies to the Yser as his father had done in 14/18, and to continue the fight or in a worst-case scenario embark part of his army for England. Since 10 May, approaching 10 per cent of the Belgian population had been killed.[1] Blanchard had known of the likely capitulation, and perhaps had not passed the information on to GQG. Weygand had known that the Belgian army was close to collapse since 15:00 the previous day, in a letter which underlined a report from timed at 12:00 on the 26th, which stated the 'The limits of the resistance are very close to being reached'. Despite the warning, the news came as a shock to the allies.[2] Once the news was known outside of the walls of Vincennes, officers and men condemned the King's decision. An officer with the 12e DIM noted 'The Belgian army has just capitulated. This is a mortal blow for the Franco-Anglian forces operating in Belgium.' With this surrender, the entire front of the Lys collapsed.[3] The direct consequence of this was that Germans were able to rush to surround Lille.

The 2nd Corps of the BEF was at Poperinge on the morning of 28 May arriving around 05:00, forced from Armentières by the Luftwaffe and German shelling: 'all the trucks and vehicles of our division lined the roadside ditches and were in flames providing a sinister spectacle' wrote one French officer. He was ordered to burn all the headquarters paperwork.[4] Lord Gort notes that later than morning:

> General Blanchard arrived at my headquarters at Houtkerque at about 11 a.m., and I read him the telegram which I had received the previous day from the Secretary of State. It was then clear to me that

whereas we had both received similar instructions from our own Government for the establishment of a bridgehead he had, as yet, received no instructions to correspond with those I had received to evacuate my troops. General Blanchard therefore could not see his way to contemplate evacuation.

I then expressed the opinion that now the Belgian Army had ceased to exist, the only alternatives could be evacuation or surrender. The enemy threat to the North-Eastern flank appeared certain to develop during the next forty-eight hours. The long South-Western flank was being subjected to constant and increasing pressure, especially at Cassel and Wormhoudt, and the arrival of the enemy heavy columns could not be long delayed. These considerations could not be lightly dismissed. While this discussion was taking place, a liaison officer arrived from General Prioux, now in command of the French 1st Army, to say that the latter did not consider his troops were fit to make any further move and that he therefore intended to remain in the area between Bethune and Lille, protected by the quadrangle of canals.

I then begged General Blanchard, for the sake of France, the French Army and the Allied Cause to order General Prioux back. Surely, I said, his troops were not all so tired as to be incapable of moving. The French Government would be able to provide ships at least for some of his troops, and the chance of saving a part of his trained soldiers was preferable to the certainty of losing them all. I could not move him. Finally, he asked me formally whether it was my intention to withdraw that night to the line Cassel-Poperinghe-Ypres.

I replied in the affirmative and informed him that I now had formal orders from His Majesty's Government to withdraw the B.E.F. and that if I was to have any hope of carrying them out, I must continue my move that night. General Blanchard's parting was not unfriendly, and when he left, I issued my orders for withdrawal to provide for that change of mind on the part of the French High Command for which I so sincerely hoped and which in fact took place later.

1st and 2nd Corps were to withdraw on the night of 28th/29th May to a horseshoe position on the line Proven-Poperinghe-Ypres-Bixschoote, with outposts on the line Ypres-Godevaersvelde . . . The 48th and 44th Divisions were in contact with the enemy on a front of over twenty miles from Bergues through Cassel to Vieux Berquin.

It was now obvious that with the Belgian army capitulating and the BEF leaving France, Dunkirk could not be held as a bastion. In reply to Gort, General de la Laurencie organised what was left of the *3e Corps d'Armée* to evacuate it through Dunkirk. De la Laurencie therefore gave the order to cross the Lys before nightfall:

> To stay there again tonight is the virtual certainty of seeing oneself surrounded and reduced to capitulation. To reach Dunkirk is to escape it. To do this, it was necessary at all costs to pass Poperinge before daylight. It's a big effort to ask of the troops who can't take it anymore. But this is the only chance of salvation.

To do so here ordered two columns were formed, protected by the remaining Panhard armoured cars. Only the 75mm guns were carried. The largest guns were destroyed so as not to fall into German hands. Route: Armentières, Bailleul, Poperinge in Belgium and Hondschoote. It was impossible to take the shortest route, as fighting raged around Hazebrouck, Cassel and Wormhoudt.[5] An officer with *Corps de Cavalerie* relates:

> At 06:15 a liaison is made with the British General Osborne; an English brigade is at Vieux Berquin in liaison with the 1re DLM; another is at Strazeele, a 3rd at Caestre. An operation is said to be in progress at Mont des Cats. General Osborne reports that he no longer has any reserves and asks that, if necessary, in the event of an enemy attack on his right (in the direction of Cassel), tanks from the 1re DLM be placed at his disposal. Orders are given to Colonel de Beauchesne, commanding the 1re DLM, to make close liaison with the British for this purpose.
>
> At 06:45 an artillery officer reports that his column was surprised by German tanks near Beau Grenier (Armentières-Lille Road); information which was confirmed by a motorcyclist. It is also reported that the enemy is at Haubourdin. The 3e DLM, with elements of the 15e DI, the 7e RI, the 32e DI and the GRCA/6, gradually moved along the Lys to Armentières after having checked the previous information by scouting parties.
>
> The enemy, increasing its pressure, gradually pushes all along the front of the CC from Vieux Berquin to Estaires. It is blocked everywhere, in particular thanks to which all the groups were able to be deployed in good time. On the right bank of the Lys, the situation is particularly confused; the traffic jam on the roads alone prevented the advance of enemy tanks.
>
> At 15:00 a German attack on Mont des Cats is repelled thanks to the tanks of the 1re DLM.
>
> At 16:00, the order is given by the *1re Armée* to storm the bridges of the Lys.
>
> The city of Bailleul suffers without interruption, an intense bombardment of aircraft throughout the day.[6]

At 17:00 General de Laurencie, in discussion with Generals Janssen and Lucas of the 12e DIM and 32e DI, on hearing of the Belgian surrender said:

'We are on the eve of a capitulation in the open country,' he said, 'and I have obtained authorization from the General Commanding the *1re Armée* to make an attempt to reach Dunkirk with the personnel who can still be saved . . . will you think about it, MM, and tell me if you consider the thing possible. If so, the withdrawal movement will continue until daylight.' The decision to be taken is of a particular gravity. Opinions are divided. A discussion begins, Generals Janssen and Lucas are the most expressly reserved and ask to consult their corps commanders . . . General de la Laurencie, leaves and returns around 7:00 p.m. he becomes more pressing 'it is the only chance of salvation that remains to you, he must, we do not have the right to neglect it. It is a question of saving fighters who will go and serve the country elsewhere. It is a question of reaching Dunkirk and embarking, that's all. If you believe you must persist in your refusal, gentlemen, you will report it to me in writing and you will retain full responsibility.' Each of the General officers, after having discussed again with his collaborators, gives his agreement in principle.

The 12e DIM and 32e DI began to retreat from Lys to Dunkirk at 19:15.[7] An officer with the 3e DLM adds:

It seems, towards the evening that, on the one hand, the enemy has cut the Army's communications between the region of Lile and that of Armentières (thus isolating the troops still on the right bank of the Lys) and that, on the other hand, he is preparing, for the next day, to make an effort on Mont des Cats to cut off the rest of the army's last route of retreat towards the sea.

Consequently, General Prioux summoned the General Commanding the CC to his HQ around 19:00. He informs him of the decision he has just taken: to have the Army Groups withdraw to Dunkirk, which are close enough to the coast to carry out this movement under the protection of the CC. The operation will be carried out under the orders of General de la Laurencie, Commander of the *3e Corps d'Armée*. General de Laurencie immediately gathered at the Steenwerk town hall the General Commanding the CC, the General Commanding the 32e DI and 12e DI. He insisted that all the elements of these divisions immediately set off despite their fatigue.

The CC would leave tanks on the Boezigne-Poperinge-Watou Line to protect the withdrawal of the infantry units and would give AMs to the generals commanding the divisions. The Movement would also be covered by British elements established at Mont des Cats and to the north by the 12e DIM, as well as by other British units.[8]

An officer with the 4e *Dragon Portés*, part of the 3e DLM, adds that the getting to Dunkirk was far from easy:

> At 14:00 Captain de l'Escalle, of the Etat Major of the 3e DLM, came to speak with the regimental HQ (west exit of Doulier) and reported that the 3e DLM. held the Estaire-La Bassée line. All day, the regiment was in contact, slightly at first, then, towards evening, much more strongly with elements of the enemy infantry, supported by tanks. An enemy tank and an armoured car were destroyed in front of Estaire by Lieutenant Becker's cannons and machine guns. The threat weighed heavily on the right of the regiment's position, which was in danger of being turned from the north. The information that arrived on the situation of the Army of Flanders was of exceptional gravity: the enemy occupied Cassel and Hazebrouck.
>
> At 21:00, Squadron Leader Amanrich received the order to withdraw to Zuydcoote, by the route: Bailleul-l'Abeele-Watou-Rondschoote-Guyvelde. The withdrawal took place from 22:00, when infiltrations had occurred between the P.A. on the right and the withdrawal took place slowly, through the rubble of Bailleul, on a route already fully used by the large units that were retreating.
>
> The regiment lost Lieutenant Boyer during the day.[9]

For others, the day was less eventful as Colonel Parent commanding the *8e Zouaves* and the 150e RI within the 12e DIM notes:

> The *8e Zouaves* arrived at Steenwerck, and around 20:00, the 150e reached Neuve-Eglise. In their exhausted state, it was out of the question to bring them into line on the Lys River at Armentières, as had been planned.
>
> At nightfall, a general retreat towards Dunkirk of a large number of formations gathered around Steenwerck – including the 12th Infantry Division – was ordered to embark at that port. The Germans pushed on Cassle, Mont-Noir, and Poperinghe, aiming to surround everything within the bend of the Lys River. It was a matter of escaping the vice while there was still time, and to do so, they would lighten their load as much as possible by abandoning their baggage.[10]

Around Lille, 40,000 French and about 50 tanks against 130,000 Germans and 435 armoured vehicles faced one another. At 16:30, Prioux gave orders to blow up all the bridges over the Deûle except for the bridge at the Moulin Rouge in Haubourdin and the bridge at the Abbey, near the prison of Loos. At the Moulin Rouge bridge, French tanks managed to cross the Deûle. Tunisian infantrymen tried to widen this bridgehead. They held out all night but had to retreat in the early morning. In Oignies, the Germans had been blocked for two days at the gates of the mining town, which was defended by a regiment of Zouaves, Moroccan infantrymen and a few British units.

Members of the 267th Infantry Division of the Wehrmacht began murdering civilians: 48 civilians were shot dead in Beuvry, 124 in Oignies, Courrières and Wahagnies. Wounded POWs were also shot. The barbarity of the German soldiers was such that Oignies was declared 'the first martyred city of the campaign of France' after the war. This time, however, they were not SS men, but regular soldiers of the Wehrmacht.

Chapter 28

DE GAULLE'S OFFENSIVE

The situation was critical, with the Belgian army having surrendered unconditionally that morning, and the BEF facing evacuation from Dunkirk. The French forces were spread thin, with some units encircled, while others were attempting to hold the line and organise a retreat. At 16:45, 28 May 1940 the newly promoted General Charles de Gaulle launched a fresh offensive. At Huppy in the Somme, nearly 6,000 French shells fell on the Germans positioned around the village. De Gaulle attacked with his tanks, his objective being to retake Abbeville and relieve German pressure on the defences of Dunkirk:

> From 22 to 24 May, the 4e DCR moved from the AISNE to the SOMME, from the region of FISMES to that of AMIENS, from the VIe to VIIe Army. The High Command planned to engage it first to the east of Amiens in conjunction with an attack by the Army of the North from ARRAS, then to the south of Amiens to reduce the bridgehead. Finally, on 27 May, he decided to launch the 4e DCR on the positions held by the enemy south of ABBEVILLE . . . On the following day, a 15-minute artillery preparation will precede the exit from the starting base. The attack, decided for 17:00., left with a delay of 30 minutes to 1 hour depending on the unit, due to the long distance that the tanks had to travel to set up. The artillery preparation must be prolonged. The tanks preceded the Infantry . . . At night, the first objective was achieved despite a very strong anti-tank defence and strong resistance at HUPPY and HUCHENNEVILLE. But the hour of attack was too late and did not allow the surprise of the enemy and the success of the attack to be exploited. In addition, the number of infantry on this 15-kilometre front was too small to attack, cleanse, defend and organise the positions.[1]

The day before at the same place, British tanks had been cut to pieces by German anti-tank guns. De Gaulle banked on the thicker armour of his B1 *bis* to give him the advantage. After two hours fighting, by 09:15 de Gaulles' tanks were short of fuel and ammunition: he had punched through the German lines. The almost total absence of an effective means of communication due the appallingly bad French radios forced French officers to communicate through motorcycle messengers. It meant de Gaulle was unable to exploit the situation. The French had taken 200 prisoners and the German units were retreating. Victory was within reach.[2]

To de Gaulle's north, fighting at Cassel was intense. During the night Colonel Vincent Christopher 'Marino' Brown OBE, DSC, Montgomery's chief of staff, was mistakenly shot dead by a British sentry. 'His death,' wrote Montgomery's liaison officer, 'was a great loss, not only for our division, but for the entire British army.'[3]

At 18:30 twenty-one new Glenn-Martin bombers took to the air, dropping 7 tonnes of bombs on German troop concentrations north of Amiens. Due to lack of fighter cover, bombers only operated at dusk and night. It meant the Luftwaffe controlled the skies during the day. At 19:40 eight Breguet 693s bombed targets along the coast. Later as darkness was falling, twenty-one Leo 45s dropped 17 tonnes of bombs on German troops stationed at the village of d'Aubigny.[4]

As the Allies fell back, the SS killed any soldiers that fell into their hands. SS men escorted about 100 British soldiers taken prisoner during the day to a place called La-Plaine-au-Bois. The British were locked in a cowshed into which the SS threw grenades. Two British officers rushed to the explosive devices to protect their men by shielding their bodies. The SS then dragged out the survivors and shot them in cold blood. Running for their lives, half a dozen British soldiers managed to escape. Some were cared for and hidden by farmers. Two of them ran to a pond to hide. They were Private Albert Evans and his captain Lynn Allen. Unfortunately, an SS soldier followed them: he shot the captain but could not find Albert Evans. Wounded in the arm, he was later arrested by Wehrmacht soldiers who took him to a medical post for treatment. When the SS left the scene, eighty British soldiers lay dead near the cowshed.[5]

Evacuation begins.

In Dunkirk, Operation Dynamo evacuated around 3,000 BEF soldiers that day: Lord Gort, summoned Colonel Humbert, the French Chief of Staff, to tell him that 'every Frenchman on board is a lost Englishman.'[6] Some French soldiers got away that evening as the adjutant of the *1re Cuirassiers* notes:

> In execution of Service Note 3872 – 3/3 of the *1re Armée* dated 26 May, the 5e B.L.M. gave the order (N°1/28 dated 6 H) to form two echelons in the Regiment: a *1er* echelon comprising officers, crews, radiomen and tank mechanics under the orders of the Colonel; a *2e* echelon with the rest of the personnel and the drivers of vehicles under the orders of the Commanding Officer of the T.R. (Lt Pruvost).
>
> The same order was prescribed to move on Zuydcoote via Izenberge – Vinken – Bulskamp – Adinkirk. The movement takes place in the middle of the day. The *1er* echelon was to embark at Dunkirk the same evening; on *2e* echelon later.
>
> At Zuydcoote, the regrouping of the column took a long time because of the extreme congestion of the roads. The cars were parked, and the staff was taken to the dunes in order to be safe from the bombings. The Brigade commander then announced that the ships on which the 1st echelon was to embark . . . was cancelled, Colonel du Vigier then sent the 2/28 order dated 11:30 which organised the defence against aircraft.
>
> However the Regiment received an order at 15:30. which prescribed to the 1st Echelon to set off on foot at 16:30 for Dunkirk . . . The march was carried out in pouring rain and without stopping; at 19:00. we reach Malo Les Bains and at 20:00. the port of Dunkirk. The General Staff and the 1st echelon embarked on the 'Sauternes'; the second group . . . could no longer find places on the 'Hird' and were embarked on the 'Douaisien'. At 20:30 p.m., the ships left the port.[7]

The adjutant continues that:

> The 'Douaisien' exploded on a mine in the middle of the night of the 28th to the 29th near Dunkirk and ran aground on a sandbank. The elements of the Regiment were evacuated at the end of the morning to the port and stayed there all day under a violent bombardment. S-Lt Depinay was killed; There are also 3 injured and 1 missing.[8]

Even getting aboard a ship was no guarantee of safety. The survivors were found space on the *Thérèse Louis* which was towed to Dover. The 2nd Echelon were placed under the command of the *2e Cuirassiers* at Zuydcoote. They were embarked for Dover on the 31st.[9]

By late evening 6,000 British and 30,000 French soldiers with 39 tanks protected Operation Dynamo against 160,000 Germans and 100 tanks. It was not until late the previous day that Weygand had learned what was happening. Darlan, commanding the French Navy, along with Weygand, believed that the Dunkirk beachhead could be sustained almost indefinitely by being supplied by sea in order to become a continuous threat to the German flank. Conversely Whitehall was intent on evacuating the BEF from Dunkirk, and since both the French and the BEF had conducted their own separate retreats and were manning their own sections of the Dunkirk perimeter, it was assumed by the Admiralty that the British would evacuate BEF troops aboard Royal Navy vessels, while French soldiers would be evacuated in French ships. Confronted with this new reality, the French were forced to revise their plans. Without the BEF to help hold the perimeter, it was impossible to hold on indefinitely, or at least till the Weygand Line was completed. The French, having come to terms months earlier with the British Admiralty, had very few warships available. This arrangement resulted in much of the French fleet being stationed in the Mediterranean, with the Channel and North Sea left to the Royal Navy. The Admiralty knew of this reality, yet simply ignored the facts, or at least conveniently overlooked them.

As part of Gamelin's concept of making Dunkirk a fortified bastion, the French navy had already gathered a force of hundreds of trawlers as part of the resupply effort, which would now be used for evacuating troops, but they lacked warships of their own. But it meant that the Royal Navy would have to help lift the French army from Dunkirk. The goal for Weygand was to evacuate the French army, re-supply in England, and then land the same men behind the Somme in early June.

Chapter 29

RETREAT TO DUNKIRK

By midnight on 28 May it was obvious to Georges and Weygand alike that after 18 days fighting the French had to pull back into Dunkirk and fortify it: the goal was to hold out and re-supply by sea. Lille was to hold out all costs. Early on 29 May, an officer with the 4e *Dragon Portés* noted:

> Around 08:00, the first elements of the regiment arrived in Guyvelde and assembled in the cemetery. The order was given to abandon the armoured cars, to sabotage the trucks and the equipment. At 13:00, German planes appeared. Until nightfall, they did not stop bombarding Bray-Dunes and the bridge over the Dunkirk canal, between Bray-Dunes and Guyvelde, without however succeeding in reaching the latter point. The British anti-aircraft artillery was in action.
>
> The regiment lost during the day, Second Lieutenant Couturier, Midshipman Bazier, Lieutenant Soye and Midshipman Perrée, missing.[1]

In Paris that morning Weygand ordered an overall disengagement. The order, which was sent via Admiral Abrial to General Blanchard, who had succeeded Billotte, read: 'Fight your way through to the coast.'[2] The columns of French soldiers who had escaped the encirclement in Lille moved up towards the coast. The progress was difficult, the Germans were on their heels and the Luftwaffe harassed them. An officer from the *Corps de Cavalerie* relates:

> The CC movement of retreat had begun . . . But soon, the march was terribly slowed down for multiple reasons: on the designated route, the first elements soon encountered obstructions and destruction created by the previous day's air bombardment. The streets of Bailleul were thus partly cut and surrounded by overturned trucks or dead horses; it was necessary to clear the road during the night and organise the passage

of cars, one by one, bypassing obstacles and bottlenecks. The drivers, tired, had difficulty avoiding these pitfalls and created traffic jams. Horse-drawn units of the CA, taking the wrong route, came to join the CC car column. Many English soldiers mingled up with our units, and obeyed none of the orders that the French traffic officers tried to give them . . . The stops of this column become more and more frequent and prolonged, the vehicles close together without any interval . . . the day is already breaking as the column is still flowing into Bailleul at the pace of a man walking while the enemy begins to attack the Mont des Cats, which is fiercely defended by a British unit.

The tanks and artillery of the CC pushed forward, are abandoned across the road to the Poperinghue to stop a possible advance of the enemy.

The movement accelerates a little with the day; it is however only in the evening that the rearguards will reach the region of Bray-Dunes without having, moreover, been worried by the enemy.

By a sort of miracle, almost no aerial attack from the Germans.[3]

Around 07:00, the column reached Poperinge in Belgium, halfway between Lille and Dunkirk. Around 08:00 the French vanguard arrived at Oost-Cappel. It was stopped by the British. An officer with the French 2e DLM writes 'Dunkirk was a veritable cemetery of tanks on the road to Bray-Dunes' and also encumbered by routed French soldiers seeking to make Dunkirk and safety.[4] Our officer continues:

Crossing the canal bridges surrounding Dunkirk we found the English had abandoned and put out of use all the trucks, cars, artillery tractors and cannons. Only a few tourists, motorcycles and tanks (not without difficulty) pass through. This sacrifice of equipment makes the organisation of the CC formations even more difficult, which until then had remained remarkably grouped in the flow of the column.

The whole afternoon is spent gathering the units; order is fairly quickly restored thanks to a remarkable action by the officers; in the evening, the DLM grouped between Ghyvelde and Bray-Dunes, exhausted but in order.

The Germans drop a few bombs on the dense crowd of troops of all arms who block roads and streets in these two localities, in particular around the beach where the English make a passage to go and embark.

General de Lafont arrived here before General Langlois, and wrote to Admiral Abrial himself to inform him that the CC had arrived and that, on the orders of General Weygand, he had to embark as a priority in order to go and reconstitute as soon as possible the motorised cavalry elements, essential for the battles that were to follow.[5]

The goal was to lift the *1re Armée* from Dunkirk to Dover: allow the men to rest and then land them behind the Somme.

The BEF's escape route from the action at the Ypres-Comines canal to Dunkirk passed through the town of Poperinge, where there was a bottleneck at a bridge over the Yser canal. Most of the main roads in the area converged on that bridge. The British wanted to evacuate their men before the French as French soldier Private Langlart remembers:

> We passed through Lille and Deûlemont and from that moment on we arrived on the road that the English reserved for themselves towards the coast and that they prevented us from taking. I witnessed several incidents between the French and the English to get through it. Especially near Les Moëres where an English sentry was guarding a bridge over a canal and wanted to prevent us from passing, which we were able to do thanks to a general whose name I have forgotten. He arrived in a [Peugeot] 402, I informed him of the difficulties we were having to cross. He ordered a tank to point its gun at the English sentry. That's how we were able to cross the canal. And on the evening of the 29th we arrived in the dunes between Bray-Dunes and Adinkerke, right on the Belgian border.[6]

On their arrival in the Dunkirk pocket, French gendarmes directed their soldiers towards the Dunes camp. There, they were divided into groups of 250, before waiting for the moment to leave for the west pier of the port or the Quai Felix Faure, the last quay still in port condition after the bombings. Getting there was risky: it was under constant fire from German artillery and aerial attack.[7]

The German bombardment of Poperinge reached its climax at 09:30. Houses were in flames and collapsing. 2nd Corps staff, housed in a farm west of the town, now came under artillery fire, the first shells landing about 20m short of the complex and a little to the left of the main building, but soon found their mark. Major Bullen Smith, who replaced Brown, was wounded by shell fragments, so too the liaison officer. Reinforced by the 7th Guards Brigade, the French clung on.[8] At Vincennes, Weygand was operating in what was becoming almost a total communications vacuum. Colonel Bourget had passed the following information to Weygand at 14:30 from the Imperial General Staff under Gort. The BEF was presumed to be in the following positions:

> Gravelines, Bergues, Nieuport: 44th Division
> Beveren, Rexpoede, Proven: 2nd Division

Proven, Poperinge – 1st and 42nd Division
Poperinge, Ypres, Bixschoote, 5th and 4th Divisions
Bergues: elements from the command of General Adam.

Weygand had now learned in detail of Operation Dynamo from Whitehall, and the need to defend the perimeter of Dunkirk to allow the evacuation of the BEF. He still hoped to use Dunkirk as a defensive bastion, but accepted the need to evacuate French soldiers. Due to communication failure, as the liaison officer noted, the French and BEF alike were unable to co-ordinate any defence of the perimeter because:

> the situation of the three other divisions (3rd, 48th and 50th) is not known; the movement of the 48th Division is dependant solely on the movements of the French . . . the position of the *1re Armée* is entirely unknown, it is presumed that they have joined the line La Bassee to Annappes, east of Lille. The pressure from the enemy continues in the regions of Bergues and at Cassel (the news is that the Germans have taken Mont des Cats).[9]

The situation was changing very rapidly. The Allies had to be able to respond in order to defend Dunkirk. The 12e DIM arrived at Dunkirk in the early evening, reduced to 8,000 exhausted men. The scene before their eyes was truly apocalyptic:

> On all sides, there are large fires, it is either houses that are burning or boats that are burning. An extraordinary armada awaits the British detachments in the port or off the beaches and we can clearly see the files of men entering the water to meet the boats. Of course, the Luftwaffe greeted them and they were constantly bombing the crossroads, the beaches, the piers and the boats . . .The long-range German artillery had just appeared and its salvos began to fall on the port, the approaches to the bastion and the ruins of the citadel.[10]

The other issue facing French operations was that 'English troops are embarking in the region of Dunkirk and have abandoned their vehicles, blocking the roads' and preventing the French army from moving. In their flight, the officers and men of the BEF had not given any thought as to how the French troops were to operate to hold up the defensive line to allow the BEF to escape.[11] Weygand gave orders to Général Georges Blanchard to establish a bridgehead south of Dunkirk-Nieuport with all troops at his disposal to ensure a quick and safe evacuation. It was still not clear, however, in what way the evacuation could be executed. Technically, Lord Gort was formally subordinate to the commander of Dunkirk, Admiral Jean Abrial.

Weygand's staff passed a long memorandum to Paul Reynaud about the problems he faced trying to secure a new front line and impose *bataille conduite*. He needed anti-tank obstacles; he needed anti-tank guns and above all else 'aircraft are essential for our success.' Copying the tactics of the Luftwaffe was the only way to clear the front and to respond. Could America or Britain supply the needed aircraft, he asked.[12] That afternoon, German columns north of Abbeville were bombed by thirty Glenn-Martin bombers, with the surrounding areas bombed by eleven LeO 45s and sixteen Breguet 693s. Amiot 143 bombers attacked St Pol as night fell, supported by antiquated Farman 222s.[13] The goal was to slow the advance of petrol, reinforcements and ammunition to Dunkirk.

Lord Gort learned that afternoon that Whitehall had conceded to Reynaud and Weygand's requests for the Royal Navy to evacuate the French. His first reaction was disbelief: he immediately telegraphed the Chief of the Imperial General Staff, Field Marshal Sir John Dill, to ask for clarification on what had been agreed. Gort did not believe the French deserved equal treatment to the BEF. Gort reminded Dill that the safety of the BEF was his primary consideration: 'every Frenchman embarked is at cost of one Englishman'.[14] Weygand had requested from Dill, that if the French were to hold the perimeter until both armies had been evacuated, he would need air support, and lots of it from the RAF.[15]

That evening in Dunkirk, the pocket was shrinking. To the east, towards Nieuport on the Belgian coast, the French 60e DI was forced to retreat in the face of assaults by two German divisions. A thousand French managed to retreat to Dunkirk. Cassel was given up, the BEF leaving behind 1,000 dead and 2,000 wounded. Arriving that evening to bolster the defences were elements of the 12e DIM, as Captain Carton explains:

> At 6:00 PM at HQ, General de la Laurencie presents the dilemma: either fight on the spot without any retreat, or escape to Dunkirk for the embarkation and subsequent regrouping.
>
> The Cavalry Corps protects the movement by leaving an echelon facing south and, on the flank, guarding the columns . . . The general decamps the column: we follow in three cars: Morin, myself, Helle, plus their adjutants from HQ. Terrible traffic jam . . . At bastion 32 (Admiral Abrial), the general receives instructions for the DI's participation in the defence of the Dunkirk bridgehead. The English regulate traffic at the

> height of the canal and force the abandonment and destruction of rolling stock. The Division HQ is set up in Malo les Bains, where we arrive on the 1st, 69, avenue de la Mer, wine and liqueurs to take away: we quickly eat some food washed down with red Bordeaux. In the afternoon, I leave with Renauldon and Bret in a sidecar for Ghivelde and the Colré canal to lead the 150th Infantry Regiment and the 8th Zouaves who . . . despite the machine-gun fire were in position by 21:30.[16]

German reprisals against civilians and prisoners continued. Around 09:00 eighty Frenchmen entrenched in a farm were taken prisoner at Emmerin, near Lille. According to local historian René-Henri Delporte, around 10:30 eleven civilians were rounded up: two men from the commune and nine Belgian refugees, among them a 15-year-old teenager. They were shot in a garden. Altogether sixty civilians including an 82-year-old woman and the eighty soldiers were murdered. The next day, three Belgian refugees were killed: a 70-year-old man and two women aged 73 and 75. Their bodies were burned in agricultural buildings, and a resident was also shot dead in the street.[17]

In Lille, the Germans overcame the defences of the Faubourg des Postes. General Juin and the rest of his troops were taken prisoner. In the Somme, General de Gaulle resumed his attack towards Abbeville. At 04:00 with 137 tanks and 14 armoured cars, the French once more broke through the German lines whose anti-tank guns could do nothing against the armour of the B1s. The 1,400 soldiers of the *7e Regiment des Dragons* were ready to deliver the coup de grace, but the order did not come. The French tanks, unlike the Germans, were sparsely equipped with radios. De Gaulle lacked precise information on the situation, nor could he order the dragoons into battle. The offensive was suspended.[18]

At Lille, René Prioux was made a prisoner along with his staff. Rommel during the previous day ordered a pontoon bridge constructed over the canal. At noon, he launched his Panzer division towards Lille to cut off the route of the Allied troops towards Dunkirk. The remnants of *1re Armée*, now to the south and west of Lille and completely surrounded, were shepherded into ad hoc divisions, and Général Jean Molinié, commander of 25ième *Division d'Infanterie Motoriseé* was put in overall command. He had the following units at his disposal:

2e Division d'Infanterie Nord-Africaine,
5e Division d'Infanterie Nord-Africaine,
25e Division d'Infanterie Motorisée,
15e Division d'Infanterie Motorisée
1re Division d'Infanterie Motorisée

These troops managed to withstand attacks from two German armoured and five infantry divisions for two days. At 01:00 on 1 June, they surrendered.

In Dunkirk, by the end of the day 47,310 more soldiers were evacuated. The destroyers HMS *Wakeful*, *Grafton* and *Grenade* were sunk. The French navy provided three light destroyers of the *Cyclone* class and five dispatch boats. The destroyers arrived in mid-afternoon, under a violent German bombardment. One eyewitness notes:

> 28 May 23: 3 p.m., at the western exit of BRAY DUNES, the congestion of the roads is such that vehicles have to be abandoned. The Battalion will reach DUNKIRK on foot; during the journey, it was diverted to MALO-les-BAINS where it arrived on 29 May at around 5 a.m.
> 29 May General FAGALDE gave at 12.15 p.m. to the 13e, 38e and 35e Battalions the order to embark.
>
> The torpedo boat CYCLONE received the 2nd Company, part of the 3rd Company and the Staff of the 13e Battalion . . . the CYCLONE set sail due to the arrival of enemy aircraft. It was subjected to a violent aerial bombardment for three quarters of an hour.
>
> The other tank elements, which remained at the port, were also bombed.[19]

The *Cyclone* got out without damage and returned to Dover that evening with 733 evacuated soldiers onboard, including 158 survivors of an English sloop picked up on the return trip. The *Siroco*, also undamaged, brought back 509 men. But the *Mistral*, badly damaged by German bombing, left Dunkirk with no French soldiers on board. In all, embarkation figures for the 29th amounted to 5,178 aboard French naval ships. The German press were in awe of the success of the Wehrmacht, boasting 'Since May 29 the BEF is in complete disintegration', reported the editor of the *NSZ Rheinfront*, who told his readers 'It has simply deserted all its vehicles and equipment and is fleeing to the sea. Swimming and on small boats, the enemy tries to reach ships lying on roadsteads, at which our Luftwaffe aims'.

Chapter 30

EVACUATION

Throughout the 29th, French soldiers had been arriving at Dunkirk. Tank crews and specialists were to be lifted off the beaches first: tanks could be replaced but not trained men. They were to be evacuated to Dover, allowed some rest and relaxation before being transport back to French soil, where it was hoped they would be ready to return to combat in new tanks. The dawn of 30 May brought salvation for the men from the *39e Bataillon de Chars de Combat*:

> 28 MAY – At 09:00., east of Bray-Dunes, the vehicles were abandoned and set on fire. At night and on foot, the detachment continued its movement along the Dunkirk-Veurne railway line, then along the Veurne Canal.
> 29 MAY. – The battalion arrived at Malo-Plage, the personnel took shelter in the dunes to the east of the city. At 15:00., the order arrived to move the detachment to the ramparts east of Dunkirk (bastion 32) occupied by the commander of the sector and the Navy. As soon as they arrived, a bombing raid by several hundred planes fell on the city. An officer of the 9e B.C.C., who had joined the battalion, was killed along with several of his men.
> At 22:00. the order was given to go to the Embectage . . . the battalion with elements of other tank units, bivouacked on the square west of the entrance to the port.
> 30 MAY. – Around 03:00 the order was given to reach Dunkirk to the embarkation points of the previous day . . . the first and third companies were embarked on the *Foudroyant*, the staff on the *Bouclier*.[1]

For others, as 30 May dawned, they had to remain at their posts to maintain the perimeter to allow their comrades a chance of escape. As the sun came up, the French had no fresh troops in fighting condition to occupy the front from Bray-Dunes to Bergues via Ghyvelde. An officer of the *4e Cuirassiers* notes:

Wednesday, 29 May:

At 03:00 the column was forced to stop 3km south of Bailleul. The road is inextricably congested. All wheeled vehicles were abandoned . . . except for about twenty tanks . . . and arrived at a place called Bray-Dunes. On 28 May, it had suffered a violent aerial bombardment at Berthen and suffered heavy losses in equipment. The basis of the 1re D.L.M. was also in Bray-Dunes.

Thursday, 30 May:

Regiment assembles on the beach of Malo-les-Bains. No boats were available to the French troops.

The tanks, under the orders of Commander Marchal, were given a mission of sacrifice: that of continuing to fight to protect the embarkation of the Army of the North.[2]

To defend the perimeter, an ad hoc armoured group was formed at Coudekerque on 30 May with all the tanks belonging to the three DLM, i.e. twenty-one S-35 and eighteen H-39 tanks marshalled together. The goal was that the tanks would be able to quickly push back any major Wehrmacht offensive against the perimeter. The BEF had abandoned or destroyed its own armour: this group was the only armour available to the Allies to hold back the Panzers. As well as marshalling tanks, what remained of the scattered French infantry divisions were ordered to defend the French sector of the perimeter.

One such was the 12e DIM. As 30 May dawned, Colonel Parent recalls:

The Dunkirk-Malo-Zuydcoote-Ghyvelde-Bray Dunes region during this period presents the desolate aspect of routed armies. French and English units wait at the seaside, on the beaches and in the dunes, for the boats that are to evacuate them . . . The intervention of English planes triggers numerous air battles with destruction of aircraft on both sides and also significant losses in the ground troops and damage to the boats. The roads and the camps are cluttered with cannons, vehicles and materials of all kinds, making all movement impossible in places, while horses and cattle wander freely. Considerable supplies of food and ammunition are lying around on the ground and are available for anyone to take, as are weapons of all French and English models.[3]

The French 12e DIM and 32e DI, under the command of General Laurencie, were holding the bridgehead at Dunkirk. The adjutant of the 12e DIM writes that the division was co-operating with the BEF and 68e DIV, adding:

> The embarkation of the English expeditionary force, taken from the 29th, continued from Panme to Dunkirk under the protection of the English war fleet and air force. A section of Anti-Aircraft Artillery was put into action. Despite the vigour of the defence, the German air force dealt severe blows to the English transport fleet. Several German planes were shot down by the Anti-Aircraft Artillery on the 29th in the afternoon above Malo-les-Bains. The embarkation operations of the English were accelerated by all means: barges, makeshift bridges and gangways, quays of circumstance. The German artillery went into action and on the morning of the 30th its first projectiles fell on the beach of Malo on the dunes and on bastion 32 in Dunkirk. General Janssen and Chief of Staff go to General Fagalde at 09:00 to explain the situation of the DIM in terms of effective strength and armament and to settle certain points concerning defence. . . . they returned to HQ at 11:00 . . . the first order from the 16th Army Corps setting out the main lines of the defence reached the DI around 14:00. This order specified that the 12th DIM was responsible for the defence of a sector extending from the North Sea to the Brander crossroads (west of Honschoote). The front limit of the position to be defended was marked by the frontier position itself on the eastern front and by the Canal de la Basse-Colme to the south. General Janssen, already oriented since his visit, General Fagalde had a summary defence order drawn up for the division. This order is inspired by the situation and what General Janssen saw on the ground the day before.[4]

Elsewhere on the perimeter, by 08:00, the 61e Division was holding the Wehrmacht in check, at least for the time being, at Yser. The road network was blocked by abandoned lorries and other vehicles from the BEF making it difficult to re-supply the French units on the perimeter, who despite the very intense aerial attacks from the Luftwaffe was putting up some resistance, albeit limited.[5] An officer with the *Corps de Cavalerie* remembers that they arrived on the beaches during the 30th:

> Despite the aerial bombardments, some 105mm shots, and the complete traffic jam of all communication routes, the DLMs formed groups of 1,000 men, divided into fractions of 250. The most complete order and the strictest discipline reigned in the formations.
>
> The English continued to embark. No departure of French troops yet.[6]

Whatever Whitehall dictated about lifting 50 / 50 French and the BEF off the beaches, the reality was very, very different. Some French troops did get out that day. Major General Howard Vyse noted:

> There are about 20 to 30,000 men, the majority are non-combatants, who have already been evacuated. Aerial operations have been of great importance over Dunkirk during the previous night: a number of destroyers laying at anchor had been sunk. One carrying 630 men was sunk by a bomb . . . There are about 20,000 men in the dunes remaining, the situation is very confused. The RAF is doing everything in their power to cover the embarkation operations.[7]

The sinking of the *Bourrasque* around 15:00 was one of the biggest tragedies that day. In mid-afternoon, shortly after the vessel had just taken on board French troops from the Quai Félix Faure along with two other destroyers, the *Bouclier* and the *Branlebas*, she came under fire from the Germans at sea off Belgium as Louis Spitaels testifies:

> Is it a mine, a bomb, a torpedo? I never knew. I rush to the deck which is strewn with corpses, the officers intervene to maintain order. The boat was seriously affected. Already, it is slowly sinking into the waves, oscillating to starboard. Soldiers, panicked, threw themselves into the water, backpacks on their backs, they sank steeply. Orders are flying from all sides. The attempt to side with each other to try to restore the balance that is seriously threatened is given in vain.

The ship had triggered a magnetic mine. German shells were also hitting the sinking ship:

> Suddenly, I felt violently thrown to the surface and I was found swimming among sailors' bags, suitcases, wood debris of all kinds, losing blood from his ears and nose. I witness atrocious scenes that remain engraved in my memory. A sailor of the Coast Battalion, the sailor Cosic, was swimming and supporting a comrade, although this asked him to let him go, he kept him on the surface anyway. They both disappeared in the waves. Everywhere there was nothing but cries and complaints.[8]

Of the 700 to 800 men on board the vessel, nearly two-thirds perished. Two English trawlers arrived less than an hour after the sinking and rescued more than 200 people. It was on one of these two trawlers that Louis Spitaels managed to get on to be taken to Dover. About fifty soldiers remained perched on the hull of the destroyer, which had completely overturned. Only thirteen were rescued at 07:00 the next day. The Luftwaffe kept up its attacks throughout the day.

The men of *Corps de Cavalerie* that evening bedded down as best they could:

> During the night, the camp of Malo-Terminus suffered a harassing fire from German 105mm artillery.
>
> While the organisation of the embarkation detachments continued in the Malo-Terminus camp, an officer from the CC was detached with the DLM liaison officers, to find Admiral Abrial (bastion 32 in Dunkirk) to organise the embarkations which were to take place, mostly on English boats, concurrently with the British troops.
>
> The embarkation was take place on the West pier, the Felix-Faure quay.
>
> The arrival of the boats is not signalled in advance, the groups of 1,000 men are made to huddle together in long lines on the quay or in the surrounding area; they embark quickly as soon as a boat presents itself.
>
> Fortunately, the Germans only fire at 105 on the quays and the city of Dunkirk. The multitude of planes, which do not stop flying over the embarkation operation during the day, hampered by a strong English Anti-Aircraft fire, only attack the ships. Many of the latter are also sunk but because of the shallows and the large number of boats, a large part of the men from shipwrecks are saved and can be transported to England.
>
> The 105 shots on Malo-Terminus increase and cause significant losses. Movements and boarding continue during the night.

The perimeter at Malo-Terminus was being defended as the day closed by General Fagalde with what remained of the *16e Corps d'Armée* and the *18e Dragons*.[9] At Bastion 32, the headquarters of Admiral Abrial, responsible for the defence of Dunkirk, Janssen, received ordered from General de La Laurencie to embark his division as quickly as possible in order to evacuate as many combatants as possible to England and from there to France to resume the fight on the Somme, was given a new mission by General Fagalde: defend the eastern flank of the bridgehead, the Moëres region, which was very much threatened by the vanguard of the 9th Panzer Division. At 19:00 Janssen issued a situation report. He was placed in command of 40,000 exhausted troops to defend the perimeter. This 56-year-old graduate of the École Polytechnique, at the head of his division since April 1939, won the esteem and affection of his subordinates for his competence.

The canal de Mardyek was defended by the 68e DI, the 42e DI covered the canal de Colme. At 11:00 elements of the Wehrmacht had occupied the village of Bierne and held the crossroads at Bergues, with patrols by 16:00 reaching the bridge at Brander and Cerf, which had yet to be destroyed. To that end the 12e DIM was to be centred at Bray-Dunes occupying the line from Uxem to Brander and also the line of the canal des Chats. The *8e Zouaves* and 150e RI were to be placed along the canal between Dunkirk and Furness. The divisions headquarters at Malo-Terminus were to be defended by the 3e GRDI. All units were to be in their allocated positions by dawn on the following day.[10] The division was to arrive at Dunkirk during the evening, it was relatively intact. The *8e Zouaves* mustered 45 officers, and 850 other ranks with 19 heavy machine guns, and the 150e RI 39 officers, 1,200 other ranks, 46 heavy machine guns, four light machine guns, three mortars, and two 25mm cannon. The brigaded artillery brought four 75mm, two 105mm, six 155mm and four 47mm artillery pieces, and five armoured cars. The biggest issue Janssen faced in getting his troops into position was the total lack of radios. He had much to say about conditions at Dunkirk and relations with the BEF:

> The 12e DLM . . . arrived in the Honschoote region with its combat equipment, but without any support elements. The order had been given to leave all its automotive assets in the Bailleuil region in order to lighten the column as much as possible and to allow it to escape by forced march from the encirclement that was leading up to its embarkation.
>
> Upon arrival in the Honschoote region, it found the bridges of the Basse-Colme Canal guarded by the British, who refused to allow any vehicles to pass, even machine-gun carriers. Despite this, we were obliged to able to force through our lorries and machine-gun carriers. Exhausted, our men fell asleep and, in the Moeres region, while they slept, English soldiers destroyed or sabotaged our heavy equipment, motorcycles and vehicles. They also killed our remaining horses . . . On learning of this, I gave orders so that as soon as possible each regiment was to searched its zone for: ammunition, rifles and others weapons, especially 25mm cannons, but I fear that little has escaped the vandalism of the English.[11]

Another eyewitness, this time the Chief of Staff of the 12e DIM, agreed that the BEF was overzealous in demanding the French destroy their vehicles, heavy artillery and artillery horses so that the Germans did not capture them. Officers of the BEF specifically demanded the French destroy their radios.[12] Basically, the BEF, in ensuring the destruction of usable military hardware in case it was captured by the Germans, 'hamstrung' the French: clearly many members of the BEF felt that the German army was moments away from capturing the perimeter and acted as they felt best. The lack of machine-gun carriers, lorries and artillery would be keenly felt over the coming days. If the perimeter was to be held as long as possible, then artillery was essential. As it was, soldiers of the BEF had robbed not only the French, but themselves their best means of defence.

Echoing Janssen's frustrations, another French officer recorded in his diary the same day, that the pillboxes and blockhouses the French were ordered to occupy by Fagalde, had been destroyed by the retreating BEF. As the BEF had pulled back to the beaches to allow the French to take over defence, cars, lorries and machine-gun carriers had been left at the crossroads to create makeshift barricades and roadblocks to stop the Germans. No thought had been given as to how the French were use the road network or defend the perimeter. Without blockhouses, the French troops were incredibly vulnerable to German machine-gun fire, aerial attack and armour. Another French officer lamented, his unit could not fulfil its objects because of the hundreds of burned-out British vehicles that blocked any line of communication and movement. 'This morning,' wrote a French officer, 'the British soldiers burned their remaining vehicles and destroyed their weapons' which he lamented could and should have been utilised in defending the perimeter. Worse still, stocks of food and ammunition had been blown up by the retreating BEF rather than be handed over to the French.[13] Defence of the perimeter was hamstrung by the retreating BEF: how much more effective could the defence have been if pillboxes and blockhouses not been demolished? How many more lives could have been saved if the French light tanks and machine-gun carriers been able to move freely against the Wehrmacht? How many lives could have been saved if food and other stores had not been destroyed by the BEF to prevent the German soldiers capturing it? No thought was given at all to the needs of the French army or of the defence of the perimeter once the BEF had retreated.

Janssen continues that the BEF in destroying its equipment impacted the defence of the perimeter far more challenging in other ways: 'the communications situation is lamentable. Everything is blocked by abandoned vehicles. I can only reach my corps leaders by solo motorcycle or on foot. I have no radio transmission.'[14]

For the men of the *8e Zouaves* and 150e RI, 'we became aware during the night that the 2nd Division of the BEF was no longer at the front; they had left to embark during the 31st.' Thus, the French, with little warning, suddenly found themselves alone and shouldering almost entirely the burden of defence of Dunkirk whilst the British Army sailed away to safety.[15] Little or no thought had been shown by officers and men of the BEF for the troops that would come to relieve them on the perimeter to allow them to escape Dunkirk.

It is unlikely that soldiers would have destroyed stocks of food, weapons and bunkers without orders (or explosives for that matter) so clearly some amongst the senior officers of the BEF were operating a scorched-earth policy that was literally Britain First: in denying resources to the Germans in case of capture (a sensible precaution), it robbed the French of food, weapons, ammunition and the ability to effectively defend the perimeter. The BEF, or more correctly Whitehall, had little interest in helping the French as 31 May dawned.

To the east of Dunkirk, on the outskirts of the Mardyck Canal, the Germans attempted an assault the canal zone. The 68e DI held this front with the support of coastal battery guns and field artillery. The 22e RI at Spycker inflicted heavy losses on the Germans around the castle of Afgand.[16] Notwithstanding all these losses, 6,363 French soldiers were embarked

Chapter 31

DISAGREEMENTS

On 30 May 1940, the French military was facing a dire situation in the Battle of France. German forces had broken through the Allied lines and were rapidly advancing, encircling Allied troops and pushing them towards the English Channel. The French army, despite some pockets of resistance, was now largely ineffective in stopping the Wehrmacht. Tens of thousands of French soldiers were heading to Dunkirk in hope of salvation. To prevent total confusion between the survivors of the BEF and French units, as more French troops arrived at beaches, officers from the BEF implemented a segregation policy on the beaches. Lord Gort agreed that was evacuating the BEF was his main priority, and the main priority of the French was to defend the perimeter to allow the BEF to get away. The beaches closest to Dunkirk were for British troops: the French were to march along the coast to the beach at Bray-Dunes. Unlike the beaches controlled by the BEF, Bray-Dunes had no anti-aircraft defences, no anti-tank obstacles and was exposed to the constant fire of German artillery and Stukas.[1] Were the French being used to draw fire from the BEF embarkation points? By relegating the French to an area to the west of the sanitorium at Zuydcoote, the assembly point hugely restricted French access to the point of embarkation, which the BEF did not face. Moreover, unlike the BEF, the French had to march to the new location under constant artillery and aerial bombardment. The new camp was almost constantly under attack.[2] Understandably, tensions between French officers and their counterparts in the BEF began to rise. The French felt that the British prioritised their own evacuation – which they had – leaving French troops to fend for themselves in more vulnerable and exposed locations. Moreover, what food and water that could be found in Dunkirk had been almost exclusively been used by the BEF who gave little thought to their allies, as we shall see.

Around 06:00, the Zuydcoote area and southern perimeter were placed under the command of General Janssen and what remained of the 12e DIM.[3] With the BEF falling back, and unable to fight back as most soldiers had dropped their rifles and ammunition, the French were spread thinly across a wide front. At 12:30, Janssen realised he lacked sufficient ammunition and men to defend the perimeter as it then existed, and sought to move back to the Canal des Chats. His beleaguered forces were reinforced by a squadron from the 13e Dragons with H-39 tanks. 'The English,' wrote the adjutant 'care only about embarking (both day and night)' adding that 'heavy aerial bombardment' was endured throughout the day, lamenting the English anti-aircraft guns were 'largely ineffective in shooting down enemy bombers'.[4] The adjutant of the 12e DIM remarked to this journal that: 'Throughout the day, the German artillery never stopped firing . . . because it had been impossible to camouflage our positions and guns or use strongpoints, the losses were experienced were very heavy . . . the enemy aircraft never ceased in their attacks.'[5]

As morning wore on, Gort didn't know yet whether he was ordered to hold out in Dunkirk as long as possible or was to see to an evacuation of the BEF as quickly as possible. Eden told Gort to continue with the evacuation and as soon as the BEF had shrunk to three divisions, he had to relinquish command over the remaining troops and have himself evacuated to England. On paper at least, Operation Dynamo was to lift 50/50 French and British off the beaches, but in fact Gort officially assigned just two ships to specifically evacuate French troops. Gort's policy of British First caused significant tension among the troops on the beaches and in the port of Dunkirk. Darlan claimed that Gort had never really been an ally of the French and had long planned for the evacuation in a terse memo written than morning. Darlan was right that evacuation had been conceived almost as soon as the campaign began.[6]

Blanchard wrote to Weygand, with news from Dunkirk: his division was holding the bridgehead at Dunkirk, with his headquarters at Fort des Dunes. He demanded an answer as why the British were not operating with the agreed plan to defend Dunkirk, but rather were evacuating only the BEF, refused to fight, and refused to take orders from the French. The BEF were acting under direct order, he was told from the government in London, either Churchill or the War Office.[7]

The structures at Fort des Dunes were partly buried beneath the sand, affording excellent camouflage. It is a remarkable example of the military architecture conceived by General Séré de Rivières. Completed in 1878, the fort is part of a series of fortifications erected following France's defeat by Prussia in 1871. It was built to defend the port of Dunkirk from an attack from the east. The Zuydcoote coastal battery, located 800m from the fort, was built in 1879 as an annex.

Chapter 32

31 MAY 1940

Just after midnight, an irate Blanchard in consort with Abrial told Weygand that if he was to get the *1re Armée* out of Dunkirk he would need four or five divisions from the BEF to cover the retreat: he insisted Weygand make these demands clear to General Dill and the British Government, as this was in breach of agreed plans. Blanchard had just five H-39 and fifteen SOMUA tanks, which desperately needed ammunition and petrol. His men needed food and bullets.[1] London replied at 04:20 that insufficient shipping existed to lift the French from Dunkirk: the British Government's priority was getting 20,000 men of the BEF off the beaches in the next 48 hours.[2] Evacuating the French was informal policy for Whitehall: the French believed it was formal policy, leading to understandable confusion and a flaring of tempers. By dawn on 31 May, the French military was facing a critical situation during the Battle of France. While the BEF was being evacuated from Dunkirk, the French forces were now engaged in fighting a desperate rearguard action to protect the withdrawal. Despite their efforts, the French army was severely weakened and facing a relentless German advance. The day marked a turning point with the evacuation of Allied troops from Dunkirk reaching its peak, but also the beginning of the end of the Battle of France.

Under pressure from Abrial and Weygand, Gort had spoken with Eden: was he to hold the perimeter as long as possible so that the maximum number of French soldiers could be lifted off the beaches or was he to withdraw when he judged the situation untenable. Eden told Gort to leave once he felt it was unsafe to remain in Dunkirk. Gort told Abrial and Fagalde that he was placing the 1st Corps of General Barker under French command, to hold the perimeter to allow time for the French reach Dunkirk and to be evacuated. Having sent his instructions to Barker and Fagalde, Gort left Dunkirk about 12:30: he was replaced by General Harold Alexander. Alexander was given the same information. Yet 24 hours earlier, General Dill, Chief of the Imperial General Staff, had told Gort – in response to pressure from Weygand – that Operation Dynamo was to lift equal number of British and French soldiers, even if it meant leaving British soldiers behind and to remain as long as possible. On assuming command Alexander took the 'safety first' option. The French were to be left behind. At 15:30 Alexander met Admiral Abrial in person to explain his planned operations in a tense meeting recorded by Abrial's secretary:

Abrial: Lord Gort has just given me a letter in which he has told me that he is leaving three British divisions in France to defend the Dunkirk bridgehead along with French forces in order to permit French and English soldiers to embark. He is putting these three divisions under the command of General Alexander, who in his turn is to serve under the General Commanding 16e Corps [General Fagalde].

Alexander: Yes [but lacking conviction.]

Fagalde: I am asking General Alexander to place these divisions after their retreat in the following places: one division in the environs of Bray Dunes to support the French 12e Division, one division in the environs of Uxem and one division east of Bergues on the Canal de la Basse Colm.

Alexander: My divisions are so tired they cannot hold the front you have specified. They are lacking in weapons due to the battles they have fought. Further, Lord Gort has not told me to hold a sector of the Dunkirk bridgehead with French troops; he has told me that all the English troops are to be evacuated.

Abrial: I do not know what Lord Gort has told you; I only know that I have this letter which we can read together to see if we are in agreement.

Fagalde reads the letter.

Alexander: Lord Gort never told me to co-operate with French troops to hold Dunkirk; he told me to save as many English troops as I can, and then to evacuate them on the boats. [Alexander's chief of staff agrees].

Fagalde: So your saying that the French army should cover the evacuation of the British Army whilst the British Army gives no assistance to the French Army for its retreat?

Alexander: I want nothing more than to co-operate with you. I am just telling that my troops will abandon their positions . . .

Abrial: If you do this, the French soldiers will not have even started to evacuate, because there have not been enough boats. The 5,000 spaces the English Navy has put at our disposal for the last two nights are insufficient to evacuate the 100,000 Frenchmen who are defending Dunkirk.

Alexander: I am sorry about this . . .

Naval officer Laperouse: No General, it is still possible to save honour. [Alexander, embarrassed looks at the table, pretending not to understand what is being said.]

Altmayer: I must insist we should act honourably. We have been fighting to save everything that can be saved, English and French, and we should not leave this place without making sure we have done our duty. We have not yet fulfilled our commitments. We can do more if the British agree to help us.

Alexander: I have received the order to evacuate at midnight.

Altmayer: But General, we have a mission which has been given to us by Admiral Abrial and by General Fagalde, and it has been explicitly confirmed by Lord Gort. It is to defend Dunkirk with all the French forces available, and with three British divisions. We must accomplish this mission.

Alexander: I have not been told this by Lord Gort.

Abrial: To sum up, the letter that Lord Gort has written, the only that in my eyes is important, has been contradicted by the verbal orders . . . I propose that we go to see Lord Gort so that we can all act in agreement. It is 16:30, and he told me he will not embark till 19:00.

Laperouse: Can you inform Lord Gort we are coming?

Alexander: There is no point, Lord Gort left at 16:00.

Abrial: Since we cannot count on English co-operation General, I will fulfil our mission using French troops. We French have a mission which is to fight to the last man to save as many soldiers as we can from Dunkirk.[3]

Weygand telegrammed London at 18:50 expressing his disgust at Alexander and that the French would be sacrificed to save the BEF. In reply, he was told Churchill was in Paris. Eden in his reply of 20:00, unaware that Gort had left France, ordered him to hold on as long as possible at Dunkirk to allow as many French soldiers to embark as possible. Gort had told Eden earlier that day that it was impossible to hold Dunkirk: his divisions were far too weak to act as a rearguard due to casualties, lack of ammunition and food; therefore, it was impossible Gort said for the BEF to hold the bridgehead to allow their French allies to embark. Eden accepted that 48 hours was the maximum time that the evacuation would continue.[4] The French were being expected to make a last stand to save the BEF, who would do nothing in return. On his part, Alexander contacted Eden around 19:15, half an hour later an emergency meeting of the War Cabinet Defence Committee met.

The Committee was in agreement that the evacuation was to end on 1 June: Alexander cautioned that Abrial could prevent access to the port if the British did not co-operate with French planning. The meeting agreed it would be 'entirely wrong to sacrifice our men by attempting to hold out longer to please the French'. The French had saved the BEF and were now expected to be killed, wounded or captured. Eden told Alexander this at 20:15 or thereabouts. Alexander's written order stated 'you should withdraw your force as rapidly as possible'. The news was passed to Abrial, who was told Alexander had to evacuate 50/50 BEF to French soldiers. At the same time, the British War Cabinet's decision, was communicated directly to the Senior Naval Officer at Dunkirk, Captain Bill Tennant, who was instructed that French soldiers were now to be evacuated alongside BEF troops in equal numbers. As noted, Gort had already left, having expressed his 'astonishment' at the French Army's lack of willingness to fight.[5] Was it not the BEF who had left the French as rearguard?

Admiral Abrial at Dunkirk telegrammed Weygand at 20:45 that General Alexander had no intension of making any dispositions to defend the bridgehead at Dunkirk:

> General Alexander, who commands the British troops that General Gort has placed at my disposal to assist in the defence of the Dunkirk headland, intends to break contact at nightfall on the 1st of June and to attempt the immediate embarkation of his troops, whatever may come.
>
> General Alexander's intentions are not in accordance with the promises I received in writing from Lord Gort this morning. I request you to order the War Office to prevent this manoeuvre, which would render the evacuation of our troops impossible and would compromise the honour of our Arms.[6]

As soon as Weyand received the telegrams, he and Admiral Darlan met at Les Invalides: they telephoned Winston Churchill who was then in Paris. The fraught conversation ended at 22:00: Weygand demanded the BEF lift the French troops off the beach and help with the defence of Dunkirk.[7]

Meantime, Abrial contacted both the War Office and Admiralty in London: 'General Alexander, placed at the disposal of Admiral Abrial, has a clear intention of embarking at night whatever happens, thus abandoning the defence of Dunkirk.'[8]

Whilst Abrial was making his panicked messages, that evening in Paris Paul Reynaud and Churchill met. Weygand allowed that the troops at Lille were in an impossible situation – remember, Gort had triggered this situation by refusing to support General René Prioux.

Churchill convinced Weygand that there was no need to hold out at Dunkirk: Reynaud complained bitterly that the British had only lifted 15,000 French troops, compared to 150,000 BEF, well below the agreed 50/50. Reynaud made it clear that the bulk of soldiers within the perimeter would be French and deserved a chance at evacuation. Admiral François Darlan, head of the French Navy, complained that the BEF rearguard would evacuate before the French: Churchill exploded, claiming the BEF and French would leave arm in arm. Eden and Alexander were both happy to sacrifice the French. Fagalde roared 'your decisions to evacuate with your three divisions represents a disgrace for England'. The meeting ended abruptly.

Eden wanted the BEF out of France and cared nothing for the fate of the French who had allowed Gort to get the BEF away to England. The total number of troops lifted off the beaches by midnight of 31 May was 171,600 members of the BEF, of which 10,600 were wounded, and just 22,600 French.[9] Close to midnight Weygand messaged Blanchard that Gort had already left France. With the French in the north in total chaos, and the BEF 'legging it' to England, Weygand stated: 'The French government has considered giving you a similar order. I cannot do so in my ignorance of the exact situation of your troops and the current organisation of their command. Your army group being dissolved, I therefore leave you free to make the decisions concerning you, once the command and embarkation of the French troops have been settled.'[10]

Blanchard was in essence told 'every man for himself. Get out if you can.' But with the BEF set to abandon their allies, what hope did Blanchard have? At 23:00 the War Office told Alexander: 'You must withdraw your forces as quickly as possible on the basis of as many French as English, endeavouring to complete your movement during the night of 1st to 2nd June. You must inform the French of this precise order.'[11] Abrial was informed by Eden that the 'the efforts for tomorrow will concentrate on the evacuation of the French.'[12]

In Dunkirk General Vernillat was placed in command of planning the French embarkation. At 15:45 he issued plans for embarkation on the following day. Eighteen columns of 250 men had arrived from the *3e Corps d'Armée,* six from the *4e Corps d'Armée* and sixteen from the *5e Corps d'Armée*. Gendarmes and army provosts were to prevent stragglers from joining the columns.[13] The individual soldiers or groups of men under 250 strong having no officers and sous-officiers with them were to be sent to a reserve camp, to be organised by the

16e *Regiment de Travailleurs,* and were to be the last body of French troops to leave. The units that still had some cohesion were to be given priority.[14] Each of the three French Army corps were to have designated assembly points and camp sites, named A to E. Vernillat wrote to the corps commanders that he had had assurance that the English would embark French soldiers from the jetty east of the fort of Dunkirk that night along with members of the BEF.[15]

Some of the French soldiers embarked that day were from the *6e Cuirassiers*:

> MAY 30, 1940
>
> In the afternoon, the order arrived to move to Malo-Terminus, where a boarding would take place. It was a difficult road among the piles of destroyed equipment, the demoralised crowd . . . the civilians relentless in looting.
>
> We spent the night in the dunes at the foot of the Terminus Hotel, under an intermittent bombardment of 77mmm shells which caused some losses.
>
> Killed: Cuirassier L.[illegible]
>
> Wounded: Marshal-des-Logis-Chef BARNAUD – Maréchal-des-Logis ROMAGEON – Trooper BULCKAEN.
>
> Four citations were awarded.
>
> MAY 31, 1940
>
> The Regiment was made up of groups of fifty men and commanded by an Officer for embarkation. It collected some elements of motorised infantry regiments, in particular the detachment DE CHAMBRUN, of the 13e R.I., with whom he has already fought. In the afternoon, it moved to the Dunkirk pier, where, despite a fairly heavy air and ground bombardment, it embarked at 7 p.m. without incident on the *Basilisk*, a British Navy destroyer. The voyage was uneventful other than the spectacle of a great naval air battle in which the flexibility of the *Basilisk*'s manoeuvres was greatly admired. Disembarkation in Dover at 11 p.m.
>
> Two citations were awarded.[16]

Another one of these lucky few Frenchmen to escape was Captain George Merac.

> At 16:00 we received the order to head to Bray-Dunes and to embark . . . we were ordered to destroy our vehicles, abandon our baggage, and to carry with us only the barest essentials . . . We had to cross 15km across the dunes, exposed the whole time to intense artillery fire. . . . progress was slow, we marched under the continuous fall of shells . . .

On arriving at the point of embarking he and his men faced angry scenes: British officers and NCOs were turning away French officers and soldiers, both able-bodied and wounded. A group of French soldiers in response to their rough treatment, threatened to open fire to break through the cordons. 'It's your country; you defend it!' was continually shouted by British soldiers as they pushed their French allies out of the way. Meric eventually found passage:

> by some miracle a small motor boat took us on board . . . we were directed to a small steam paddle wheeler and put aboard; this was the *Sandown*, launched in 1898. A Royal Navy Officer drew his revolver and demanded to know who I was – I explained my comrades and I were officers . . . the night had no moon . . . the fire was all along the coast, immense flames and black smoke billowed from the oil tanks at Mazout . . . there was continual explosions, the banging or mortars, the falling of German bombs.

The *Sandown* left Dunkirk at 01:00 on 1 June 1940 and landed at Ramsgate at 11:00.[17]

At 20:00 Janssen issued orders in reply to Gort's planned evacuation:

> I. The bulk of the British forces in the Furness region will gradually withdraw during the night of May 31st to June 1st to embark.
>
> During the night and into the morning of June 1st, two British Divisions are to cross the position held by the 12th Infantry Division:
>
> – 4th Infantry Division to the north for the Duynhock-Bray-Dunes road (it will then regroup towards Bray-Dunes beach).
> – 3rd Infantry Division to the south on N1 40 towards Dunkirk. This withdrawal will be covered by small infantry tanks, which will be the last to land.
>
> In addition, some infantry elements will withdraw along the coast of La Panne towards Bray-Dunes.
> II. Consequently:
>
> 1. The 12th Infantry Division's front between Ghyvelde and Bray-Dunes may be exposed, and enemy contact may be established during the morning.
> 2. When the last troops arrive, there will be reason to deploy demolitions and lay the mines prepared for this purpose.

A British officer must be stationed on each route and indicate when demolitions and mines may be effective.

3. The artillery must be very attentive, and as soon as the British officers have warned of the arrival of the last troops, it must be ready to fire with the aim of slowing the enemy's approach.

III. All this concerns the withdrawal of troops from the Furness region. Later instructions will specify the organisation of the division's defensive position.[18]

At midnight Weygand was sent a telegram from London. He was told that during the course of the day 22,000 French soldiers had been evacuated from Dunkirk, and that the evacuation of the two armies was to carry on despite the heavy German bombardment. He was told:

> General Alexander believes, like Lord Gort, that the troops available to hold the zone occupied by the two armies are not sufficient to resist the serious attempts at infiltration, the pressure of which is already gradually being felt. The increasing fire from enemy artillery makes embarkation on the beaches and quays of Dunkirk more and more difficult. In these circumstances, we are making every possible effort to complete the evacuation this evening, and to save as many French and British troops as possible while conditions are still favourable.[19]

That night German artillery stepped up its bombardment of Bray-Dunes and Zuydcoote. At first light swarms of Stukas descended on the camp: houses at Zuydcoote were burning, cars, lorries and vehicles of every kind, an eyewitness remembered, were burning.[20] Despite these forty-eight French ships of all kinds from the merchant marine brought back 9,984 men. In spite of pockets of French forces fighting bravely and even achieving some tactical victories, they were ultimately unable to stem the German tide due to a combination of factors, including strategic miscalculations, operational and tactical shortcomings, and a lack of decisive leadership when it was most needed. 'The retreat is like an escape', wrote the editor of the German newspaper *Der Führer* of 31 May. He continued: 'There are no rules, no more military order. There's only one command: save yourself if you can. The British have experienced a lot in their military history on the Continent, but never this completely hopeless stranglehold and total destruction. Dunkirk will remain a bad memory for proud Albion for hundreds of years. The French are now completely alone.'

Chapter 33

1 JUNE 1940. GET OUT WHILE YOU CAN

As 1 June dawned, with the last of the BEF falling back to Dunkirk and leaving the perimeter, the only option for the French was to reduce the size of the perimeter. Captain Carton reports that at dawn on 1 June: 'General Fagalde, commanding the 16th Army Corps, was surprised by the withdrawal of the line along the Canal des Chats (finally agreed by General Janssen). The morning was initially calm . . .'[1]

By 06:00 the Luftwaffe began operations as did the German heavy artillery. One salvo of 105mm shells killed three officers and wounded others. Because of the shellfire,

> it was decided to transfer HQ to the Fort des Dunes. I went there with the battalion commander and Farthouat to conduct reconnaissance and sketches for where we were to fall back. At the rear we witnessed the departure of General Blanchard, who embarks that same evening . . . The last British detachments left the anti-tank trench around 07:00.[2]

To bolster the French position at Zuydcoote, General Janssen ordered a squadron of H35 tanks from the *Corps de Cavalerie* to the section which had been placed at the disposition of the 12e DIM. The armour was to be positioned so as to intervene rapidly along the Dunkirk-Furness canal.[3]

The adjutant of the 12e DIM recorded:

> During the course of the night of 31 May to 1 June, activity by both artillery's was unceasing: the Germans direct their fire to harass Bray-Dunes, Ghyveldt, Malo les Baines and Dunkirk.
>
> The enemy made contact with the front of our division at 08:00.

> At 07:00 the last elements of the British forces had fallen back from Nieuport and Furnes and left their positions. They had ceased firing and our division was ready for combat.[4]

As the adjutant notes, the hastily dug anti-tank position at Ghyveldt, now being defended solely by the *8e Zouaves*, came under fierce attack by 150 German soldiers. The Germans had tried to attack along the undefended beach to try and outflank the Zouaves. The Zouaves fought back, taking forty-five Germans as prisoners. The perimeter was holding by midday.[5] A second attack against the perimeter, this time in the sector held by the 150e RI, was repulsed by 14:00, with around fifty German prisoners taken.[6]

Elsewhere the situation was not as optimistic. As the Germans stepped up the attack, at 09:30 Zuydcoote was abandoned: it was impossible to remain, remembered a French soldier. Roads leading from Zuydcoote were blocked by burning vehicles, collapsed houses and bomb-cratered roads. It was not till after midday that the last of the French soldiers escaped. The ordeal was not over: at Bray-Dunes the artillery fire and attacks by the Luftwaffe were almost constant, and lasted into the night. The soldiers had no cover, no food and no water.[7] But the Luftwaffe did not have everything all its own way: forty-seven aircraft were shot down by the French on 1 and 2 June.[8] Janssen issued a situation report at midday:

> The crossroads at Zuydcoote were blocked by engineers demolishing houses to prevent German tanks moving easily in the area by 11:00.
>
> The crossroads at Noorenberghe were blocked at 11:30.
>
> An anti-tank ditch was being dug across the road Ghyvelde, to create a stop line.
>
> The Germans are following the retreating English units very closely. Fighting was now along the Ghyvelde – North Sea front.[9]

Along the coast, an officer with the *Corps de Cavalerie* noted: 'The circling of planes continues without interruption above the ships; some English fighter raids come as far as Dunkirk, but the city begin to be bombed more effectively from 10:00.'[10]

The western sector held by the 68e DI, was also attacked as Lieutenant Mennesson an artillery officer with the 89e RI recounts:

> Towards the middle of the afternoon, gunfire began to spread nearby. A French infantryman ran up to announce the arrival of German infantrymen from the armoured units, whose uniforms were dark. Then

suddenly, with no other warning than the burning of a nearby haystack, the observation post was surrounded by German infantrymen uttering hoarse cries. On the other bank of the canal, others were beginning to put a barge across. After a quick consultation, Commander Nevue and Captain Lemonnier gave Captain Bieche the order to fire. After consulting the map, the latter grabbed the telephone, rang his battery, and gave him the following order: '8th Battery, Attention! Get ready to fire with shrapnel shells . . .' At the battery, Lieutenant Durand immediately understood that things were going badly. Before giving the final order to fire, he checked his map. Without a doubt, he was going to fire on the observation post. He called his captain back on the phone: 'Hey, Bieche, it seems to me you're making us fire on the op?' 'You . . . I know that. Shoot anyway!'

The 75mm cannon is certainly the ballistic weapon that makes the most noise, but this noise is even more piercing, more alarming when the muzzle is behind you . . . at 1,000 meters. The crackle of the bullets hitting the ground had a magical effect. In an instant, the swarming of Germans was replaced by absolute stillness. Where were all these people? Bieche's guns barked regularly. Clearly, the fire was well aimed from the start, and the observation post received its share of shrapnel, just like the German infantry. The attack seemed to have stalled, so the battery was ordered to suspend fire and the remaining officers were ordered to fall back near the guns so that their presence would be more useful.[11]

The French rearguard were controlling the perimeter and buying time for the last of the BEF to get away.

For Abrial, it was still not certain that the British government would save any of the French army trapped at Dunkirk: many were being killed to save the BEF and the chance of the French army being taken off the beaches was still looking slim. At 09:00 Abrial had a telegram from General Alexander; It conformed his worst fears. He messaged Darlan at 09:30 telling him what he had been told: Alexander had told Eden that the evacuation would end at midnight that day, adding:

That before the 20,000 French in line can be withdrawn, 30,000 French and 20,000 British remain to be evacuated.

This operation cannot be completed before the evening of June 2, orders are to be given to the French troops in line to resist in their positions despite the departure of the British.

I ask that for our departure, every means of transport be provided and that air protection be ensured.[12]

Darlan took Abrial's concerns that the French would be sacrificed by Whitehall to Weygand; Weygand transmitted them to London. At 10:30 Weygand received the following message:

> Under the present circumstances we are making every effort to complete the evacuation tonight and to save as many French and British troops as possible while conditions still permit. End. The circumstances mentioned are intended to point out the dangers of enemy attacks.
>
> General Alexander now commands all the British troops in the sector and has his Headquarters with those of General Fagalde and Admiral Abrial.
>
> General Barker who left Dunkirk yesterday evening considers that the elements of the 12th, 23rd and 62nd DI as well as the 1st, 2nd and 3rd French DLM hold part of the perimeter or are behind it but their situation is weak and communications very bad. It is therefore impossible to obtain confirmation.[13]

At 11:30 Gort told the War Cabinet it was impossible to hold out in Dunkirk, adding that British troops should evacuated from Dunkirk rather than holding the perimeter with the French. At 16:00 Weygand was told that the Royal Navy did not believe it could remain beyond midnight. The French were told that six Royal Navy ships and three torpedo boats had been sunk during the course of the morning, and the Navy supported by General Dill wanted to end the evacuation.[14]

Neither Weygand nor Abrial had given up hope of changing the minds of the British. Weygand messaged London at 12:45 that Abrial 'requests with great insistence that General Alexander be kept alongside the French troops in order to allow the embarkation to be completed, as the Prime Minister of England has given his assurance to the President of the French Council'.[15]

In reply, the War Office told Weygand at 17:15:

> It seems perfectly obvious from a naval and military point of view that every effort must be made to complete the evacuation this very night. It is urgent that Admiral Abrial receive instructions to cooperate in these efforts in the interest of our two armies. As the present situation is under the fire of enemy guns, this may put a definitive end to any daytime evacuation.[16]

Weygand told Abrial at 17:56:

> The Chief of the British Imperial Staff had said that efforts must be made to complete the evacuation next night from June 1st to 2nd, evacuation at night may become impossible due to the action of enemy artillery.

> Make every effort to try to complete this evacuation tonight including that of the personnel of the Northern maritime forces.
> If you do not succeed we will try to continue the following night.[17]

Yet by evening Churchill had softened his line in abandoning the French, and ordered that the defence of Dunkirk was to continue as long as the perimeter held, even with the loss of shipping. Alexander was once more told to obey Admiral Abrial: Churchill told Weygand that Abrial was to use his judgement when to end the defence of the perimeter. At 21:30 Eden messaged Alexander: 'We are not setting you any time for the evacuation. Hold on as long as possible so that we can evacuate as many French and British troops as possible. It is impossible to judge the situation from here. You must therefore act according to your own judgment in close collaboration with Admiral Abrial.'[18]

Meantime at Dunkirk, the situation for the French was getting desperate as the Wehrmacht piled on more pressure along the perimeter. At 15:50 Janssen recorded:

> At 14:30, Colonel Fabre reported that his troops had been hit by infantry fire at Bray-Dunes. He was ordered to withdraw his troops to the Dune camps.
> Officers communicated with the HQ of the 12e DIM, which was located there, with the liaison officer of the i. Enemy light infantry units, about two companies, having infiltrated since 11:00 had turned and forced passed the line of outposts and were now attacking the strongpoint at Bray-Dunes (Grande Mare Farm). The 3rd Brigade, which was in front, was completely exposed on its left flank. There was no communication with the 150e RI south of the canal.
> To the south, the British units were on the Canal des Chats.
> The general commanding the 12e DIM ordered his artillery to intervene vigorously and verbally ordered the colonel of the *8e Zouaves* to hold this line at all costs until the day after tomorrow morning. He would, as much as possible, keep the tanks he had been given for a possible counter-attack tomorrow.[19]

An eyewitness noted:

> On the evening of June 1st, General Janssen set up his headquarters at Fort des Dunes, east of Dunkirk. This location made it easy to command the sector assigned to the 12th Division, whose fort occupied a position almost in the centre of our lines.

From that day on, enemy pressure increased; although bombarded relentlessly by aircraft and artillery, the fort had remained intact until then, and the general had set up his headquarters in one of the rooms on the first floor of the southern building. We all gathered there. The night of June 1st to 2nd was quite eventful. June 2nd was a Sunday, and at 08:00, a mass was celebrated by Father Roche.[20]

Along the coast, an officer with the *Corps de Cavalerie* noted that around midday:

the last elements of the CC begin to leave their positions (including staff of the 3rd DLM), General Langlois and his staff went down to the quay Felux-Faure to embark on the torpedo boat *Foudroyant* which was announced as coming to take us to Dover. Unfortunately, we waited in vain and we learnt, around 14:00 that it has been sunk. At 18:00 the torpedo boat *Bouclier* arrives, on which General Blanchard, General Langois with part of their staff and 300 men embark. Narrowly escaping a 105mm shot and two series of bombs, the torpedo boat quickly left the port and set off at full speed for Dover where the docking took place without incident around 21:00. The English fighters, flying low over the water, protected the crossing for the greater part of it.[21]

In total 38 French ships had evacuated 7,483 men. Of the forty-three ships which had started out, five were sunk off Dunkirk, including the *Foudroyant* by a magnetic mine and three minesweepers sunk by the Luftwaffe.

Evacuation was not just at Dunkirk. At Cherbourg three British boats lifted 3,000 men and three Dutch boats picked up another 3,000 men. During the following day, it was planned to lift a further 5,000 British soldiers, and on the 3rd, a final 5,000 men.[22]

Chapter 34

2 JUNE 1940. PRESSURE MOUNTS

Late on 1 June and into the early hours of 2 June, a vast transit camp was established for the French, as a participant in the evacuation from the 1re DIM remembers:

> It consisted several hectares of dunes, located west of the large lock of the new oil port. The camp extended along the coast to the rockwork of the western jetty. The protective jetty of the Channel of this lock, called Embecquetage, constituted the mooring pier. Medium tonnage boats (ships, torpedo boats) could dock to the east of the access channel to the lock. Only very shallow draft boats (minesweepers, trawlers) could dock to the west, and even then, they ran the risk of running aground on the sand of the beach.
>
> On June 2nd, the units moved from Malo and Bray-Dunes towards the Embecquetage camp. A police post had been set up at the lock crossing to turn back isolated individuals coming from Dunkirk; the burning oil basin and refineries of St-Pol blocked the passage to the south. From the west, where Fort Mardyk still stood, only a few people came. Everyone dug their own hole to shelter from the Stukas: the camp quickly took on the appearance of a vast cemetery.
>
> Captain Matha, quartermaster of the 1st DIM, had placed some supplies at our disposal in Malo-les-Bains, and we sent two convoys through Dunkirk to resupply the men of this division. A wagon from the 43rd Infantry Regiment was available . . . there was still a little water in a tank near a lighthouse. A quartermaster from the 1st Army having told us that there were barrels of biscuits in a train of destroyed wagons on one of the Freycinet quays, we managed to bring it back to the camp with the help of some volunteers from the 43rd Infantry Regiment.[1]

Very early that morning the men of the 12e DIM were woken by bullets zipping over their heads: one officer noted at dawn 'a very strong attack was launched against the front of the 8e Zouaves.'[2] The centre of the attack, supported by artillery and wave after wave of Stukas' came along the canal de la Basse Colme. Men of the *8e Zouaves* hastily fortified themselves in the villages of Bergues.[3] If the canal was crossed, the perimeter would have fallen, and any hope of evacuation ended. The attack that morning was not just against the *8e Zouaves*. The 150e RI in the centre of the 12e DIM positions was attacked in force, but pushed back. The *Chef d'Etat Major* (Chief of Staff) of the 12e DIM adds in a memo hastily scribbled on pages from a school textbook at 09:00 that morning that the 92e GRDI had replaced the BEF at the bridge of Holie-Koncke and at Uxem, where they engaged enemy troops at dawn. At Notres-Dame-des-Neiges, German light tanks were observed moving up with infantry.[4]

To try and hold the perimeter, about 06:00 the French attempted a counter-attack to push the Germans back beyond the canal de la Basse Colme: the French dragoons and their few remaining H-39 tanks rattled forward, with battalions from the 137e and 224e RI moving up behind.[5] Lieutenant Sigogne, and officer with the 137e RI whose headquarters were at Notes-Dame-des-Neiges, writes:

> It was around 07:00. on June 2, 1940. The open and flooded terrain made it impossible to dig in, and losses were severe: many were killed and wounded. Moreover, no contact was possible with neighbouring units, which had not responded. Repeated requests for ambulances went unanswered.
>
> At 08:00, 25 wounded were crammed into a cellar. The hamlet of Notre-Dame-des-Neiges was on fire. The positions were held were mercilessly attacked; we were still holding out despite the arrival of numerous enemy reinforcements. Only two machine guns remained in the 4th Platoon; the others had been destroyed. The AMD Panhard 178 armoured car placed at my disposal was pierced by several anti-tank shells, and the driver was killed. We had to withdraw under the most violent fire.
>
> At 8:30 I was wounded a second time, by a shell fragment in the right thigh. At my side, Sergeant Pierre Crouzet was seriously wounded in the leg and was suffering seriously, but he refused to leave me.
>
> At 9:30 a shell fell near us and wounded us both again, his right arm and me in the left arm. The projectile pulverised my rifle. By 10:00, we were still holding out with a handful of men under very heavy bombardment. The air force joined in and poured a deluge of bombs . . . It was hellish, more wounded, more moans, more dead. At 10:30, exhausted with help from Crouzet, we both arrived at the first aid station; It was necessary to cover 1,500 meters and cross two small streams.[6]

Not seen by our lieutenant, the French tanks and some of the accompanying infantry not only secured the canal line, but succeeded in pushing the German troops back at Benkies Mill bridge between Hoymille and Warhem. Agreeing with our lieutenant, the adjutant of the 12e DIM noted in his report that it took the intervention of fifty German bombers at around 10:00 to stop the advance of the French tanks.[7] So much for the French not being able to fight!

At 08:30 on 2 June, Abrial told Whitehall that French 25,000 troops were defending the Dunkirk bridgehead, and he estimated there were still around 20,000 French soldiers at Bray Dunes. He added it would be impossible to lift these men off the beaches with the remaining British contingent on the night of 2/3 June. As more elements of the French army arrived at Dunkirk, the number of soldiers needed to be evacuated rose to above 60,000 by the end of the day. If the French army was to be saved, more time was needed, he pleaded. He told Whitehall that the French, although outnumbered were successful holding the perimeter.[8] At 09:00, General Janssen commanding the 12e DIM issued the following order:

> The British have fallen back during the night. In consequence, the bridges at Honke and d'Uxen are not defended.
>
> Enemy light troops have infiltrated positions 2 ½km from Bergen.
>
> To defend from the menace of enemy troops in the southern sector, the 150e RI are to deploy a battalion to the sector, their destination to be fixed by the field commander there. A squadron of Hotchkiss are to be moved to this sector with a peloton under the command of the Groupe de Reconnaissance in the sector. A liaison officer to be stationed 300m south-west of the crossroads of Moulin Vernemann. The 150e RI and *8e Zouaves* to be remain at Ardouin-Dumazet.[9]

During the afternoon of 2 June, before the ships had arrived to lift the rearguard of the BEF off the beaches, a message from Abrial arrived in London at 13:45:

1. I ask you to urgently convey to Mr. Churchill by Ambassador that Admiral Abrial hopes to be able to embark all the British troops tonight.
2. Contrary to what Mr. Churchill himself had asked the Supreme Council, the French are therefore the last to defend Dunkirk. It is thanks to their defensive action that the British troops will be able to embark.
3. I consider that the impossible must be done to evacuate them on the night of 3 to 4 and I urgently request the assistance of the British Admiralty and the RAF until the end.[10]

Weygand informed London via Koeltz:

> There are 25,000 troops who are defending the Dunkirk bridgehead, there are still around 22,000 French soldiers. All the British soldiers are leaving tonight. We are hoping to evacuate these 22,000 men during the coming night; there will still be 25,000 defenders here tomorrow. In consequence, Admiral North has stated he will remain in Dunkirk and that he was delaying the traffic jam. He is asking that as many British aircraft and ships as possible be given to him tomorrow evening Monday; in order to evacuate the 25,000 combatants who by remaining on site would therefore allow the last British contingents to take to the sea.
>
> Insist in the most urgent manner in the name of the General Commander-in-chief that satisfaction be given to the request of the North Admiral and emphasise that the solidarity of two armies that the French rearguard is not sacrificed.[11]

The Wehrmacht stepped up its operations as day turned to dusk. Rather than infantry, in the eastern sector it was the Luftwaffe that stepped up pressure as one eyewitness notes:

> At around 6:45 p.m., six German planes appeared above Fort des Dunes, diving quickly, and descended on us. Arriving at the end of their dive, each of the Heinkel's dropped a torpedo [*sic*]; the last two exploded in the small courtyard where the cars were located . . . We hurried down into the courtyard. General Janssen was found slumped at the door, had a large wound in his head and showed no sign of life; next to him we found, Captain Helle and Captain de Varine. Both were dead. Captain Bourgerie of the artillery was seriously wounded, and Adjutant Chief of the Engineers Princet lay dead close by.

Bombing by the Luftwaffe lasted until nightfall, when General Janssen and the other dead officers were buried by Father Roche.[12] It transpired that Janssen was stood smoking his pipe in the doorway to the courtyard when the bombs exploded, killing him instantly. As the cars and other vehicles in the courtyard exploded, flying shrapnel 'gravely wounded' Captain Schan 'to the face who was taken to a dressing station: he died before he received medical treatment'. Princet had been torn to pieces by the blast. Colonel Blanchon was placed in command of the 12e DIM.[13]

General Vernillat issued orders at 18:00 for that evening's embarkation. For principal embarkation, Abrial ordered there were to be two points of embarkation: the eastern jetty for the *5e Corps d'Armée* and loading dock which was to be shared with the BEF and French soldiers from the

3e Corps d'Armée. The quay Felix Faure was to act as the second point of embarkation for the *4e Corps d'Armée*. In theory 109 ships were to lift the French to Dover and Folkestone. The BEF was to be given priority over the *3e Corps d'Armée*, to ensure that 'the totality of the British troops are embarked, probably by 22:30'.[14] As the men arrived at the embarkation points, what stocks of food that remained was to be issued from military stores, so each man had two days' rations.[15]

At 22:00 embarkation began, but 'boarding operations' for the French troops 'was very limited during the first night because very few boats arrived, mostly units of the French Navy.'[16] A fleet of 57 ships of all sizes arrived to embark the 26,500 soldiers who were lined up at Dunkirk to be lifted off the beaches, 20,000 of which were French. Due to a total communication breakdown, the French soldiers who had been sent to Dunkirk from Bray-Dunes learned that they needed to be at the mole. By the time the soldiers marched back to the mole area, constantly under German artillery fire and from aerial attack from Stukas, the British ships had been and gone. General Fagalde's aide, Commandant René Lehr, noted in his note book the anger and frustration of the soldiers he met. He noted 'entire columns of soldiers had been annihilated by the bombardment. Not far from bastion 32 lay a line of bodies, all fallen on top of each other: it was as if a gust of wind had blown over a row of wooden soldiers.' The roads to Dunkirk were blocked with debris from collapsed buildings, abandoned equipment as well as bodies of dead soldiers: many of these corpses were rendered to almost nothing by the passage of cars and lorries over them. The 32e DIV had expected to be evacuated on the night of 1 to 2 June, yet were still on the beaches as the day wore on.[17] Instead of being evacuated the demoralised men were sent into action to defend the perimeter at 04:00 on the morning of 3 June. It was, to quote one officer, 'a suicide mission'.[18]

At 23:00 the last British soldiers left Dunkirk on the *Saint-Helier*; Operation Dynamo was officially over. But on the dunes or in the ruins of Dunkirk there were still 66,000 French soldiers. General Vernillat, commanding the 43e DI, who had masterminded the French evacuation, writes:

> For the evening of May 30, subject to absolute priority for the mechanised cavalry corps, sixty detachments, or 15,000 men, were to take the road to the port. The day had been very eventful. On the beaches the English suffered heavy losses, but the camp at Dunes was spared. However, the journeys to the port were very difficult and only part of the sixty detachments could be embarked during the night. This is why Admiral Abrial returned in person to my HQ on May 31 to study with me the

> possible improvements to this organisation. It was decided to organise embarkation posts on the beach from Dunkirk to Bray-Dunes and the soldiers were ordered to set up makeshift landing stages using trucks. During the night of May 31 to June 1, the remainder of the first sixty detachments of the mechanised cavalry corps embarked, plus twelve others of the same formation and eight of the 3rd, 4th, 5th Army Corps of the 1st Army. On the morning of June 1, I managed to send off fifteen detachments of the 4th and 5th Army Corps and ten of the 3rd Army Corps, or another 10,000 men, while for the night we had to prepare seventy-two more. On the morning of June 2, the decision was taken to stop daytime embarkations. There were only 15,000 men left at the Dunes camp, and the C D E zones were suppressed to tighten up the system so that I transported my HQ to Malo itself to have faster connections with the admiralty. The English evacuation having been completed, all the usable positions became available to the French.
>
> The embarkations of the night of June 2–3 were done in a very orderly manner and without loss. The English had to complain that 10,000 places had been lost on their ships due to the lack of French troops at the embarkation positions. This is exactly the figure given in my report for these men who could not embark that night due to the lack of boats . . . the only explanation is obviously that these men were delayed en route and presented themselves too late on the quays.[19]

That evening 43 French ships had embarked 6,474 men.

Chapter 35

3 JUNE 1940. LAST MEN STANDING

Before dawn on 3 June, an officer of the *18e Dragons* noted:

> At 03:30 Commander MARCHAL's HQ embarked on a small fishing boat 'Le Ciel de France' bound for Ramsgate (S.E. coast of England) where he arrived at 09:00. From there, he was transported by rail to Bournemouth on the south coast of England to the N.W. of the Isle of Wight where he stayed until 7 June.
>
> Captain De SALINS' detachment disembarked at La Bonneville at 07:00. From there, it was transported by train to La Bretonnière (3km N.W. of La Bonneville). Cantonment in this village until 7 June inclusive.
>
> Lieutenant De VANDIERES' tanks counter-attacked again south of Teteghem at 04:30. in conjunction with the 134e RI and again reached the line they had left the previous evening, but they could go no further, the enemy was considerably reinforced which prevented any further movement of our Infantry; moreover the terrain was impassable for tanks outside the metalled because of the surrounding fields had been flooded.
>
> The position was nevertheless maintained until noon; then it was necessary to retreat by covering the Infantry who unfortunately prematurely blew up a bridge where the tanks had to pass which had to be abandoned and destroyed on the south bank of the Teteghem canal. A few moments before, Lieutenant De VANDIERES was wounded in the left arm and leg by a burst of machine-gun fire while out of his tank, he wanted to make sure that our Infantry was well withdrawn.
>
> He was nevertheless able to escape, but he was taken prisoner the next day in the hospital in Zuydcoote, where he had been transported.
>
> No crew of the SOMUA Squadron was able to embark and all these valiant men were taken prisoner after fighting to the extreme limit of their means.

> Lieutenant De VANDIERES was able to escape later, his wounds barely closed; but Lieutenants ARDISSON, De LAVERNE and BOIDIN remained in the hands of the enemy. All of them were more or less wounded during these last fights.
>
> The HOTCHKISS tank squadron placed at the disposal of the 12e DIM was distributed by platoon among the various units. No information could be gathered on 3 of these platoons; the 4th platoon, that of Lieutenant De FERRY of the 4th *Cuirassiers* (Commanders of tanks: Maréchal-des-Logis-Chef Le TORZEC of the 4th *Cuirassiers;* Marechal des logis THIERRY, HUMEAU and BOUTIN of the 2nd Squadron of the 18th Dragoons) was first assigned to the 1st Battalion of the 8th Zouaves until June 3 at 3:30 p.m. and then at the 92e G.R.D.I. (Lieutenant-Colonel De BOISSY) which is clinging in the region east of Leffrinckoucke on the Canal des Chats. He supported the defence of this unit until 9 p.m.[1]

Defending the perimeter was the 12e DIM and what remained from the 38 BCC. The adjutant of the 12e DIM recalls 'the night of 2 to 3 June was relatively calm'.[2] An officer with the 38e BCC recalls:

> 3 JUNE. – 5 a.m. – Last offensive effort. A counter-attack was mounted with two infantry battalions
>
> - on the right one from the 143e R.I.
> - on the left one of the 122e R.I.
>
> Six SOMUA, four Hs of 38e and eight Hs of a DLM.
> The enemy unleashed accurate artillery fire, combined with a bombing of aircraft. However, the tanks advanced to the outskirts of Notre-Dame-des-Neiges, the friendly infantry advanced towards the Moeres canal, then withdrew to the north, leaving the elements of the 137e RII.
> The group of tanks that covered the right flank of the attack was violently attacked by anti-tank guns placed in the Boomkems farm which had been abandoned during the night by the infantry (without notifying the command). Only one tank from this group entered our lines.
> In the other group, two tanks of the 38e and four SOMUA were destroyed.[3]

Despite being considered a suicide mission, the counter-attack early that morning at Teteghem won sufficient time to delay the German attack on the north bank of the Dunkirk Canal. As the day wore on, it was increasingly evident that the perimeter would crumble. At midday the Germans attacked again, the situation being stabilised by 16:00 by committing the last reserves of ammunition and men.[4] Our officer from the 38e BCC again: 'At 5:30 p.m., north and north-west of Bergues, the enemy increased its pressure, the troops of the S/Teteghern sector were ordered to retreat in leaps and bounds, delaying the enemy advance to the Dunkirk Canal on the south-eastern edge of Rosendaël. Position which was occupied at 7:30 p.m.'[5]

Howard-Vyes informed Weygand that 'up to 06:00 hours 3rd June' 69,000 French soldiers had been evacuated along with 795 wounded adding, 'it is hoped to continue the evacuation tonight. British Naval losses since 1st June have been 3 destroyers, 5 small naval craft and 2 transports sunk. 6 destroyers and 3 small naval craft damaged.'[6]

General Vernillat, commanding the 43e DIV, notes: 'On the morning of June 3, it was necessary to think about preparing the disengagement and embarkation of the defenders of the entrenched camp. After having envisaged this operation for the night of June 4–5, it was necessary to admit that that of June 3-4 was an extreme limit, which one was not even certain of reaching.'[7]

During the night, five large transports had turned back, which could have carried a further 10,000 French soldiers: the other problem the French faced was, the British ships arrived where the French were not ready. Surgeon-Major Jacques Mordal of the French navy recollects: 'It was broad daylight, but freezing like the dawn of a beautiful summer day, and this Monday, June 3rd, promised to be incomparable. We were not well at all. Cold, sleepy, hungry . . .'[8]

Colonel Parent adds:

> In the afternoon, enemy aircraft bombed Fort des Dunes again, but with larger projectiles. They destroyed the fort's entrance arch, the exit from the transfer arch, and one of the casemates. About 150 men were buried in the ruins.
>
> The German infantry increased its pressure on the southern front of the bridgehead and captured Kateghem. The 150th Infantry Regiment was to provide a counter-attack company to the 94th Reconnaissance Group, which was beginning to retreat before the two infantry units. These units were employed to hold the Diernes Canal crossings, towards which the German infantry was beginning to infiltrate. It was in these circumstances that the General Commanding the 16th Army Corps ordered the troops at the Dunkirk bridgehead to break off combat during the night and, after having rendered armament and ammunition unusable, to reach the port of Dunkirk to be embarked.[9]

Colonel Basse concurs, noting that from midday the Luftwaffe increased its operations, dropping 'enormous bombs' that destroyed casemates and forced troops to evacuate these places of shelter on fear of being trapped or killed in the debris. The men had to shelter as best they could in the dunes, exposed to machine-gun fire: 'it was a miracle' that any order was maintained.[10] With less and less men on the perimeter it was only a matter of time before it collapsed as Abrial explained to Weygand:

> Enemy pushed back to starting position by counter-attack east of Bergues; enemy attacked again and advanced towards bridgehead. Counter-attack regained lost ground and will continue tomorrow. Partial attacks pushed back in environs of the bridgehead.
>
> The Enemy occupies Bergues but has made no move. General Janssen has been killed.
>
> British elements embark on the high tide. In case of active operations on June 3, the ammunition situation will become critical and may require the departure of defence troops before total embarkation is completed.[11]

Once in Dover, General Alexander telephoned Eden in Whitehall, conveying his concerns for the British wounded that had been left behind at Dunkirk. He also argued that not evacuating the French rearguard would be 'a breach of faith'. There were an estimated 47,000 French troops remaining in the pocket, of which 25,000 were directly engaged in the defence of the port.[12]

Admiral Ramsay assured Alexander that he would do what he could for the remaining French. Ramsay issued instructions to destroyer and minesweeper crews involved in the operation, to prepare themselves to go across the English Channel one last time for the sake of their ally: 'We cannot leave our Allies in the lurch, and I call on all officers and men detailed for further evacuation tonight to let the world see that we never let down our Ally . . .'[13] Royal Navy warships crossed to Dunkirk to evacuate French soldiers waiting on the mole. That afternoon, the Wehrmacht reached Rosendal, at the entrance of the Dunkirk perimeter.[14]

In Dunkirk, at 14:30 orders were issued concerning the sequence of embarkation: the eastern mole was the assembly point for the *16e Corps d'Armée,* 12e and 60e DI, the port of Dunkirk for the 32e and 68e DI.[15] Having committed their lasty reserves to shore up the perimeter, an hour after orders for embarking had been issued, the French rearguard ran out of ammunition and were virtually unarmed.[16] It was now a race against time to hold the perimeter with the minimum number of men and get as many French soldiers away to the south coast of England as possible. In an untimed order Colonel Blanchon stated, after liaison with Abrial and Fagalde: 'The 12e Division will disengage during the night of 3 to 4 June and will embark during the course of the same night at the mole east of the Port of Dunkirk (the mole is situated 1km west of Malo-les-Bains).'[17] Clearly, Abrial and Ramsey had concluded some form of timetable for the evacuation of the remaining French troops at Dunkirk, but this is sadly not to be found in the French Army Archives in Paris. Ramsey was well aware of the numbers remaining to be evacuated, and where the ships were needed; however, as we shall see, 'wires got crossed' in what was being organised between the Royal Navy and the French rearguard.

In his orders, Blanchon, now commanding the 12e DIM, stressed that the principal line of resistance was to be evacuated by midnight, the troops were to be at their embarkation points by 01:00 on the morning of 4 June, movement beginning at 21:30. At 21:40 destruction of crossroads, strongpoints and other buildings to provide road blocks and barricades was to commence organised by the remaining French engineers. Once the bridge at Zuydcoote was crossed, it was to be demolished not later than 01:10. The retreat was to be conducted in total silence Blanchon ordered, with no torches or fires to be lit. Light tanks and equipment not capable of being carried was to be destroyed, headquarters was to be evacuated at 23:30.[18]

Already French stragglers were crowding onto the beaches expecting to be evacuated to safety. As men huddled on the beaches of Bray Dunes, a wave of twenty-nine German bombers flew over Zuydcoote. Their target was Fort des Dunes. Three of the principal galleries were destroyed, which were used as first aid stations, with hundreds trapped or killed. Three casemates were also destroyed.

> Everything was on fire, the head of the first aid teams was amongst those burned alive . . .the losses were serious – the situation became extremely difficult] lamented the adjutant of the 12e DIM, 'from then on it was almost impossible to command the division and the Etat-Major . . . at 18:30 Fort des Dunes came under heavy German artillery fire, we had to evacuate the fort and we set up a new HQ in a school.[19]

Staff officer Billard adds that he heard with horror the cries of those trapped in the debris of the fort. It was a scene of total horror, he adds, as he and fellow officers scrambled through the rubble to escape.[20] By 18:30 the leading elements of the Wehrmacht were 4km from eastern mole as an officer of the *2e Bataillon* of the 137e RI led by Colonel Miquel recalls:

> At all levels, the defenders have reached the very limit of their resistance capacity. The front is shaken, there are no more reserves, no more

> ammunition, no more food for several days already, no more fuel. The enemy is becoming more and more pressing along the entire front, its activity does not cease, night and day. It is exasperated by achieving only partial and local successes.
>
> For our part, it seems that on this day of June 3rd, a kind of torpor and weariness has descended upon the entire defence zone. Besides, why make plans for the future? Everyone knows that the resistance is reaching the end of its tether; it would take a miracle to be able to sufficiently hold the enemy back, disengage, and embark by the next night . . . General Fagalde decides to organise a final barrage behind the canal bordering the southern edges of Dunkirk. He gave this mission to the general commanding the 32nd Infantry Division, who had only the few remaining elements and reinforcements from a company of mobile guards, those assigned to guard the HQ. The German attack began with the 10th Army Corps, led by the 18th Infantry Division. It was particularly violent along the Bergues Canal. In the afternoon, the enemy crossed the Moeres Canal at its junction with the Bergues Canal, but Colonel Marlot's reconnaissance group, in a magnificent display, pinned them to the ground at the edge of Couderkeque Branch. The losses were extremely heavy . . . in the eastern part of the perimeter, the fighting was violent and confused around Teteghem, defended by several battalions. The artillerymen fighting among the infantry fired on the attackers on sight. Local attacks and counter-attacks followed. In the afternoon, overwhelmed from the west, the defenders of Teteghem withdrew to the Dunkirk-Furnes Canal, where they were caught by the last barrage under the command of General Lucas, commander of the 32nd Infantry Division.[21]

By 17:00 the village of Téteghem was taken. This is where Jacques Duquesne and his family were forced to take refuge. He remembers 'Two (French) officers had arrived . . . One of them had hung a white handkerchief on a kind of cane. We had already heard the word "Ceasefire" circulated in a low voice. But nothing was guaranteed.' With the perimeter collapsing, at 19:00 Weygand messaged Abrial to leave: Abrial's staff and General Fagalde evacuated Bastion 32 and boarded motor torpedo boat *VTB 25* at 22:00.[22] With no senior French officers remaining on the beaches or in Dunkirk, there was almost no possibility of co-ordinating the evacuation of the French: chaos was the inevitable result. In Dunkirk, in cellars or shelters such as those on Place de la République and Place Jean-Bart, the civilian population was still holed up. The sub-prefect Le Gentil wrote in his memoirs that he had tried to protect these inhabitants from the deserting soldiers who often reigned terror until the end.

'As events unfolded around Dunkirk, the city was plagued by looting and excesses of all kinds,' he describes. 'There were individuals of all kinds, deserters of all arms, a plebs such as one only sees in troubled hours . . . But these brutes were armed and threatened anyone who dared to make an observation. The central commissioner Preuilh, who bravely faced these madmen, was wounded by one of them during a cleaning operation in one of these shelters.' In his novel *Week-end à Zuydcoote*, Robert Merle, then a liaison officer in the Dunkirk pocket, also describes this violence when his hero, the soldier Julien Maillat (played by Jean-Paul Belmondo in Henri Verneuil's film) saves a young girl from rape by killing two soldiers.

At 20:30 orders were issued to evacuate. Mordal again:

> We will embark this evening on the *Emile Deschamps*, somewhere near the Felix Faure quay unless it is at the Armement quay, with the transmission people and some other crews without boats.
>
> At 18:00 here we are at the Felix Faure quay. The *Emile Deschamps* is opposite, at the Armement quay, dry land by the way because the tide is low, but it is starting to rise. It will not be long before it floats. A few more hours of patience . . . the Germans are not there yet . . . we wait for the time to embark, or that of the 105 which will come to conclude the adventure.
>
> At 20:30. finally the *Emile Deschamps* stirs. Here it is, docking near us. All that remains is to embark . . . there are even a few women, a baby. We couldn't put a pin on board. And yet there are still some on the quay. But there will be other boats.
>
> It must have been between 21:30. and 22:00 when the *Emile Deschamps* cast off. The falling night gave a renewed glow to the glow of the fire. The port in ruins, sinister with the carcasses of the burnt-out hangars that looked like gibbets.[23]

Another eyewitness wrote:

> During the day, new groups had joined in; elements of the 1st Army . . . A total of 15,000 men. Other units nominally placed under the command of Colonel Chevillard were sent by Bastion 32 to embark at the same time as those under the orders of Colonel Sabathie. The isolated units were pouring in, and to maintain order, they were formed into a group of 250 under the command of officers. By the end of the evening, the men collected by Chevillard also comprised nearly 15,000 men . . . newcomers were sent to the area of the camp located behind the HQ barracks. Order was maintained. Except for a few who were lobbying to get a better position in the boarding lines, everyone understood that discipline was the necessary condition for the boarding that night to be success: this was our last chance.

> A battery of anti-aircraft guns manned by the Marines was installed a little east of the lock. Around 20:30, they received Admiral Abrial's order to disengage and having been firing violently. Then they fell silent, and the sailors, led by an ensign, were seen arriving at the lock . . . Colonel Sabathie had asked Colonel Prevot of the 1st Army to line his men up at the foot of the jetty. When the first boats arrived around 22:00, the columns set off one after the other in perfect order. At the end of the jetty, Colonel Sabathie, assisted by Lieutenant Robez-Pagillon, received the admissible strength from the boat commanders, and the groups of 250 men only crossed the provost's cordon as the embarkation progressed. This was very rapid and the boats numerous. No individual boarding could be made, each column forming a protective cordon. An attempt was made, however, by a group coming from the west and having followed in remarkable order behind the last group of the 2nd column. The liaison officers warned us in time. When the group arrived at the jetty, an officer made it turn right instead of left, go along the lock, and line up behind the column, without the men having understood the subterfuge. Around 23:00, we saw General Lucas, commanding the 32nd Infantry Division, arrive. The infantry had probably left their positions around 20:30 and had fallen back towards our camp. Shortly after, we saw German shells falling, this time coming from the west, on the last groups of the columns. They informed us that they had a lot to do to contain the new arrivals who were planning to embark immediately.[24]

An officer with the French anti-aircraft guns defending the embarkation remembered:

> Despite the large number of ships that arrived in Dunkirk on the night of the 3rd to the 4th, the means were insufficient to ensure the embarkation of the troops. It is certain, moreover, that a good number of men, faced with the considerable risks and difficulties that embarkation presented, gave up on it . . . Arriving in Folkestone, I was directed to Bournemouth with the officers and the group of men of the DAT who embarked with me. The quarters were comfortable. The personnel were very well received, with good food and we had our clothing washed and cleaned.[25]

As ordered the 12e DIM began leaving the front line at 21:30, leaving behind the barest minimum of a rearguard. A company of the *8e Zouaves* remained at the artillery emplacement at Zuydcoote, with another company left behind at Bray-Dunes. The 150e RI posted men along the Canal de Dunkerque at Funes and at the bridges of Zuydcoote and Rosendale. Any remaining ammunition was issued to these men, who knew they were going to be killed or made POW. The men of the *8e Zouaves* and 150e RI took six hours to cross 4km of ground 'constantly attacked' by the Luftwaffe and German shells 'which inflicted heaving loses on the column.'[26] General Barthélémy, commander of the fortified sector of Flanders, described the scene at the point of embarkation 'floods of soldiers came out from everywhere and converged towards the eastern jetty, forming by their junction, an immense tide of people! All were motivated by the announcement that these were the last chances.' Captain Partiot was one of these men. He remembers 'we walked along the pier which seemed to be at least two kilometres long. We stepped over the corpses of dead soldiers . . . When we reach the end, we had to fight against those who claim to take our places under the most diverse and false pretexts.' Desperation drove deserters and civilians to flee: priority was given to formed units of soldiers.[27]

Despite the best efforts of the Luftwaffe, many French troops did manage to escape the chaos to Dover. At 22:30 the ships began to leave Dunkirk. That night, the last 26,175 French soldiers managed to embark. General Vernillat: 'I received the order at 22:00 on June 3rd at the east jetty with my staff to embark in turn . . . considering the very difficult circumstances one can say that the execution of these movements was as correct as one could hope. Except for a few incidents the embarkations took place in good order.'[28]

Others were not so lucky. One of those Frenchmen who hoped to be lifted off the beaches was Captain Carton of the 12e DIM:

> At 16:00 and notice for embarkation on night 3 of the 4th arrived. . . At 17:25 the second bombardment of Fort de Dune began, this time with heavy bombs with delayed fuses – they crushed the casemates – vehicles were burning – 150 men from the train buried alive . . . we left the fort through the breach and jumped into the moat: as we climbed the counterscarp we were met by artillery fire. Finochi; had an arm torn off . . . am in charge of regulating the retreat of the division to St Malo. Morin meets me there at the crossroads at 19:30. The traffic jam slowed out movement.[29]

When they arrived, the boats had gone: 63 ships from the French merchant marine had evacuated 10,120 French soldiers.

Chapter 36

4 JUNE 1940. THE END

As 4 June dawned, it became obvious to the French troops at Dunkirk that any hope of salvation was gone. Colonel Parent again:

> Colonel Parent was sent at 7:00 PM to the headquarters of the 16th Army Corps at Bastion 32, Fortification Dunkirk, to finalise the details of the division's embarkation. There, he contacted Colonel Estreme, Chief of Staff.
>
> The enigmatic attitude of this senior officer and the very vague instructions given by the maritime authority did not leave a favourable impression. Embarkation was to begin at 22:00 . . . based on this information, head of column of the 12th DIM, arrived at 23:30 at the eastern Mole . . . a detachment of sailors – among whom we recognise a few women in sailors' uniforms – passed ahead, having been given priority. No naval officers or staff officers were visible. We advance slowly, tramping hard all night long on the jetty, in the darkness where a few German shells burst here and there, and where the flashes of fire from the harbour organisations occasionally illuminate the rushing crowd.[1]

Pierre Billard remembered that he and the 12e DIM had been assured by Admiral Abrial that they would embark for England that night, and had arrived at the Port of Dunkirk at 22:00: no ships were to be seen. At 03:00 the port was rocked by a violent explosion; the Royal Navy had begun sinking ships to block the harbour.[2] The *18e Dragons* were amongst the last to escape, having:

> remained in position until 12:10 a.m. before retreating but not without inflicting losses on the enemy who sought to infiltrate under cover of night.

The platoon reached Malo-Terminus where it destroyed its tanks in accordance to orders and at 08:00 it was able to leave the port of Dunkirk on an abandoned pilot's boat, the engine of which it was able to start, bringing back with it about thirty other Horsemen and Artillerymen and reach the port of Dover without incident around 16:00. Only Marechal des Logis Chef BOERC and his driver AUVRAY, having been lost in the region of Malo, could not be found, were not brought back.

From Dover, the detachment was transported by rail to Southampton.[3]

The men of the *18e Dragons* were lucky. The 12e DIM had arrived on time at its embarkation points at 01:00. In the clamour to escape, stragglers and deserters had rushed onto the waiting ships in advance of the 12e DIM and other units from the rearguard. The lack of command and control at the embarkation points meant that when the 12e DIM arrived, the ships had left or were close to capacity to take on many more men: 'the spectacle of the ships leaving writes one eyewitness lit by the gigantic torches of the burning oil refineries is unforgettable'.[4]

Captain Carton again:

the last boats were leaving before our eyes. We arrived at the mole – we attempted to embark in lifeboats but arrival of German motorcycles and armoured cars at the mole stopped the attempt to embark.[5] Some men had managed to get into the small boats, but 'only about ten officers – among them I was – and about eighty men who, in small sailing or rowing boats, were able to escape, were able to reach the English coast before the arrival of the Germans.[6]

Lieutenant Colonel Cope, commanding the engineers of 12e DIM, noted many officers, NCOs and men swam out to sea to try and climb on to the boats to escape being killed or made prisoner by the Germans, desperate to get to Dover or Folkestone, after it had been announced it was too late for to embark.[7] If it was too late for the 12e DIM to embark, it was far too late for the men of the 137e and 38e BCC still defending the perimeter:

The last tanks fight in the ranks of the 137e RI. The personnel without equipment continued the fight with the infantry and then arrived on the eastern quays of Dunkirk around 4:30 am. Since 3:30 a.m., the Channel has been blocked by two sunken boats across the Channel. No order was given for embarkation and the Commander of the S.F.F. took his place in the last launch.

> 6 a.m. – No boat appears on the horizon. No defence could be envisaged, all that remained with the survivors was the individual armament that had been collected and ammunition was scarce.
>
> The air force continued to fly over Dunkirk and Malo-les-Bains. The German artillery was almost silent. The German infantry continued its advance and reached the piers where the troops without means of defence had piled up. DUNKIRK is taken.[8]

As dawn broke on 4 June, about 34,000 French soldiers had been left behind on the beaches of Dunkirk. The adjutant of the 12e DIM released at 05:00 'there was to be no embarkation . . . all eyes turned to the sky, watching for the reconnaissance aircraft of the enemy'. Some 25,000 men were gathered at the east mole and the port of Dunkirk, having spent a night on the beaches cold and very hungry.[9] Colonel Parent again:

> At first light, we can see that there are no vessels in the Channel, nor at sea, to embark troops. We only see two small steamers flying the British flag, which come to position themselves in the middle of the Channel near a third similar one that was already there and are sunk in an explosion. When it became clear that everything that remained on the jetty (several thousand men) was now abandoned to the mercy of the Germans who were going to lead the officers to bring their men back to the Malo beach and the glacis of the Dunkirk fortifications where they found the units of the Flanders defensive sector of the 68th Division whose embarkation came after that of the 12th Division.[10]

Quartermaster Carton, one of the French naval gunners of a bastion at Dunkirk, acknowledged:

> When the last boats had left the port, the Germans were arriving from all directions. Resistance proved impossible. The guns were destroyed and the breechblocks removed: due to lack of time, the ammunition could not be blown up. . . . two machine guns were put into battery and resistance was organised, while the German infantrymen manned the top of the cliff and the tanks patrolled at the foot. The sailors held out for two hours and then had to surrender; they had not suffered any losses.[11]

As the sun came up and no ships were obvious, men started shouting 'we have been abandoned!' Around 07:00 Colonel Blanchon commanding the 12e DIM, arm yourselves with whatever weapons and ammunition you can find 'if the division is to be sacrificed, we will fight on!' Blanchon went to Bastion 32 to meet with Admiral Abrial and

General Fagalde: Blanchon did meet General Tesseyre commanding the 60e DI who had expected to find Abrial and obtain orders. All the paperwork had been burned: whilst the French officers were shouting at each other about what do to next, at 07:45 German motorcycle troops arrived in Dunkirk. Blanchon surrendered at 08:30.[12]

They were made POWs along with half a million of their comrades trapped in the 'Flanders pocket'. Those remaining at Dunkirk were angry, and felt betrayed by their allies who had, to quote one officer, 'shamefully fled behind the English Channel'. Another condemned the British as cowards for not standing and fighting.[13]

The remaining men from the 12e DIM became prisoners of war.[14] Losses amongst the 12e DIM were heavy: 400 men had given their freedom and lives to save the BEF during the course of 3 June. The remaining 4,100 men were amongst the 35,000 other French soldiers captured on the morning of 4 June.[15]

All was lost, save honour. Abrial estimated that some 25,000 remained, but he did not know for sure, but noted 23,000 men had been lifted off the beaches on the 3-4 June. Crucially he told Ramsay that any further evacuation would be useless. Abrial estimated that 112,000 French soldiers and other Allied personnel were lifted by the Royal Navy during Operation Dynamo.[16] The last word goes to the adjutant of the 38e BCC:

> The officers and men of the 38e fought with great bravery, showed remarkable tenacity, unfailing physical resistance, exemplary sense of discipline, unrestricted devotion and admirable patriotic faith. And yet the moral conditions were particularly painful. Almost all of them come from the Nord and Pas-de-Calais. From 18 to 24 May, they fought at home, some even in their fields, in their villages. What an atrocious situation for the boys of the land to cooperate in the destruction of their homes, to know that their loved ones are in danger, on the roads, and cannot ensure their protection.
>
> They did everything they could to avoid falling into the hands of the enemy, and exhausted all means of combat. They had been promised to take them on board, to save them, and they were abandoned. They did not deserve the fate that was reserved for them.
>
> It was thanks to the spirit of sacrifice of the last defenders that 300,000 combatants, including the entire British army, were able to be embarked.
>
> The help they gave to their comrades, the infantrymen, was an example of solidarity and Major Miquel, commander of the 1/137, eloquently expressed to them all the gratitude for which his unit was indebted to them. 'I would like to draw your attention,' he said, 'to the brilliant conduct of two officers of your battalion, Captain Renard and

Lieutenant Spriet, as well as their crews who remained at my disposal with their tanks from June 2 at noon to June 4 at 4 a.m., and who, despite the intense, repeated and prolonged bombardments of the enemy, have always brought to my battalion, at the appropriate time, all the support I had a right to expect from them.

In particular, at the critical moment of the day of June 3rd, when around 5 p.m., the Colonel Commandant of the Regiment had just been taken prisoner with his staff, and what remained of the 1re and 3e battalions, a soldier came to summon me to surrender with my men.

'It was because I had the total and absolute support of your tanks that I was able not only to repel this offensive, but to break the attempt to encircle my position and then to participate effectively until 4 a.m. on June 4 in the defence of Dunkirk by containing the enemy beyond the Veurne Canal.'

When it was time to surrender, Commander Miquel found the words that could express the most beautiful tribute to his companions in misery.

'The tradition has been maintained by the 38e BCC and that of 137e RI of Verdun, in 1916, it had not been forgotten by the generation of 1940.'[17]

As the French surrendered at Dunkirk, the Luftwaffe flew over Paris. The raid, part of the larger German offensive against France, involved 155 planes, with 83 bombing Paris directly. Forty-five civilians were killed. The French nightmare from the 1930s of cities being eviscerated by aerial bombing seemed to be coming true. This day also saw the conclusion of the Battle of Abbeville with a German victory. A new phase in the war was just beginning.

Of those who made it to Dover, after weeks rest, these men would be back in France, re-embarking on French naval vessels, and once issued new tanks and weapons, they would be fighting for the survival of their homeland. This story is yet to be told.

Chapter 37

EPILOGUE

Since 1940 the British myth of Dunkirk has painted defeat as inevitable, and pointed the blame directly at the French army. The French army, goes the myth as told by Field Marshal Bernard Law Montgomery, 'was an accident waiting to happen' and the soldiers ran away, leaving the valiant, BEF to fight a re-run of Thermopylae or Rorke's Drift alone, and snatched victory from the jaws of defeat. Nazi propaganda films produced in the wake of the battle shows wave after wave of German armour and aircraft moving unopposed through the French countryside. These images were quickly circulated across the globe: as Goebbels had hoped they would, they had considerable influence in shaping the narrative of why and how France fell so quickly. Goebbels' propaganda has for the last 80 years shaped the erroneous conviction that the French army was overwhelmed by an industrial tidal wave of tanks and soldiers. The Vichy government also supported this propagandised version of events: from 22 June 1940, the French army were at pains to blame socialists, atheists, trade unionists, the 'corrupt' Third Republic and Maurice Gamelin for the fall of France. Politicians had entered a war that could not be won; politicians had not heeded the words of the army and it was Gamelin's fault re-armament was slow and ineffective. Gamelin was imprisoned at the Château de Chazeron alongside Blum, Daladier, Georges Mandel and Reynaud. He was placed on trial four times between September 1940 and September 1941 as part of the Riom Trials. 31 March 1943 he was transferred to a hunting lodge attached to Buchenwald concentration camp, near Weimar. He was liberated by United States Army troops after the Battle of Castle Itter. Vichy re-wrote the story of how France fell, to exonerate the army and blame Daladier, Reynaud and Gamelin. This view has become solidly entrenched in French and Anglo-phonic studies of the war: Gamelin since May 1940, like Marshal Emmanual de Grouchy, have received unsympathetic comment whilst Weygand receives more sympathetic treatment: perhaps this text will show Gamelin, like Grouchy, is 'more sinned against than sinning'. For British Nationalist views of Dunkirk, blaming the French for everything that is wrong in the world, contributes in a major way to British views of self. By blaming Gamelin, Lord Gort, Eden, Chamberlain and others who agreed to Gamelin's thinking, who offered no other strategic vision, demanded *7e Armée* was to be subsumed into the front line and then compounded this by refusing to negotiate with Belgium, caused Dunkirk to happen, made Gamelin their scapegoat. Much of the blame for the fall of France stems from decisions made in Whitehall. The French soldier in 1940 fought as bravely and as well as his father or grandfather had done on the Somme or at Verdun.

Between 26 May and 4 June 1940, 30,000 French soldiers, supported by perhaps 6,000 soldiers from the BEF opposed 160,000 men of the Wehrmacht. The losses amongst the French army were appallingly high:

Lost shipping: total 58
Principal fleet 10
Auxiliary fleet 28
Commercial fleet: 20
591 men killed or lost at sea, 300 wounded. 150 French naval personnel killed at Dunkirk.
Naval Aircraft:
34 aircraft lost in combat over Dunkirk
Army:
5,000 soldiers killed defending the perimeter, 1,500 French soldiers drowned when embarkation vessels sunk.
123,000 French soldiers evacuated
48,474 French Naval personnel evacuated (3, 936 disembarked at Cherbourg or Le Havre)[1]

In total the British and French navies had obtained 484 naval and civilian vessels to evacuate the men trapped at Dunkirk: 519 were British registered, 300 French and 29 were Dutch. The Royal Navy lost 112 ships or civilian craft, the French Navy 123. Of these 59 were sunk. It is time in the 80th anniversary year of VE Day to remember the brave French sailors killed in those tumultuous days in 1940.

In all, 245,211 soldiers were lifted from Dunkirk by the Royal Navy and British civilian boats, while the French and Dutch evacuated

102,570. Perhaps because Dunkirk is such an important myth in the British psyche, popular films, commemorations and books all ignore the considerable contribution made by the French and Dutch; they are almost entirely forgotten in all commemorations of Dunkirk. In total 224,686 British soldiers were saved and 123,095 French. During the campaign to Dunkirk British, Belgian and Dutch military losses combined reached 50,300 soldiers hors de combat (13,900 killed and 36,400 wounded): 15,897 French were killed or wounded defending Dunkirk to allow the BEF to evacuate: the sacrifice of the French has been almost forgotten by British National Myth. Between 10 May and 25 June, the French fighter force had flown 20,410 operational sorties. The bomber force flew 2,130. Of the 1,300 aircraft committed to action in that period, 1,247 were destroyed. In the same period, 541 pilots were killed and 364 wounded with a further 105 disappeared; some 1010men. Overall, this was an attrition rate of 40 per cent of officers and 20 per cent for NCOs and men. For the Luftwaffe, of the approximately 3,500 aircraft engaged, 1,428 were destroyed, 2,668 aircrew killed, 4,191 wounded and 2,923 missing, totalling 9,782 aircrew lost, primarily from the reconnaissance and bomber forces

Overall, from 10 May to 26 June 1940 the Luftwaffe lost in total 1,428 aircraft shot down, and a further 1,616 aircraft in the Battle of Britain. By the time of the Battle of Britain, the Luftwaffe had not been able to restore its strength in terms of fighters, bombers and personnel to that of 10 May 1940. The Luftwaffe was short of pilots, aircraft and was demoralised. The losses before 26 June in pilots and aircraft outstripped production and training: it meant when the Battle of Britain came, the RAF with its English, Scots, Welsh, Canadian, American, Indian, French, Polish and Czech pilots, to name a few of the nationalities involved, had the advantage. Britain never stood alone against Nazi Germany. The sacrifice of the French permitted Churchill to continue to fight on.[2]

After the initial checks at Gembloux and Sedan, the French carried on the fight: Gamelin had proved himself capable of high command. Had his order of 19 May been carried out by either fighting back to the Somme or shipping the BEF and French *1re Armée* from Dunkirk by sea to the Somme, as did happen, the outcome of the Battle of France could have been very different. Had Gamelin not been ousted, had the BEF and inter alia Whitehall fully supported Gamelin and Weygand in their planning for counter-attack at Arras and then Cambrai rather than concentrating their effort on retreating, then the outcome of the Battle of France may have been different. A failure of co-operation doomed France and Europe to five more years of war. Despite all its failings, the French army fought well: during the six weeks of fighting from May–June 1940, German military losses were proportionately higher than the first six months of the war on the Russian front in 1941: 4,711 German soldiers were killed or wounded per day in May–June 1940 compared to 4,222 in June-November 1941. The total Allied and German-Italian military losses in May–June 1940 were also heavier than the three months of the Battle of Normandy in June–August 1944: 610,500 Allied and German-Italian soldiers out of action (killed or wounded) in May–June 1940, compared with 466,000 German and Allied military casualties (killed or wounded) in June–August 1944.

Another fact that has gone unremarked is that the slaughter of May–June 1940 was proportionally higher than the Battle of Verdun in 1916 and that of Stalingrad in 1942–3: 13,566 Axis and Allied soldiers were killed or wounded per day in May–June 1940, compared to 3,000 in Verdun in February–December 1916 and 8,600 in Stalingrad in September 1942–February 1943! From 10 May to 25 June 1940, the German army suffered 212,000 soldiers hors de combat (49,000 killed and 163,000 wounded), 1,800 tanks destroyed or damaged out of 3,039 engaged, not to mention 1,559 aircraft shot down or damaged out of 3,900 engaged. The French army had 342,000 soldiers out of action (92,000 killed and 250,000 wounded), 1,900 tanks lost out of 2,262 engaged and 892 aircraft out of 1,300 engaged.

By 23 May, Hitler had lost 30 per cent of his tanks: 612 had been destroyed and 179 damaged beyond repair. For his part, General Heinz Guderian stressed that 'despite the enormous tactical errors of the Allied command, the French soldiers of 1940 put up an extremely tough resistance, with an extraordinary spirit of sacrifice, worthy of the *poilus* of Verdun in 1916.'[3] Yet we are told the French could not fight: who then destroyed the tanks causing Hitler to issue the famous stop order? The idea that the French didn't fight in 1940 is a common misconception. In reality, the French army fought fiercely during the Battle of France, suffering nearly 90,000 military casualties in just six weeks: the political and military leadership – led by Marshal Philippe Pétain – opted to seek an armistice rather than fight to the death or continue the war from the French colonies. While the metropolitan government in Vichy ultimately chose capitulation, tens of thousands of French soldiers continued to fight under Charles de Gaulle's Free French Forces.

NOTES

Chapter 1: To War

1. Robert Young, 'La Guerre de Longue Dureé: Some Reflections of French Strategy and Diplomacy in the 1930s', in Adrian Preston (ed.), *General Staffs and Diplomacy Before the Second World War* (Croom Helm, London: 1978), pp. 46–9.
2. Ibid. p. 58.
3. Peter Jackson and Joseph Maiolo, 'Strategic Intelligence, Counter-Intelligence and Alliance Diplomacy in Anglo-French Relations Before the Second World War', *Militärgeschichtliche Zeitschrift* 65, no. 2 (2006), pp. 453–4.
4. Martin S. Alexander and William J. Philpott (ed.), *Anglo-French Defence Relations Between the Wars* (Palgrave Macmillan, New York: 2002), pp. 106, 211.
5. The National Archives [hereafter TNA] Cabinet Papers [hereafter CAB] 80/104, Notes of a Meeting at the Headquarters of Gamelin, 21 September 1939.
6. Norman Dixon, *On The Psychology of Military Incompetence* (Pimlico, London: 1994).
7. Nick Smart, *British Strategy and Politics During the Phony War: Before the Balloon Went Up* (Praeger, Westport, CT: 2003), p. 86.
8. TNA War Office [hereafter WO] 106/1684, War Office to British Military Attaché, 4 September 1939.
9. TNA Cabinet Papers [hereafter CAB] 53/4-5, 'Defence Plans', Chiefs of Staff (COS) Committee, 125th and 133rd Meetings, 4 May and 9 October 1934 and CAB16/209 'Strategical Appreciation Sub Committee of the Committee of Imperial Defence (CID), minutes of the 1st, 2nd and 3rd meetings, 1, 13 and 17 March 1939.
10. TNA WO 106/1684, Director of Military Operations and Plans, Notes of a Meeting Held at the Headquarters of General Gamelin, 9 November 1939.
11. TNA WO 106/1684, Hore-Belisha Note, 21 September 1939.

12. Service Historique de la Armée du Terre [hereafter SHDDT] GR/7/N/3697 le problème militaire français' 1 Juin 1936.
13. SHDDT GR/1/N/36 'Note résumant l'expose fait par le général Gamelin à la réunion du 4 avril 1936'.
14. SHDDT 1K/224/74 Dossier 7: 'L'Art de la guerre. Doctrine et procédés. Expose fait par le général Gamelin au Centre des Hautes Etudes Militaires en Avril 1937'.
15. SHDDT GR/7/N/23 'Résumé de la note sur l'instruction en 1939'.
16. SHDDT GR/32/N/134/ 23e Division etat major.
17. SHDDT GR/29/N/435/rapports sur le moral (Janvier 1940).
18. TNA WO 167/40, Swayne Mission War Diary, 8–9 September 1939.
19. TNA WO 167/41. No 2 Military Mission War Diary, 26 March 1940.
20. Ibid.
21. TNA CAB 80/104, Ironside Memo, 24 January 1940.
22. TNA CAB 80/3, General Gamelin's Observations, 27 September 1939; CAB 80/3, Chiefs of Staff Committee, Comments on General Gamelin's Observation on our Appreciation on the Possible Course of the War, 2 October 1939; and Gamelin to Daladier, 7 January 1940.
23. Ministère de la Guerre, *Instruction sur l'emploi tactique des Grandes Unités* (Librairie Militaire Berger-Levrault, Paris: 1937), p. 30.
24. SHDDT GR/7N/4025 Dossier 12, Notions stratégiques suite aux manoeuvres générales du 24-29 Juin, 1935.
25. Ibid., p. 31.
26. Ibid., p. 90.
27. TNA WO 106/1684, Director of Military Operations and Plans, Notes of a Meeting Held at the Headquarters of General Gamelin, 9 November 1939.
28. TNA CAB 80/105, Chiefs of Staff Committee, German Invasion of Holland: Allied Policy Draft Memorandum, no date.
29. TNA CAB 80/3, French Permanent Military Representatives, Note Relative to Operations in Holland, Belgium, and Luxembourg, 24 September 1939.
30. TNA CAB 66/1/44, Conversation with M. Daladier and General Gamelin, 21 September 1939.
31. TNA WO 106/1684, Dewing to Pownall, 23 September 1939; WO 106/1684, British Chiefs of Staff Draft Letter to Gamelin, September 1939; and WO 106/1684, General Staff Criticism of General Gamelin's Plan, September 1939.
32. Jacques Minart, *P.C. Vincennes, Secteur 4* (Editions Berger-Levrault, Paris: 1945), Tome I, Titre II, pp. 151–2.

Chapter 2: Command and Control

1. SHDDT GR 13 YD 1279 Dossier 2. Dossier du Personnel, Maurice Gamelin.
2. TNA Foreign Office [hereafter FO] 'Record of Leading Personalities in France', 17 January 1934.
3. TNA WO 106/4989. Major General Sir Richard Howard-Vyse, letter to DMO, 26 April 1940.
4. Ibid.
5. SHDDT GR/1K/224 Dossier 15, Gamelin's apologia, p. 5.
6. TNA WO 167/50, Swayne Mission War Diary, 16 November 1939.
7. Christophe Bertrand, *Comme en 40* (Gallimard, Musee de l'Armée: 2020), pp. 40–5.

Chapter 3: Communications

1. Thomas Christofferson and Michael Christofferson, *France during World War II: From Defeat to Liberation* (Fordham University Press: 2006), p. 18.
2. David French, *Raising Churchill's Army* (Oxford University Press, Oxford: 2000), p. 165.
3. Vincent Arbarétier, *L'école de la guerre, Sedan 1940: Ou la failite du système de commandement français* (Economica, Paris: 2000), p. 33.
4. SHDDT GR/2/N/262 dossier 1, Conseil Supérieur de la Défense Nationale, 'Approvisionment de'Armée d Terre, en material de TSF', 15 Novembre 1935, pp. 2–4.
5. SHDDT GR/29/N/18 dossier. 2. Note from Colonel Coussillan to Alombert, 8 Septembre 1939.
6. SHDDT GR/ 7/N/3997 dossier 3. Lettre, 21 Janvier 1940.
7. Robert A. Doughty, *The Breaking Point: Sedan and the Fall of France, 1940* (Stackpole Books, Mechanicsburg: 1990), p. 25.
8. Karl Heinz Frieser, *The Blitzkrieg Legend* (Naval Institute Press, Annapolis: 2012), pp. 237–8.
9. Ibid., p. 575.
10. SHDDT GR/2/N/262 Réalisation du programme de 1939 d'amélioration de transmissions nécessaires aux besoins de la Défense nationale, 12 Fevrier 1940.
11. SHDDT GR/2N/231 Note du Conseil Supérieur de la Défense nationale au président du Conseil, 4 Janvier 1940.
12. SHDDT GR/9/N/253 Rapport du commandant Labat, réalisation d'un matériel adapte à la liaison radiotélégraphique, 29 Mai 1940.

13. SHDDT GR/30/N/264, dossier 6. Lettre, Prioux à Blanchard, 26 Septembre 1939.
14. Ibid. dossier 11. Corps de Cavalerie, Note de Service, 11 March 1940.
15. SHDDT GR/9/N/325 dossier 2. Rapport par général Riegel, Inspecteur Technique des Transmissions, Télégraphie Militaire and Transmissions, 1938, p. 27.
16. Ibid. pp. 28–9.
17. SHDDT GR/7/N/3983 dossier 1. Section du Material de Transmissions, par Captain Romon 'au sujet des manoeuvres des Transmissions de 1939', p. 3.
18. SHDDT GR/2/N/261 coopération franco-britannique dans le domaine des télécommunications, 5 Avril 1940.
19. SHDDT GR/2/N/261 Amélioration des moyens de transmissions, 31 Mai 1940, pp. 8–9.
20. Martin S. Alexander, 'Radio Intercepts, Reconnaissance and Raids: French Operational Intelligence and Communications in 1940', *Intelligence and National Security* 28 (2013), p. 345.
21. Ibid., pp. 348–50.
22. SHDDT GR/2/N/262 dossier 3. 'Câbles téléphoniques souterrains à grande distance', Gamelin à Chefs d'Etats Major Generals de la Marine et de l'Air 27 June 1938, pp. 1–2.
23. Miles Reid MC, *Last on the List* (London, Leo Cooper: 1974), pp. 26–7.
24. R. F. H. Nalder, *The History of the British Army Signals in the Second World War* (Royal Signals Institution, London: 1953), p. 32.
25. SHDDT GR/2/N/261 dossier 6. 'Note sur la creation projetée d'un Comité Interallié des Transmissions', 18 July 1939, p. 1.
26. SHDDT GR 7/N/3983/8 dossier 1. Annex IV, 'Notes sur l'appareil emetteur-recepteur portatif d'Infanterie de l'Armée Britannique (Poste Radio no. 8)', p. 6.
27. SHDDT GR/2/N/262 dossier 1, Conseil Supérieur de la Défense Nationale, 'Approvisionment de'Armée d Terre, en material de TSF', 15 Novembre 1935, pp. 2–4.
28. SHDDT GR/2/N/262 dossier 3. Note from General Jullien to President du Conseil, Ministre de la Défense Nationale et de la Guerre, 12 Fevrier 1940. See also further correspondence from Jullien dated 25 May 1940; ibid GR/6N/ 352 dossier 3.
29. SHDDT GR/9/N/18 dossier 2. Colonel Goetschy à Colonels Commandants des Transmissions des groupes d'Armées, des Armées, 18 Septembre 1939.
30. TNA WO 106/1678. Captain Miles Reid, report to Lieutenant Colonel P Gregson Ellis on First French Army, 29 May 1940.

31. Reid, *Last on the List*, pp. 26–7.
32. French, *Raising Churchill's Army*, p. 180.
33. Reid, *Last on the List*, pp. 29–30.
34. L. H. Harris, *Signal Venture* (Gale & Polden Ltd, Aldershot: 1951), p. 133.
35. SHDDT GR/27/N/188 dossier 5. Colonel de Cardes, la Mission Française de la Liaison à Lt Colonel Noiret, Chef du 3eme Bureau N.E, 27 Juin 1940.
36. Ibid. dossier 9. Mission Militaire Française de Liaison, Capitaine Ciriez, Commandant le Détachement de Liasion du 2eme CAW à Capitaine Furby, Officier-Rapporteur, Laval, undated 1940.
37. T. B. Gravley, *The Second World War 1939-1945: Signal and Communications* (War Office, London: 1950), p. 32.

Chapter 4: The Problem of Belgium

1. SHDDT GR/7/N/8 Dossier 1 lettre de président Daladier au général Gamelin, 18 Octobre 1939.
2. Pierre Le Goyet, *Le Mystère Gamelin* (Plon, Paris: 1957), pp. 217–20.
3. TNA (WO) 208/88: lA WO and Military Attache, 19 January 1940; see also ibid., 3a 9 April 1940.
4. TNA CAB 65/11, annex 15 in reference to the Mechelen Affair and the Allies armies moving into Belgium: 'King Leopold had expressed his belief in the genuine character of the documents which had been captured. No doubt the documents, if published, would be repudiated, but nevertheless Germany would make tremendous capital of the fact if Belgian neutrality were violated by Great Britain and France.'
5. TNA CAB 65/11, annex 13.
6. TNA FO 371/24277: C896 (W.M.(40) 15th Conclusions, 16 January 1940.
7. SHDDT DE/2016/SA/68, 2ème Bureau: Rapport à l'État-Major de L'armée de Terre, 20 Fevrier 1940.
8. SHDDT DE/2016/SA/67, Gamelin, Instruction Personelle et Secrète no. 11, 12 Mars 1940.

Chapter 5: The Breda Hypothesis

1. SHDDT GR/7/N/3006. Untitled report from the French military mission to Poland, 12 September 1939.
2. Ibid., French Military Mission to Poland Report, 2 October 1939.
3. Ibid., Report by General Faury to General Gamelin, 9 October 1939.
4. TNA CAB 80/104, Notes of a Meeting Between Gamelin and CIGS, 6 October 1939.

5. Ibid., General Billotte: Étude sur la possibilité d'une intervention en Hollande, 30 Novembre 1939.
6. Max Schiavon (ed.), *Les Carnets secrets du Général Huntziger, 1938-1941* (Éditions Pierre de Taillac, Paris: 2019), p. 105.
7. Martin S. Alexander, '"Fighting to the Last Frenchman"? Reflections on the BEF Deployment to France and the Strains in the Franco-British Alliance, 1939-1940', in Joel Blatt (ed.), *The French Defeat of 1940: Reassessments* (Berghahn Books, Oxford: 1998), p. 308.
8. SHDDT DE/2016/SA Dossier 68, General Giraud: 'Étude sur une intervention éventuelle de la VIIème armée en Hollande méridionale (région Bréda), 3 Décembre, 1939; Ibid, Synthèse du G.Q.G. 3ème Bureau 7 Janvier 1940
9. Ibid.
10. Ibid. Note by General Blanchard: Objet: Hypothèse Canal Albert, 11 Fevrier 1940.
11. SHDDT GR/1K/224 Dossier 15, Extraits d'une lettre du Général Georges, 14 Avril 1940.
12. SHDDT DE/2016/SA Dossier 68, 2ème Bureau: Note sur les mesures militaires prises par la Hollande, 3 Octobre 1940 ; Ibid. 2ème Bureau: Rapport à l'État-Major de L'armée de Terre, 20 Fevrier 1940.
13. Paul Baudoin, *Neuf Mois au Gouvernement (Avril-Décembre 1940)* (Éditions de la Table Ronde, Paris: 1948), p. 33.
14. SHDDT 1K 224/10 Dossier 4, Gamelin, Journal de Marche, 16 Mars 1940.
15. Ibid. Lettres Personelles du Général Gamelin, Reynaud à Gamelin 10 Mai 1940.
16. TNA WO 106/1684, Dewing to Pownall, 23 September 1939; WO 106/1684, British Chiefs of Staff Draft Letter to Gamelin, September 1939; and WO 106/1684, General Staff Criticism of General Gamelin's Plan, September 1939.
17. TNA CAB 80/104, Ironside Memo, 24 January 1940.
18. Ibid.
19. TNA WO 197/44, Swayne to Pownall, 7 November 1939.
20. Maurice Gamelin, *Servir* (Plon, Paris: 1946), vol. 3, p. 401; TNA WO 197/44, Georges to Gort No, 770 3/O9 19 Mars 1940 @ 14:30.
21. Jeffrey Gunsburg. 'The Battle of Gembloux, 14–15 May 1940: The "Blitzkrieg" Checked', *The Journal of Military History*, Vol. 64, No. 1 (January 2000), pp. 97–140.
22. TNA WO 197/44 Witts to Gort, 6 April 1940; ibid, Gort to Georges No. GR/217/0 19 April 1940.
23. TNA WO 197/44 M.M/14, 20 April 1940.

24. TNA WO 197/44 Georges to Gort, No. 1178/3/0p 22 Avril 1940 @ 16:00; Georges to Gort, No. 1180/3/0p 22 Avril 1940 @ 20:00; Gort to Georges GR/217/0.
25. TNA WO 197/44 Gort to Georges, GR/217/8 2 May 1940.
26. SHDDT GR/1K/224 Dossier 15, Maurice Gamelin à Edouard Daladier, 12 Avril 1940, p. 2.

Chapter 6: Carry On Regardless

1. TNA CAB 80/10, Chiefs of Staff Committee, Allied Action in the Event of a German Attack on the Netherland Islands, 1 May 1940.
2. SHDDT GR/27/N/3 lettre No. 799, 15 Avril 1940.
3. Paul Baudoin, *Neuf Mois au Gouvernement (Avril-Décembre 1940)* (Éditions de la Table Ronde, Paris: 1948), p. 36
4. SHDDT GR/1K/224/10 Dossier 4 Journal de Marche, 7 Avril 1940.
5. TNA CAB 80/105, Chiefs of Staff Committee, German Invasion of Holland: Allied Policy Draft Memorandum, 5 April 1940; CAB 80/105, Chiefs of Staff Committee, German Invasion of Holland: Air Policy Report, 8 April 1940.
6. François Bedarida, *La Stratégie Secrète de la drôle guerre* (Presse FNSP: 1979), pp. 179, 338, 383, 439.
7. TNA CAB 80/105, Chiefs of Staff Committee, German Invasion of Holland: Air Policy Report, 8 April 1940.
8. Ibid., WO 106/1684, Dewing to Pownall, 23 September 1939; WO 106/1684, British Chiefs of Staff Draft Letter to Gamelin, September 1939; and WO 106/1684, General Staff Criticism of General Gamelin's Plan, September 1939.
9. Minart, *P.C. Vincennes, Secteur 4,* Tome I, Titre II, pp. 151–2.
10. TNA CAB 66/2/50, 2nd Bureau, Note on the Available Personnel of Germany, 14 October 1939; TNA CAB 80/104, Ironside Memo, 24 January 1940.
11. Gamelin to Georges, 15 April 1940, cited in Gamelin, *Servir*, vol. 3, p. 343.
12. TNA WO 106/1684, Notes of a Meeting Held at the Headquarters of General Gamelin, 9 November 1939; WO 106/1684, General Staff to C.I.G.S., 20 April 1940.
13. SHDDT GR/27/N/81 Journal du Marche du 48e DIF, p. 6.
14. TNA CAB 80/10, Chiefs of Staff Committee, Allied Action in the Event of a German Attack on the Netherland Islands, 1 May 1940.
15. TNA CAB 80/105, Chiefs of Staff Committee, German Invasion of Holland: Allied Policy Draft Memorandum, 5 April 1940; CAB 80/105, Chiefs of Staff Committee, German Invasion of Holland: Air Policy

Report, 8 April 1940; and CAB 80/10, Chiefs of Staff Committee, Allied Action in the Event of a German Attack on the Netherland Islands, 1 May 1940.

16. TNA CAB 66/1/44, Conversation with M. Daladier and General Gamelin, Note by the Secretary of State for War and Lord Hankey, 21 September 1939.
17. SHDDT GR/5/N/580, Plan de guerre pour le printemps 1940, 26 Fevrier 1940.
18. Ernest May, *Strange Victory: Hitler's Conquest of France* (I B Taurus & Co, New York: 2009), p. 385.
19. SHDDT GR 5N 580, Decisions of the Supreme Council, 17 Novembre 1939; TNA 106/1684, Director of Military Operations and Plans, Notes of a Meeting Held at the Headquarters of General Gamelin, 9 November 1939.

Chapter 7: 10 May 1940

1. Julian Jackson, *The Fall of France: The Nazi Invasion of 1940* (Oxford University Press, Oxford: 2003), pp. 37–8.
2. SHDDT GR/32/N/76 Dossier 1 'Journal du Marche de la 12e DIM 10 Mai – 14 Juin 1940', p. 7.
3. SHDDT GR/31/N/38 Dossier 5. Rapports Mauberge, p. 1.
4. Ibid., p. 189.
5. SHDDT A1/3/D/498; 'Dossier 1. Aviation de Bombardment Française pendant le campagne 1939-1940', p. 19.
6. Ibid. p. 24.
7. Greg Baughen, *The Rise and Fall of the French Air Force* (FontHill Media, Stroud: 2019), p. 190.
8. Ibid., pp. 187–8.
9. Ibid., p. 189.
10. SHDDT GR/30/N/260. Dossier Journal de Marche du Corps de Cavalerie. 10 Mai 1940, p. 1.
11. SHDDT GR/32/N/76/Dossier 1 'Journal du Marche de la 12e DIM 10 Mai – 14 Juin 1940', p. 8.
12. Ibid., p. 9.
13. SHDDT GR/32/N/47 Rapport 9e Division d'Infanterie 15 Mai 1940.
14. Ibid., ordre du jour 10 Mai 1940.
15. Ibid., Rapport 9e Division d'Infanterie 15 Mai 1940,
16. Ibid., ordre 10 Mai 1940.

17. Ibid., Rapport 9e Division d'Infanterie 15 Mai 1940.
18. Ibid., ordre 10 Mai 1940.
19. Baughen, *The Rise and Fall of the French Air Force,* p. 190.
20. Frieser, *The Blitzkrieg Legend,* p. 45.

Chapter 8: 11 May 1940

1. SHDDT GR/32/N/47 Ordre du Jour 13 Mai 1940.
2. Baughen, *The Rise and Fall of the French Air Force,* p. 193.
3. Ibid. p. 194.
4. Frieser, *The Blitzkrieg Legend,* p. 360.
5. Ibid., p. 198.
6. SHDDT GR/32/N/76/Dossier 1 'Journal du Marche de la 12e DIM 10 Mai – 14 Juin 1940', p. 11.
7. SHDDT GR/30/N/260. Dossier Journal de Marche du Corps de Cavalerie. 10 Mai, p. 2.
8. Baughen, *The Rise and Fall of the French Air Force,* p. 198.
9. SHDDT GR/30/N/260. Dossier Journal de Marche du Corps de Cavalerie, p. 3.
10. SHDDA 3/D/498 Dossier 1. Aviation de Bombardement Française pendant le campagne 1939-1940, pp. 25–6.
11. SHDDT GR/30/N/260. Dossier Journal de Marche du Corps de Cavalerie, p. 3.
12. SHDDA 3/D/498 Dossier 1. Aviation de Bombardement Française pendant le campagne 1939-1940, p. 27.
13. Ibid., p. 29,
14. Frieser, *The Blitzkrieg Legend,* p. 606
15. John Buckley, 'The Air War in France,' in Professor Brian Bond and Michael Taylor (eds), *The Battle for France & Flanders: Sixty Years On* (Barnsley: Leo Cooper, 2001), pp. 109–26.
16. SHDDA 3/D/498 Dossier 1. Aviation de Bombardement Française pendant le campagne 1939-1940, p. 27.
17. Ibid., pp. 32–47.
18. Ibid., p. 29.
19. SHDDT MR/31/1001111/51 Journal du Marche, pp. 2–3.
20. SHDDT GR/30/N/260. Dossier Journal de Marche du Corps de Cavalerie, p. 3.

Chapter 9: 12 May 1940

1. SHDDA 3/D/498 Dossier 1. Aviation de Bombardement Française pendant le campagne 1939-1940, p. 30.
2. SHDDT GR/30/N/260. Dossier Journal de Marche du Corps de Cavalerie, p. 3.
3. SHDDT GR/27/N/81 Rapport 20 July 1940, p. 1.
4. SHDDT GR/32/N/76 Dossier 1 'Journal du Marche de la 12e DIM 10 Mai – 14 Juin 1940', pp. 12–13.
5. SHDDT GR/30/N/260. Dossier Journal de Marche du Corps de Cavalerie, p. 4.
6. SHDDT GR/34/N/457 Rapport 24 Avril 1940, p. 1.
7. SHDDA 3/D/498 Dossier 1. Aviation de Bombardement Française pendant le campagne 1939-1940, pp. 30–5.
8. SHDDT GR/30/N/260. Dossier Journal de Marche du Corps de Cavalerie, p. 4.
9. SHDDA 3/D/498 Dossier 1. Aviation de Bombardement Française pendant le campagne 1939-1940, pp. 30–5.
10. SHDDT GR/30/N/260. Dossier Journal de Marche du Corps de Cavalerie, p. 4.
11. SHDDT GR/32/N/76/Dossier 1 'Journal du Marche de la 12e DIM 10 Mai – 14 Juin 1940', pp. 12–13.

Chapter 10: 13 May 1940

1. Baughen, *The Rise and Fall of the French Air Force*, p. 196.
2. SHDDT GR/32/N/47 ordres 13 May 1940.
3. SHDDT GR/27/N/81 Rapport 20 Juillet 1940, pp. 1–2.
4. SHDDT GR/32/N/76/Dossier 1 'Journal du Marche de la 12e DIM 10 Mai – 14 Juin 1940', p. 15.
5. SHDDT GR/30/N/260. Dossier Journal de Marche du Corps de Cavalerie, p. 5.
6. Baughen, *The Rise and Fall of the French Air Force*, p. 204.
7. SHDDT GR/30/N/260. Dossier Journal de Marche du Corps de Cavalerie, p. 6.
8. Ibid. Dossier La premier bataille de chars blindes de l'histoire Mondiale, pp. 4–8.
9. Ibid. Dossier Journal de Marche du Corps de Cavalerie, p. 7.
10. Ibid. Dossier La premier bataille de chars blindes de l'histoire Mondiale, p. 8.
11. Baughen, *The Rise and Fall of the French Air Force*, pp. 204–05.

12. Érik Barbanson, *Les 2e et 3e divisions légères mécaniques, t. 1: Hannut-Gembloux 10-15 mai 1940: la première bataille de chars de l'histoire* (Arès, Toul: 2017).

Chapter 11: 14 May 1940

1. SHDDT GR/30/N/260. Dossier Journal de Marche du Corps de Cavalerie, p. 7.
2. SHDDT GR/32/N/76 Dossier 1 'Journal du Marche de la 12e DIM 10 Mai – 14 Juin 1940', p. 16.
3. Baughen, *The Rise and Fall of the French Air Force*, p. 215.
4. SHDDT GR/30/N/260. Dossier Journal de Marche du Corps de Cavalerie, p. 7.
5. SHDDT GR/31/N/38 Dossier 5. Rapports Mauberge, p. 1.
6. SHDDT GR/27/N/81 Diverse, p. 3.
7. SHDDT GR/5/N/580 Dossier1, Rapport de l'État-Major de l'Armée, 14 Mai 1940.

Chapter 12: 15 May 1940

1. Alistair Horne, *To Lose a Battle: France 1940* (Macmillan, London: 1969), pp. 444–5.
2. SHDDT A1/3/D/498; Dossier 1. Aviation de Bombardment Française pendant le campagne 1939-1940, p. 45.
3. TNA CAB 79/4/33.
4. Horne, *To Lose a Battle*, pp. 445–7.
5. SHDDT A1/3/D/498; Dossier 1. Aviation de Bombardment Française pendant le campagne 1939-1940, pp. 45–7.
6. Vic Flintham, Close Call: RAF Close Air Support in the Mediterranean. Volume I Defeat in France to el Hamma 1939-1943 (Crecy: Manchester, 2021), p. 40.
7. SHDDT MR/31/1001111/51 Journal du Marche, p. 53.
8. SHDDT GR/32/N/76, Dossier 1 'Journal du Marche de la 12e DIM 10 Mai – 14 Juin 1940', pp. 19–20.
9. SHDDT GR/30/N/260. Dossier Journal de Marche du Corps de Cavalerie, p. 8.
10. Horne, To Lose a Battle, pp. 429–30.
11. SHDDT GR/30/N/260. Dossier Journal de Marche du Corps de Cavalerie, p. 8.
12. SHDDT GR/27/N/81 Diverse, p. 4.

13. SHDDT GR/27/N/81 opérations sur les lignes de communications britanniquee, p. 2.
14. TNA CAB 80/3 General Gamelin's Observations, 27 September 1939; CAB 80/3 Chiefs of Staff Committee, Comments on General Gamelin's Observation on our Appreciation on the Possible Course of the War, 2 October 1939; ibid. Gamelin to Daladier, 7 January 1940.
15. TNA CAB 65/13/20.
16. Titre V. p. 11.
17. Bruno Chaix, *En mai 1940, fallait-il entrer en Belgique?* (Economica, Paris: 2000), pp.282–3.

Chapter 13: Flavion

1. SHDDT GR/31/N/38 Dossier 5. Rapports Mauberge, p. 3.
2. SHDDT GR/27/N/112 Journal de marche 28eme Bataillon du Chars du Combat, Mai à Juin 1940, pp. 17–21.
3. SHDDT GR/30/N/260. Dossier Journal de Marche du Corps de Cavalerie, p. 10.
4. SHDDT GR/31/N/38 Dossier 5. Rapports Mauberge, pp. 3–4.
5. SHDDT A1/3/D/498 ; Dossier 1. Aviation de Bombardment Française pendant le campagne 1939-1940 pp. 46–8.
6. Ibid., pp. 4–5.
7. SHDDA 3/D/498 Dossier 1. Aviation de Bombardement Française pendant le campagne 1939-1940. p. 53.
8. SHDDT GR/32/N/76/Dossier 1 'Journal du Marche de la 12e DIM 10 Mai – 14 Juin 1940' pp. 19–24.
9. SHDDT A1/3/D/498 ;'Dossier 1. Aviation de Bombardment Française pendant le campagne 1939-1940, pp. 53–4.
10. https://france3-regions.francetvinfo.fr/
11. Flintham, *Close Call*, pp. 40–1.
12. Ibid. p. 43.
13. https://france3-regions.francetvinfo.fr/
14. SHDDT GR/27/N/81 Diverse, p. 5.
15. SHDDT GR/27/N/81 Madert, p. 2.
16. SHDDT GR/27/N/81 opérations sur les lignes de communications britanniquee, pp. 2–3.
17. SHDDT GR/34/N/437 45e Bataillon des Chars de Combat, Rapport Commandant Bezanger, 16 Mai 1940, p. 2. See also SHDDT GR/34/N/439, Journal de Marche et Operations du 49eme Bataillon de Chars de Combat, pp. 7–9.

18. Baughen, *The Rise and Fall of the French Air Force*, p. 217.
19. SHDDT GR/27/N/85 Dossier 16 Chars de Combat, Emploi des chars, p. 15.

Chapter 14: 17 May 1940

1. SHDDT GR/32/N/76/Dossier 1 'Journal du Marche de la 12e DIM 10 Mai – 14 Juin 1940', pp. 24–6.
2. https://france3-regions.francetvinfo.fr/ accessed 29 July 2025.
3. Ibid.
4. SHDDT GR/27/N/85 Dossier 16 Chars de Combat, Emploi des chars, pp. 16–22.
5. SHDDT A1/3/D/498 Dossier 1. Aviation de Bombardment Française pendant le campagne 1939-1940, p. 55.
6. Ibid., p. 58.
7. SHDDT GR/31/N/38 Dossier 5. Rapports Mauberge, p. 5.
8. SHDDT GR/32/N/76 Dossier 1 'Journal du Marche de la 12e DIM 10 Mai – 14 Juin 1940', p. 29.
9. SHDDT GR/30/N/260 Dossier Journal de Marche du Corps de Cavalerie, p. 11.
10. Ibid., p. 12.
11. SHDDA A1/3/D/498 Dossier 1. Aviation de Bombardment Française pendant le campagne 1939-1940, p. 59.
12. Flintham, *Close Call*, p. 43.
13. SHDDA A1/3/D/498 Dossier 1. Aviation de Bombardment Française pendant le campagne 1939-1940, pp. 56–60.

Chapter 15: 18 May 1940

1. Richard Vinen, *The Unfree French: Life under the Occupation* (Allen Lane, London: 2006); Douglas Porch, *Defeat and Division: France at War, 1939–1942* (Cambridge University Press, Cambridge: 2022), pp. 180–4; Martin S. Alexander, *Soldiers and Socialists: the French officer corps and leftist government, 1935–7* (Cambridge University Press, Cambridge: 2009).
2. Anna von der Goltz and Robert Gildea, 'Flawed saviours: the myths of Hindenburg and Pétain', *European History Quarterly* 39.3 (2009), pp. 439–64; Jacques Szaluta, 'Marshal Pétain and French nationalism: The interwar years and Vichy', *History of European Ideas* 15.1–3 (1992), pp. 113–18; Charles Williams, *Pétain: How the Hero of France Became a Convicted Traitor and Changed the Course of History* (Palgrave Macmillan, London: 2005).

3. SHDDT GR/27/N/85 Dossier 16 Chars de Combat, Emploi des chars, pp. 17–18.
4. SHDDT GR/31/N/38 Dossier 5. Rapports Boulogne sur Mer, p. 1.
5. SHDDT GR/31/N/38 Dossier 5. Rapports Mauberge, pp. 3–4
6. SHDDA A1/3/D/498 Dossier 1. Aviation de Bombardment Française pendant le campagne 1939-1940, p. 63.
7. Ibid., pp. 67–8.
8. SHDDT MR/31/1001111/51 Journal du Marche, pp. 2–3.
9. SHDDT GR/27/N/81 opérations sur les lignes de communications britanniquee, p. 5.
10. SHDDT GR/30/N/260. Dossier Journal de Marche du Corps de Cavalerie, p. 12.
11. Chaix, *En mai 1940, fallait-il entrer en Belgique?* pp. 282–3.
12. Horne, *To Lose a Battle*, pp. 549–50.

Chapter 16: Weygand takes Charge

1. TNA CAB106/274 folios 52-53A.
2. Ibid.
3. General G. Roton, *Années Cruciales: La Course aux Armements (1933-1939), La Campagne (1939-1940)* (Charles Lavauzelle, Paris: 1947), p. 302.
4. SHDDT GR/27/N/81 order General Georges, 19 Mai 1940 No.1615/3/op.
5. TNA CAB106/279 French Army, folios 6-11; SHDDT GR/1/K/224 Journal du cabinet General Gamelin, 19 Mai 1940.
6. SHDDA A1/3/D/498 Dossier 1. Aviation de Bombardement Française pendant le campagne 1939-1940, p. 74.
7. SHDDT GR/27/N/81 The Ninth Queen's Royal Lancers, p. 1.
8. SHDDT GR/27/N/81 Diverse, p. 7.
9. SHDDT GR/30/N/260. Dossier Journal de Marche du Corps de Cavalerie, pp. 13–14.
10. SHDDT GR/31/N/38 Dossier 5. Rapports Boulogne sur Mer, p. 1.
11. SHDDT GR/31/N/38 Dossier 5. Rapports Maubeuge, p. 7.
12. SHDDA AI/3/D/498 rapport 21 Mai 1940.
13. SHDDT GR/32/N/47 Journal du Marche de la 4eme DCR, pp. 17–18.
14. SHDDT GR/30/N/260. Dossier Journal de Marche du Corps de Cavalerie, p. 14.
15. Baughen, *The Rise and Fall of the French Air Force*, pp. 229–30.

Chapter 17: 20 May 1940

1. TNA CAB 79/4/41.
2. Schiavon (ed.), *Les Carnets secrets du Général Huntziger, 1938-1941*, p. 131.
3. SHDDT GR/5/N/580 Dossier1, Rapport de l'État-Major de l'Armée, 14 Mai 1940.
4. SHDDT GR/31/N/38 Dossier 5. Rapports Maubeuge, p. 9.
5. Ibid.
6. SHDDA A1/3/D/498 Dossier 1. Aviation de Bombardment Française pendant le campagne 1939-1940, pp. 70–3.
7. SHDDT GR/30/N/260 Dossier Journal de Marche du Corps de Cavalerie, p. 10.
8. SHDDT GR/27/N/81 message téléphonique, 20 Mai 1940.

Chapter 18: 21 May 1940

1. Baughen, *The Rise and Fall of the French Air Force*, pp. 230–1.
2. SHDDT GR/27/N/81 Diverse, p. 7.
3. SHDDT GR/5/N/580 Dossier 21 Mai 1940.
4. SHDDT GR/27/N/81 telegramme 6763 21 Mai 1940.
5. SHDDT GR/27/N/81 HVI 204 21/5/1940.
6. SHDDT GR/27/N/81 traduction d'un Telegramme 21 Mai 1940. No.1161 D/3.
7. SHDDT GR/31/N/38 Dossier 5. Rapports Maubeuge, p. 9.
8. SHDDA A1/3/D/498 Dossier 1. Aviation de Bombardement Française pendant le campagne 1939-1940, p. 78.
9. SHDDT GR/30/N/260. Dossier Journal de Marche du Corps de Cavalerie, pp. 15–16.
10. SHDDT GR/27/N/81 Le Corps Expéditionnaires Anglais en France en 1939-40, pp. 3–4.
11. SHDDT GR/30/N/260 Dossier Journal de Marche du Corps de Cavalerie, pp. 15–16.
12. SHDDT GR/27/N/81 Le Corps Expéditionnaires Anglais en France en 1939-40, pp. 3–4.
13. SHDDA 3/D/498 Dossier 1. Aviation de Bombardement Française pendant le campagne 1939-1940, p. 78.
14. Site visit 1 March 2025.
15. Jacques De Launay, *Major Controversies of Contemporary History* (Pergamon Press, London: 1965), pp. 228–9.
16. Testimony of General Maxime Weygand, former Commander-in-Chief of the French Army in 1940, for the program 'Le Magazine du Passé' on RTF in 1960.

Chapter 19: The Battle of Arras

1. SHDDT GR/27/N/81 The Ninth Queen's Royal Lancers, pp. 1–2.
2. SHDDT GR/30/N/260. Dossier Journal de Marche du Corps de Cavalerie, p. 17.
3. Ibid., p. 18.
4. SHDDT GR/27/N/81 traduction d'un un Telegramme 22 Mai 1940. No.1170 D/3.
5. SHDDA 3/D/498 Dossier 1. Aviation de Bombardement Française pendant le campagne 1939-1940, p. 78.
6. Ibid., p. 80.
7. Site visit 1 March 2025. The memorial to the massacre of 22 May 1940 in Aubigny-en-Artois.

Chapter 20: 23 May

1. SHDDT GR/27/N/81 Message passe Amiral Odenhal pour Amiral Abrial, 21:30 23 Mai 1940.
2. SHDDT GR/27/N/81 Message prive du General Ironside reçu par le General Georges, 23 Mai 1940.
3. SHDDT GR/27/N/81 Madert, p. 3.
4. SHDDA A1/3/D/498 Dossier 1. Aviation de Bombardement Française pendant le campagne 1939-1940, p. 82.
5. SHDDT GR/30/N/260. Dossier Journal de Marche du Corps de Cavalerie, pp. 19–20.

Chapter 21: 24 May 1940

1. SHDDA A1/3/D/498 Dossier 1. Aviation de Bombardment Française pendant le campagne 1939-1940, pp. 83–5.
2. SHDDT GR/27/N/81 The Ninth Queen's Royal Lancers, pp. 1–2.
3. SHDDT GR/27/N/81 Chenu Diverse, pp. 1–2.
4. SHDDT GR/27/N/85 Dossier 16 Chars de Combat, Emploi des chars, p. 20.
5. SHDDT GR/27/N/81 Chenu Diverse, pp. 1–2.
6. SHDDT GR/30/N/179 rapoort Fauvelle, p. 2.
7. SHDDT GR/27/N/81 traduction d'un Telegramme 24 May 1940 No. 1179 D/3.
8. SHDDT GR/30/N/260. Dossier Journal de Marche du Corps de Cavalerie, p. 20.
9. Ibid., p. 21.
10. SHDDT GR/30/N/179 rapport Fauvelle, pp. 2–3.

11. Sir Edward Spears, *Assignment to Catastrophe* (William Heinemann Ltd, London: 1955), volume 1, p. 188.
12. Ibid., pp. 187–92.
13. SHDDT GR/30/N/179 rapport Fauvelle, pp. 2–3.
14. SHDDA A1/3/D/498 Dossier 1. Aviation de Bombardment Française pendant le campagne 1939-1940, p. 87.
15. SHDDT GR/27/N/81 Madert, p. 3.
16. SHDDT GR/31/N/38 Dossier 5. Rapports Boulogne sur Mer, p. 2.

Chapter 22: On the Job Training

1. SHDDT GR/27/N/85 Titre III, pp. 185–7.
2. Frieser, *The Blitzkrieg Legend*, p. 39.
3. SHDDT GR/27/N/85 Weygand, telegramme 1142, 24 Mai 1940.
4. SHDDT GR/27/N/85 Keller, 25 Mai 1940.

Chapter 23: 25 May 1940

1. SHDDT GR/27/N/81 traduction d'un Telegramme 25 May 1940 No. 1135 D/3.
2. SHDDT GR/27/N/81 Telegramme 25 May 1940 @ 03:15.
3. SHDDT MR/31/1001111/51 Journal du Marche, pp. 2–3.
4. May, *Strange Victory*, p. 268.
5. SHDDT GR/27/N/81 traduction d'un Telegramme 25 Mai 1940 No. 1194/D4.
6. SHDDT GR/27/N/81 traduction d'un Telegramme 25 Mai 1940 No. 1196 D/3.
7. SHDDT GR/31/N/38 Dossier 5. Rapports Calais, pp. 1–2.
8. SHDDT GR/31/N/38 Dossier 5. Rapports Boulonge sur Mer, p. 1.
9. SHDDT GR/27/N/81 Diverse, p. 8.
10. SHDDT GR/27/N/81 traduction d'un télégramme du Lieutenant-Colonel Desroche, 25 Mai 1940 @ 06:25.
11. SHDDT GR/27/N/81 Message General Dill au General Swayne 25 Mai 1940.
12. SHDDT GR/27/N/81 traduction d'un telegramme, No. 811 25 Mai 1940 @ 18:25.
13. SHDDT GR/27/N/81 traduction d'un telegramme, No. 810 25 Mai 1940 @ 16:30.
14. SHDDT GR/27/N/81 traduction d'un Telegramme 25 Mai 1940 No. 1198 D/3.

15. SHDDT GR/30/N/260. Dossier Journal de Marche du Corps de Cavalerie, p. 21.
16. SHDDT GR/27/N/81 traduction d'un telegramme, 26 Mai 1940 @ 06:25.
17. SHDDA 3/D/498 Dossier 1. Aviation de Bombardement Française pendant le campagne 1939-1940, p. 91.
18. SHDDT GR/27/N/81 traduction d'un telegramme, 26 Mai 1940 @ 06:25.
19. SHDDT GR/30/N/260. Dossier Journal de Marche du Corps de Cavalerie, pp. 21–2.
20. SHDDT GR/27/N/81 Message General Dill au General Swayne 25 Mai 1940.
21. SHDDT GR/27/N/81 traduction d'un telegramme, No. 7043 25 Mai 1940 @ 19:10.
22. SHDDT GR/30/N/260. Dossier Journal de Marche du Corps de Cavalerie, p. 22.
23. SHDDT GR/27/N/81 traduction d'un telegramme, No. 7056 26 Mai 1940 @ 09:10.
24. Baughen, *The Rise and Fall of the French Air Force*, pp. 237–9.

Chapter 24: 26 May 1940

1. SHDDT GR/27/N/85 Weygand, telegramme No. 1184 26 Mai 1940.
2. SHDDT GR/27/N/81 Le Corps Expéditionnaires Anglais en France en 1939-40, pp. 5–6.
3. SHDDT GR/27/N/81 traduction d'un telegramme, No. 1275 D/3 26 Mai 1940 @ 08:35.
4. SHDDT GR/30/N/260. Dossier Journal de Marche du Corps de Cavalerie, pp. 23–4.
5. SHDDA A1/3/D/498 Dossier 1. Aviation de Bombardement Française pendant le campagne 1939-1940, pp. 94–5.
6. SHDDT GR/27/N/85 Dossier 16 Chars de Combat, Emploi des chars, pp. 52–3.
7. Ibid., pp. 95–6.
8. SHDDT GR/27/N/81 traduction d'un telegramme, No. 1219 D/3 26 Mai 1940 @ 20:20.
9. SHDDT GR/27/N/81 Le Corps Expéditionnaires Anglais en France en 1939-40, p. 5.
10. SHDDT GR/31/N/38 Dossier 5. Rapports Calais, p. 2.

Chapter 25: Dunkirk

1. Dominque Lormier, *La Bataille de Dunkerque* (Flavie Memet, Paris: 2011), pp. 74–8.

2. Horne, *To Lose a Battle*, p. 550.
3. Gamelin, volume 1, p. 245.
4. SHDDT GR/27/N/12/4 Gamelin, 'Note . . . ', 12 Oct. 1939; SHD 28N14/1Prételat to Georges, 19 Nov. 1939; Ibid. Gamelin to Georges, 21 Dec 1939.
5. SHDDT GR/27/N/85 Georges telegramme No. 2149 27 Mai 1940.
6. Ibid.
7. SHDDT A1/3/D/498 Dossier 1. Aviation de Bombardment Française pendant le campagne 1939-1940, p. 99.
8. Op cit.

Chapter 26: Fighting Continues

1. SHDDT GR/27/N/81 Le Corps Expéditionnaires Anglais en France en 1939-40, pp. 5–6.
2. SHDDT GR/30/N/260. Dossier Journal de Marche du Corps de Cavalerie, pp. 24–5.
3. Site visit 28 February 2025. Memorial in tribute to the 97 men of the Royal Welsh Fusiliers who died in the vicinity of Saint-Venant between 23 and 27 May 1940.
4. Site visit 28 February 2025. The memorial dedicated to the victims of the SS, on 27 May 1940, at the site of the Paradis massacre in Lestrem.
5. SHDDT GR/27/N/81 The Ninth Queen's Royal Lancers, pp. 3–4.
6. SHDDT GR/27/N/81 The First Armoured Division, p. 6.
7. SHDDT GR/27/N/81 Rapport Julotte, p. 4.
8. Roger Keyes, *Un règne brisé* (Paris-Bruxelles, Duculot: 1985); Edmond de Fabribeckers, *La Campagne de l'Armée Belge en 1940* (Rossel: 1978).
9. SHDDT GR/27/N/81 telegramme @ 23:15 27 Mai 1940.

Chapter 27: 28 May 1940

1. Lormier, *La Bataille de Dunkerque*, p. 66.
2. https://www.maisondusouvenir.be/campagne_et_reddition_armee_belge.php.
3. SHDDT GR/32/N/47 Journal du marche de 12e DIM, p. 55.
4. SHDDT GR/27/N/81 Diverse, p. 11.
5. SHDDT GR/27/N/81 Note par le Laurencie, p. 1.
6. SHDDT GR/30/N/260. Dossier Journal de Marche du Corps de Cavalerie, pp. 25–6.
7. SHDDT GR/32/N/47 Journal du marche de 12e DIM, pp. 58–60.

8. SHDDT GR/30/N/260. Dossier 3 Journal de Marche du Corps de Cavalerie, pp. 25–6.
9. SHDDT GR/34/N/471 Dossier 3 Journaux des marches et opérations des corps de troupe 1 Septembre 1939 à 25 Juin 1940, pp. 55–7.
10. SHDDT GR/32/N/76 Dossier 21 Rapport Commandant Parent 10 Mai – 1 Juin 1940, pp. 7–8.

Chapter 28: De Gaulle's Offensive

1. SHDDT GR/32/N/47 Journal du Marche de la 4eme DCR, pp. 20–2.
2. SHDDT GR/27/N/85 Journal du marche, p. 23.
3. SHDDT GR/27/N/81 Diverse, p. 11.
4. SHDDA A1/3/D/498 Dossier 1. Aviation de Bombardement Française pendant le campagne 1939-1940, p. 103.
5. From the memorial plaque tribute to the victims of the massacres in the reconstructed cow shelter at the La-Plaine-au-Bois memorial site.
6. SHDDT GR/27/N/81 Diverse B, p. 12.
7. SHDDT GR/34/N/462 Dossier 4, Rapports d'officiers, faits d'armes, propositions de citations, rapport 28 Mai 1940, p. 1.
8. Ibid., pp. 1–2.
9. SHDDT GR/27/N/113 Journal de Marche du 1re Cuirassiers, 10 Mai à 1 Aout 1940, pp. 32–40.

Chapter 29: Retreat to Dunkirk

1. SHDDT GR/34/N/471/3 Journaux des marches et opérations des corps de troupe 1 Septembre 1939 à 25 Juin 1940, pp. 57–8.
2. SHDDT GR/27/N/113 Journal de Marche du 1re Cuirassiers, 10 Mai à 1 Aout 1940, p. 33.
3. SHDDT GR/30/N/260. Dossier Journal de Marche du Corps de Cavalerie, pp. 27–8.
4. SHDDT GR/27/N/81 Diverse, pp. 13–15.
5. Ibid., p. 28.
6. 'Dunkirk 1940' directed by Bernard Claeys and broadcast on May 28, 1978 in the programme 'Hexagonal, Histoire de France' (FR3).
7. Ibid.
8. SHDDT GR/27/N/81 Diverse, pp. 13–15.
9. SHDDT GR/27/N/81 Note par le Colonel Bourget, p. 1.
10. SHDDT GR/32/N/47 Rapport Pommerueil, 29 Mai 1940.
11. SHDDT GR/27/N/81 Telegramme No. 7246, 29 Mai 1940 @ 13:05.

12. SHDDT GR/27/N/85 Weygand, 29 Mai 1940.
13. SHDDA A1/3/D/498 Dossier 1. Aviation de Bombardement Française pendant le campagne 1939-1940, p. 106.
14. TNA WO 106/1613. Gort to Dill, 29 May 1940.
15. Ibid. Air and Naval Cover, Dunkirk.
16. SHDDT GR/32/N/76 Dossier 25 Rapport Capitaine Carton 10 Mai – 1 Juin 1940, p. 6.
17. Site visit 28 February 2025. Emmerin Civilian Victims Memorial.
18. SHDDT GR/27/N/85 Journal du marche, p. 24.
19. SHDDT GR/34/N/425/7 Journaux des marches et opérations de 13ème bataillon de chars de combat, pp. 33–4.

Chapter 30: Evacuation

1. SHDDT GR/34/N/435/18 Journaux des marches et opérations des 39e Bataillion de Chars de Combat, p. 35.
2. SHDDT GR/34/N/463 Journaux des marches et opérations des corps de troupe 2 Septembre à 8 Juillet 1940, p. 75.
3. SHDDT GR/32/N/76 Dossier 21 Rapport Commandant Parent 10 Mai – 1 Juin 1940, pp. 7–8.
4. SHDDT GR/32/N/47 Journal du marche de 12e DIM, pp. 65–6.
5. SHDDT GR/27/N/81 Telegramme No. 3779 30 Mai 1940 @ 08:00.
6. SHDDT GR/30/N/260. Dossier Journal de Marche du Corps de Cavalerie, p. 29.
7. SHDDT GR/27/N/81 Note par le Colonel Bourget, p. 1.
8. Nord-Maritime, 29 Septembre 1942, p. 2.
9. SHDDT GR/30/N/260. Dossier Journal de Marche du Corps de Cavalerie, p. 29.
10. SHDDT GR/32/N/47 ordre 30 Mai @ 19:00.
11. SHDDT GR/32/N/47 Situation de la 12e DIM à la date du 30 Mai 1940, p. 1.
12. SHDDT GR/32/N/76 Amicale de la 12e Division Motorisee General Janssen, Bulletin No, 21, Mai 1968, p. 10.
13. SHDDT GR/32/N/47 Situation de la 12e DIM à la date du 30 Mai 1940, par Colonel Parent.
14. Op cit., p. 2.
15. SHDDT GR/32/N/76 Dossier 25 Rapport Capitaine Carton 10 Mai – 1 Juin 1940, p. 7.
16. Ibid.

Chapter 31: Disagreements

1. SHDDT GR/32/N/47 Situation de la 12e DIM à la date du 30 Mai 1940, p. 1.
2. SHDDT GR/31/N/40 Dossier 5, Journal du Marche de FTA, p. 8.
3. SHDDT GR/32/N/47 ordre 31 Mai 1940 @ 17:30.
4. SHDDT GR/32/N/47 Journal du Marche, 10 Mai à 4 Juin 1940, p. 72.
5. Ibid., p. 73.
6. John C. Cairns, 'De Gaulle Confronts the British: The Legacy of 1940', *International Journal – Canada's Journal of Global Policy Analysis*, Vol. 23, No. 2 (1968), pp. 187–210.
7. SHDDT GR/27/N/81 Telegramme No. 880 31 Mai 1940 @ 04:20.

Chapter 32: 31 May 1940

1. SHDDT GR/27/N/81 Telegramme No. 7361 31 Mai 1940 @ 00:15.
2. SHDDT GR/27/N/81 Telegramme No. 7337 31 Mai 1940 @ 05:30.
3. SHDDT GR/30/M/179 rapport General Fagalde.
4. SHDDT GR/27/N/81 Telegramme No. 889 31 Mai @ 20:00.
5. John C Cairns, 'The French View Dunkirk', Bond and Taylor (eds), *The Battle for France & Flanders: Sixty Years On*, p. 94.
6. SHDDT GR/27/N/81 Telegramme No. 7460 31 Mai 1940 @ 20:45.
7. Ibid.
8. SHDDT GR/27/N/81 Telegramme No. 7476 31 Mai 1940 @ 22:55.
9. SHDDT GR/27/N/81 Telegramme No. 72732 31 Mai 1940.
10. SHDDT GR/27/N/81 Telegramme No. 72728 1 Juin 1940.
11. SHDDT GR/27/N/81 Telegramme No. 72746 1 Juin @ 18:45.
12. SHDDT GR/27/N/81 Telegramme No. 1290 31 Mai.
13. SHDDT GR/32/N/221 Dossier 11 Embarquement Dunkerque: notes du 30 mai au 2 Juin 40. Ordre 31 Mai 1940 @ 15:45.
14. SHDDT GR/32/N/221 Dossier 11 Embarquement Dunkerque: notes du 30 mai au 2 Juin 40. Ordre 31 Mai 1940.
15. SHDDT GR/32/N/221 Dossier 11 Embarquement Dunkerque: notes du 30 mai au 2 Juin 40. Ordre 31 Mai 1940 A.
16. SHDDT GR/34/N/464 Journaux des marches et opérations des corps de troupe du 6e régiment des Cuirassiers. 2 Septembre 1939 à 8 Juillet 1940, p. 75.
17. SHDDT GR/27/N/81 Diverse, pp. 14–16.
18. SHDDT GR/32/N/47 ordre 31 Mai 1940 @ 20:00.
19. SHDDT GR/27/N/81 Telegramme No. 72734, 1 Juin 1940.
20. SHDDT GR/31/N/40 Dossier 5, Journal du Marche de FTA, p. 6.

Chapter 33: 1 June 1940. Get Out While You Can

1. SHDDT GR/32/N/47 ordre 1 Juin 1940 A.
2. SHDDT GR/32/N/47 Journal du Marche, 10 Mai à 4 Juin 1940, p. 72.
3. SHDDT GR/32/N/47 ordre 1 Juin 1940 A.
4. SHDDT GR/32/N/47 Journal du Marche, 10 Mai à 4 Juin 1940, p. 73.
5. SHDDT GR/32/N/76 Dossier 25 Rapport Capitaine Carton 10 Mai – 1 Juin 1940, pp. 7–8.
6. SHDDT GR/32/N/47 Journal du Marche, 10 Mai à 4 Juin 1940, p. 74.
7. SHDDT GR/31/N/40 Dossier 5, Journal du Marche de FTA, p. 6.
8. SHDDT GR/31/N/40 Dossier 5, Notes sur le Groupement DDT p. 2.
9. SHDDT GR/32/N/47 ordre 1 Juin 1940 B.
10. SHDDT GR/30/N/260. Dossier Journal de Marche du Corps de Cavalerie, p. 30.
11. Lormier, *La Bataille de Dunkerque*, pp. 101–02.
12. SHDDT GR/27/N/81 Chiffre 1 Juin 1940.
13. SHDDT GR/27/N/81 Telegramme No. 7529 1 Juin 1940: 16:00.
14. SHDDT GR/27/N/81 Telegramme 1 Juin 1940.
15. SHDDT GR/27/N/81 Telegramme 1 Juin 1940.
16. SHDDT GR/27/N/81 Telegramme No. 7254 1 Juin 1940 @ 17:15.
17. SHDDT GR/27/N/81 Telegramme No. 7243 1 Juin 1940 @ 17:56.
18. SHDDT GR/27/N/81 Telegramme No. 7552 1 Juin 1940 @ 21:30.
19. SHDDT GR/32/N/47 ordre 1 Juin 1940 @ 15:50.
20. SHDDT GR/32/N/76 Dossier 21 Rapport Colonel Basse. Retrait de la 12e DIM. 10 Mai – 1 Juin 1940, pp. 1–2.
21. SHDDT GR/30/N/260. Dossier Journal de Marche du Corps de Cavalerie, p. 30.
22. SHDDT GR/27/N/81 Telegramme No. 901 1 Juin 1940 @ 19:30.

Chapter 34: 2 June 1940. Pressure Mounts

1. SHDDT GR/32/N/38 Dossier 2 10 Mai – Juin 1940, Notes sur les journées de 2 et 3 Juin 1940, p. 1.
2. SHDDT GR/32/N/47 Journal du Marche, 10 Mai à 4 Juin 1940, p. 74.
3. Ibid., p. 75.
4. SHDDT GR/32/N/76 Dossier 11, rapport 2 Juin 1940 @ 09:00.
5. SHDDT GR/32/N/47 Journal du Marche, 10 Mai à 4 Juin 1940. p. 76.
6. Lormier, *La Bataille de Dunkerque*, pp. 104–05.

7. SHDDT GR/32/N/47 Journal du Marche, 10 Mai à 4 Juin 1940. p. 76.
8. SHDDT GR/27/N/81 Telegramme No. 7616 2 Juin 1940 @ 08:30.
9. SHDDT GR/32/N/47 ordre 2 Juin 1940 @09:00.
10. SHDDT GR/27/N/81 Telegramme No. 7618 2 Juin 1940 @ 13:45.
11. SHDDT GR/27/N/81 Telegramme No. 1328 2 Juin 1940 @ 17:15.
12. SHDDT GR/27/N/81 Telegramme No. 901 1 Juin 1940 @ 19:30.
13. SHDDT GR/32/N/76 Dossier 21 Quelques souvenirs du Lieutenant P. Billard, p. 32.
14. SHDDT GR/32/N/221 Dossier 11 Embarquement Dunkerque: notes du 30 mai ay 2 Juin 40. Ordre 2 Juin 1940 @ 18:00.
15. Ibid. Ordre du jour, 2 Juin 1940.
16. SHDDT GR/321N/38 Dossier 2 Rapport Capitaine 10 Mai – Juin 1940, Notes sur les journées de 2 et 3 Juin 1940, p. 1.
17. SHDDT GR/34/N/141 Le 3e Bataillon du 143e à la Contre-Attaque de Teteghem, 3e Juin 1940.
18. SHDDT GR/32/N/202 Dossier 3 'Role du 3eme bataillon du 122e constute en bataillon de march sous les ordres du Captain Arbola, 2e et 3e Juin 1940'.
19. Lormier, *La Bataille de Dunkerque*, pp. 151–3.

Chapter 35: 3 June 1940. Last Men Standing

1. SHDDT GR/34/N/476 Dossier 9 Journaux des marches et opérations des corps de troupe 3 Septembre 1939 – 23 juin 1940, p. 70.
2. SHDDT GR/32/N/47 Journal du Marche, 10 Mai à 4 Juin 1940, p. 77.
3. SHDDT GR/34/N/435 Dossier 14 Rapports d'officiers, riches de renseignements 38eme Bataillon de Chars de Combat Septembre 1939 à Juin 1940. Rapport 3 Mai 1940.
4. SHDDT GR/32/N/47 Journal du Marche, 10 Mai à 4 Juin 1940, p. 77.
5. SHDDT GR/34/N/435 Dossier 14 Rapports d'officiers, riches de renseignements 38eme Bataillon de Chars de Combat Septembre 1939 à Juin 1940. Rapport 3 Mai 1940.
6. SHDDT GR/27/N/81 H.V.0/242.
7. Lormier, *La Bataille de Dunkerque*, pp. 151–3.
8. Ibid., pp. 170–1.
9. SHDDT GR/32/N/76 Dossier 21. Retraite leur 12e DIM, p. 2.
10. SHDDT GR/27/N/81 Telegramme No. 901 1 Juin 1940 @ 19:30.
11. SHDDT GR/27/N/81 Telegramme No. 1328 3 Juin 1940 @ 07:34.
12. TNA WO 106/1613, Record of Phone Conversations with Generals Alexander & Lloyd, 3 June 1940.

13. Hugh Sebag-Montefiore, *Dunkirk: Fight to the Last Man* (Harvard University Press, Cambridge MA: 2006), p. 448.
14. TNA WO 106-1613, Admiral Ramsay (Vice-Admiral Dover) to Admiralty: Admiral Abrial's message, the closing Dynamo & dispersal of task force, 4 June 1940.
15. SHDDT GR/32/N/47 Journal du Marche, 10 Mai à 4 Juin 1940, p. 78.
16. TNA WO 106-1613, Admiral Ramsay (Vice-Admiral Dover) to Admiralty: Admiral Abrial's message, the closing Dynamo & dispersal of task force, 4 June 1940.
17. SHDDT GR/32/N/76 Dossier 11, ordre du jour 3 Mai 1940.
18. SHDDT GR/32/N/47 Ordre du Jour, 3 Mai 1940.
19. SHDDT GR/32/N/47 Journal du Marche, 10 Mai à 4 Juin 1940, p. 80.
20. SHDDT GR/32/N/76 Dossier 21 Rapport Lieutenant Billard 10 Mai – 4 Juin 1940, p. 23.
21. Lormier, *La Bataille de Dunkerque*, pp. 106–07.
22. SHDDT GR/32/N/76 Rapport, 3 Mai 1904 @ 22:00.
23. Lormier, *La Bataille de Dunkerque*, pp. 170–1.
24. SHDDT GR/31/N/38 Dossier 2 Rapport 10 Mai – Juin 1940, Notes sur les journées de 2 et 3 Juin 1940, p. 2.
25. SHDDT GR/3/1N/38 Dossier 2 Rapport Chef d'escadron Ziegler, p. 3.
26. SHDDT GR/32/N/47 Journal du Marche, 10 Mai à 4 Juin 1940, p. 80.
27. Archives Communales de Dunkerque 18Z – Témoignages et récits sur les deux guerres mondiales.
28. Lormier, *La Bataille de Dunkerque*, pp. 151–3.
29. SHDDT GR/32/N/76 Dossier 25 Rapport Capitaine Carton 10 Mai – 1 Juin 1940, pp. 7–8.

Chapter 36; 4 June 1940. The End

1. SHDDT GR/32/N/76 Dossier 21 Rapport Commandant Parent 10 Mai – 1 Juin 1940, pp. 8–9.
2. SHDDT GR/32/N/76 Dossier 21 Rapport Lieutenant Billard 10 Mai – 4 Juin 1940, p. 23.
3. SHDDT GR/34/N/476 Dossier 9 Journaux des marches et opérations des corps de troupe 3 septembre 1939 – 23 juin 1940, p. 74.
4. SHDDT GR/3/1N/38 Dossier 2 Rapport 10 Mai – Juin 1940, Notes sur les journées de 2 et 3 Juin 1940, p. 3.
5. SHDDT GR/32/N/76 Dossier 25 Rapport Capitaine Carton 10 Mai – 1 Juin 1940, pp. 8–9
6. SHDDT GR/27/N/81 Telegramme No. 901 1 Juin 1940 @ 19:30.

7. SHDDT GR/32/N/76 Dossier Lt-Colonel Cope, p. 2.
8. SHDDT GR/34/N/435 Journaux des marche du 38e BCC 2 Septembre 1939 à 8 Juin 1940, p. 70 .
9. SHDDT GR/32/N/47 Journal du Marche, 10 Mai à 4 Juin 1940, pp. 82–3.
10. SHDDT GR/32/N/76 Dossier 21 Rapport Commandant Parent 10 Mai – 1 Juin 1940, pp. 9–10.
11. SHDDT GR/32/N/47 Journal du Marche de la 4eme DCR, pp. 47–8.
12. SHDDT GR/32/N/47 Journal du Marche, 10 Mai à 4 Juin 1940, pp. 82–3.
13. SHDDT GR/32/N/76 Dossier 27 Rapport Retrait du 12e DIM Mai – 1 Juin 1940, pp. 9–10.
14. SHDDT GR/32/N/76 Dossier 25 Rapport Capitaine Carton 10 Mai – 1 Juin 1940, pp. 8–9.
15. SHDDT GR/32/N/76 Dossier 21. Lettre 23 Janvier 1941.
16. TNA WO 106/1613, Evacuation of Dunkirk Area: Total number of troops (British, Allies, Fit, Wounded) evacuated from 20 May to 4 June, 1940.
17. SHDDT GR/34/N/435 Journaux des marche du 38e BCC 2 Septembre 1939 à 8 Juin 1940, p. 70.

Chapter 37: Epilogue

1. SHDDT GR/31/N/38 Dossier 2 Rapports. Interrogatoire du quartier-maitre carton, pp. 1–2.
2. Dominique Lormier *Mai-Juin 1940: Les causes de la Défaite* (Aliso Histoire, Paris: 2020), pp. 143–51.
3. Ibid.

BIBLIOGRAPHY

Primary Sources

Archives Nationales de France
AN 4/DA7/14 3748 (S/3), 'Etude sur l'emploi des chars'
AN 496 4/DA7/folio 3 A7/Dr.3: compte-rendu de la *2e* Division Cuirassée

Archives Communales de Dunkerque
18Z – Témoignages et récits sur les deux guerres mondiales

The National Archives, Kew
Cabinet Papers 66, 80
Foreign Officer Papers 371/24277 General correspondence
War Office Papers 106, 160, 167, 202, 203

Liddell Hart Centre for Military Archives
Dill correspondence and papers

Service Historique de la Armée de l'Air
1A/11Z/12938
1A/3/D/498

Service Historique de la Armée du Terre
DE/2016/SA/65
GR 13YD 837, 1279 (Général d'Armée: Gamelin, Maurice Gustave)
GR/1K/224 Fonds Gamelin
GR/1/K713 papiers General Marty
GR/1/N/34
GR/1/N/67
GR/2/N/261
GR/2/N/262
GR/5/N/580

GR/6/T/952
GR/7/N/3
GR/7/N/8
GR/7/N/2292
GR/7/N/3006
GR/7/N/3017
GR/7/N/3983
GR/7/N/3997
GR/7N/4025
GR/9/N/18
GR/9/N/157
GR/9/N/253
GR/9/N/325
GR/27/N/3
GR/27/N/80
GR/27/N/81
GR/27/N/85
GR/27/N/105
GR/27/N/112
GR/27/N/113
GR/27/N/155
GR/27/N/188
GR/28/N/2
GR/29/N/18
GR/29/N/430
GR/29/N/439
GR/30/N/82
GR/30/N/92
GR/30/N/123
GR/30/N/260
GR/30/N/264
GR/31/N/38
GR/32/N/47
GR/32/N/76
GR/32/N/204
GR/32/N/253
GR/34/N/132
GR/34/N/425
GR/34/N/435
GR/34/N/437

GR/34/N/439
GR/34/N/430
GR/34/N/435
GR/34/N/457
GR/34/N/462
GR/34/N/463
GR/34/N/471
GR/34/N/476
MR/31/1001111/51

Printed Sources

Alexander, Martin S., *The Republic in Danger: Maurice Gamelin and the Politics of French Rearmament* (Cambridge University Press, Cambridge: 1993).

Alexander, Martin S., 'In Defence of the Maginot Line: Security policy, domestic politics and the economic depression in France' in Boyce, Robert (ed.), *French Foreign and Defence Policy, 1918-1940: The Decline and Fall of a Great Power* (Routledge, London: 1998), pp. 163–93.

Alexander, Martin S., '"Fighting to the Last Frenchman"? Reflections on the BEF Deployment to France and the Strains in the Franco-British Alliance, 1939-1940' in Joel Blatt (ed.), *The French Defeat of 1940: Reassessments* (Oxford, Berghahn Books: 1998).

Alexander, Martin S., 'Prophet without Honour? The French High Command and Pierre Taittinger's Report on the Ardennes Defences, March 1940', in *War and Society* IV (1986), pp. 53–71.

Alexander, Martin S. and William J. Philpott, ed., *Anglo-French Defence Relations Between the Wars* (Palgrave Macmillan, New York: 2002).

Arbarétier, Vincent, *L'école de la guerre – Sedan 1940: Ou la faillite du système de commandement français* (Economica, Paris: 2000).

Barbanson, Érik, *Les 2e et 3e divisions légères mécaniques, t. 1: Hannut-Gembloux 10-15 mai 1940: la première bataille de chars de l'histoire* (Arès, Toul: 2017).

Baudoin, Paul, *Neuf Mois au Gouvernement (Avril-Décembre 1940)* (Éditions de la Table Ronde, Paris: 1948).

Baughen, Greg, *The Rise and Fall of the French Air Force* (FontHill Media, Stroud: 2019).

Bedarida, François, *La Stratégie Secrète de la drôle guerre* (Presse FNSP: 1979).

Bell, P. M. H., *A Certain Eventuality: Britain and the Fall of France* (Saxon House, Farnborough: 1974).

Bertrand, Christophe, *Comme en 40* (Gallimard: Musee de l'Armée: 2020).

Blonde, Louis, *Historique des transmissions de l'armée de Terre, Des Origins a 1940* (Musée de la Armée, Sartory: 1995).

Bock, Fedor von. *The War Diary 1939-1945* (Schiffer Publishing Ltd, Atglen, PA: 2004).

Bond, Brian, and Michael Taylor (eds), *The Battle for France & Flanders: Sixty Years On* (Leo Cooper: Barnsley 2001).

Botquin, Gaston, *The Morane Saulnier 406*. (Profile Publications Ltd., Leatherhead: 1967).

Boog, H., 'The Luftwaffe's Assault', in Paul Addison and Jeremy Crang, *The Burning Blue: A New History of the Battle of Britain* (Faber and Faber, London: 2011), pp. 39–54.

Bourachot, Andre, *De Sedan à Sedan: Une histoire de l'armée Francise 1870-1940* (L'artilleur: 2022).

Brindley, John, *French Fighters of World War Two* (Hylton Lacy, London: 1971)

Cairns, John C., 'De Gaulle Confronts the British: The Legacy of 1940', in *International Journal – Canada's Journal of Global Policy Analysis* (1938), Vol. 23, No. 2, pp. 187–210.

Carrer, Claude, *Historie du ministre de la Defense et des departments ministeriels militaires* (Lazuavelle: Paris, 2001).

Chaix, Bruno, *En mai 1940, fallait-il entrer en Belgique?* (Economica, Paris: 2000).

Christofferson, Thomas, and Michael Christofferson, *France during World War II: From Defeat to Liberation* (Fordham University Press: 2006).

Clarke, Lloyd, *Blitzkrieg: Myth, Reality, and Hitler's Lightning War: France 1940* (Atlantic Books, New York: 2017).

Coates, John, *The Hour Between Dog and Wolf* (Fourth Estate, London: 2012).

Conquet, Général Alfred, *L'énigme des blindés 1932-1940* (Nouvelles Éditions Latines, Paris: 1956).

Crémieux-Brilhac, Jean-Louis, *Les Français de l'An '40* (Folio, Paris: 2020)

Danchev, Alex, and Dan Todman (eds), *War Diaries 1939-1945: Field Marshal Lord Alanbrooke* (Weidenfeld & Nicholson, London: 2001).

Danel, Raymond, *The Dewoitine 520: Aircraft in Profile Number 135* (Profile Publications Ltd, Windsor: 1971).

Danel, Raymond, *The Potez 63 Series Aircraft in Profile Number 195* (Profile Publications, Leatherhead, Surrey: 1967).

Deist, Wilhelm, *Germany and the Second World War* (Clarendon Press, Oxford: 1990)

Delpla, François, *Les Papiers Secrets du General Doumenc: Un Autre Regard sur 39-40* (Olivier Orban, Paris: 1992).

Dixon, Norman, *On The Psychology of Military Incompetence* (Pimlico: London, 1994).

Dutailly, Henri, *Les Problèmes de l'Armée de Terre Française, 1935-40* (Service Historique de l'Armée, Paris: 1980).

Fabribeckers, Edmond de, *La Campagne de l'Armée Belge en 1940* (Rossel, 1978).

Facon, Patrick, 'Slowing Down Blitzkrieg – A Curtiss Fighter Ace in the Battle of France', *AIR FAN International*, Publitek Ltd (March 1996), pp. 54–62.

Faury, Louis, 'La Pologne Terrassée', *Revue Historique de l'Armée* 9:1 (1953), pp. 131–52.

Ferrard, Stéphane, 'Du Char B à l'ARL 44, un long cheminement (II). 1937-1940: Ce Mal Aimé. Le char B1ter', *Histoire de Guerre, Blindés & Matériel* 109 (2014), pp. 67–78.

French, David, *Raising Churchill's Army* (Oxford University Press, Oxford: 2000).

Frieser, Karl Heinz, *The Blitzkrieg Legend* (Naval Institute Press, Annapolis: 2012).

Flintham, Vic, *Close Call: RAF Close Air Support in the Mediterranean. Volume I Defeat in France to el Hamma 1939-1943* (Crecy: Manchester, 2021).

Fussell, Paul, *The Great War and Modern Memory* (Oxford University Press, Oxford: 1975).

Gamelin, Maurice, *Servir* (Plon, Paris: 1947).

Gauché, Maurice Henri, *Le Deuxième Bureau au Travail* (Amiot, Paris: 1952).

Gravley, T. B., *The Second World War 1939-1945: Signal and Communications* (War Office, London: 1950).

Guderian, Heinz, *Panzer Leader* (Penguin, London: 2009).

Gunsburg, Jeffrey, 'The Battle of Gembloux, 14–15 May 1940: The 'Blitzkrieg' Checked', in *The Journal of Military History* Vol. 64, No. 1 (January 2000).

Halder, Franz, Charles Burdick, et al., *The Hadler War Diary 1939-1942* (Greenhill Books, London: 1989)

Hamilton, Nigel, *Monty: The Making of a General, 1887–1942* (McGraw-Hill, New York: 1981).

Harris, L. H., *Signal Venture* (Gale & Polden Ltd, Aldershot: 1951).

Harvey, A. D., 'The French Armée de l'Air in May–June 1940: A Failure of Conception', *Journal of Contemporary History*, vol. 25, no. 4 (1990), pp. 447–65.

Horne, Alistair, *To Lose a Battle: France 1940* (Macmillan, London: 1969).

Jackson, Julian, *The Fall of France: The Nazi Invasion of 1940* (Oxford University Press, Oxford: 2003).

Jackson, Peter and Joseph Maiolo, 'Strategic Intelligence, Counter-Intelligence and Alliance Diplomacy in Anglo-French Relations Before the Second World War', *Militärgeschichtliche Zeitschrift* 65, no. 2 (2006), pp. 450–65.

Jordan, Nicole, 'Strategy and Scapegoatism: Reflections on the French National Catastrophe, 1940', in Blatt, Joel (ed.), *The French Defeat of 1940: Reassessments* (Berghahn Books, New York: 2001).

Jordan, Nicole, *The Popular Front and Central Europe: The Dilemmas of French Impotence, 1918-1940* (Cambridge University Press, Cambridge:1992).

Keyes, Roger, *Un règne brisé* (Paris-Bruxelles, Duculot: 1985).

Kirkland, Faris R., 'French Air Strength in May 1940', *Air Power History*, vol. 40, no. 1 (1993), pp. 22–34.

Launay, Jacques De, *Major Controversies of Contemporary History* (Pergamon Press, London: 1965).

Le Goyet, Pierre, *Le Mystère Gamelin* (Plon, Paris: 1957).

Lormier, Dominique, *Mai-Juin 1940: Les causes de la Défaite* (Aliso Histoire, Paris: 2020).

Lormier, Dominique, *La Bataille de Dunkerque* (Flavie Menet, Paris: 2011).

Lormier, Dominique, *La Bataille de Stonne Ardennes, mai 1940* (Edition Perrin, Paris: 2010)

Lormier, Dominique, *La Bataille de France Jour Apres Jour. Mai-Juin 1940* (Le Cherche Midi, Paris: 2010).

Lormier, Dominique, *Commes des Lions: Mai Juin 1940. Le sacrifice héroïque de l'Armée Française* (Carmen Levy, Paris: 2005).

May, Ernest, *Strange Victory: Hitler's Conquest of France* (I B Taurus & Co, New York: 2009).

Minart, Jacques, *P.C. Vincennes, Secteur* 4 (Editions Berger-Levrault, Paris: 1945).

Ministère de la Défense Nationale, *Règlement des unités de Chars de Combat, 2ème Partie: Combat* (École des chars de combat, Paris: 1939).

Ministère de la Guerre, *Instruction sur l'emploi tactique des Grandes Unités* (Librairie Militaire Berger-Levrault, Paris: 1937).

Nalder, R. F. H., *The History of the British Army Signals in the Second World War* (Royal Signals Institution, London: 1953).

Pelletier, Alain, *French Bombers of World War II in Action. Aircraft No. 189* (Squadron/Signal Publications, Carrollton, Texas: 2003).

Porch, Douglas, *Defeat and Division: France at War, 1939–1942. Armies of the Second World War* (Cambridge University Press, Cambridge: 2022).

Porch, Douglas, *The French Secret Services* (Oxford University Press, Oxford: 1997).

Prioux, Général, *Souvenirs de Guerre* (Flammendon, Paris: 1947).

Reid, Miles, *Last on the List* (Leo Cooper, London: 1974).

Rocelle, Colonel Pierre, *La guerre de 1940* (Armand Colin, Paris: 1990).

Rothenberg, Gunther E., *The Art of Warfare in the Age of Napoléon* (Indiana University Press, Bloomington, Indiana: 1978).

Roton, General G., *Années Cruciales: La Course aux Armements (1933-1939), La Campagne (1939-1940)* (Charles Lavauzelle, Paris: 1947).

Saint-Martin, Gerard, *L'Arme blindée français tome 1 Mai-Juin 1940: Les blindés français dans la tourmente* (Economica, Paris: 1998).

Sarmant, Thierry, 'Prélude à Juin 1940: Le Commandement Français et les enseignements de la Campagne de Pologne de Septembre 1939', in *Guerres mondiales et conflits contemporains* No. 192 (Décembre 1998), p. 122.

Schiavon, Max, ed., *Les Carnets secrets du Général Huntziger, 1938-1941* (Éditions Pierre de Taillac, Paris: 2019).

Schuker, S. A., 'Seeking a Scapegoat: Intelligence and Grand Strategy in France', in Jonathan Haslam and Karina Urbach (eds), *Secret Intelligence in the European States System, 1918–1989* (Stanford, Stanford University Press: 2014), pp. 111–12.

Sebag-Montefiore, Hugh, *Dunkirk: Fight to the Last Man* (Harvard University Press, Cambridge MA: 2006).

Shuster, Richard J., *German Disarmament of Germany after World War I: The Diplomacy of International Arms Inspection, 1920–31* (Routledge, London: 2006).

Smart, Nick, *British Strategy and Politics During the Phony War: Before the Balloon Went Up* (Praeger, Westport, CT: 2003).

Spears, Sir Edward, *Assignment to Catastrophe* (William Heinemann Ltd, London: 1955).

Stehlin, Paul, *Témoignage Pour l'Histoire* (Robert Laffont, Paris: 1964).

Stolfi, R. H. S., 'Equipment for Victory in France in 1940', *History*, vol. 55 (1970), pp. 1–20.

Taylor, A. J. P., *The Origins of the Second World War* (Hamish Hamilton, London: 1961).

Todman, Daniel, *Britain's War: Into Battle 1937-1941* (Allen Lane, London: 2016).

Tournoux, Général P. E., *Défense des Frontières: Haut Commandement – Gouvernement 1919-1939* (Nouvelles Editions Latines, Paris: 1960).

Vidalenc, J., 'Les Divisions de serie 'B2 dans l'armee francaise dans la campagne de France', in *Revue Historique des Armees*, IV (1980), pp. 106–26.

Webster, Charles and Noble Frankland, *The Strategic Air Offensive Against Germany: 1939-1945* (Her Majesty's Stationery Office, London: 1961).

Young, Robert, 'La Guerre de Longue Dureé: Some Reflections of French Strategy and Diplomacy in the 1930s,' in Preston, Adrian (ed.), *General Staffs and Diplomacy Before the Second World War* (Croom Helm, London: 1978), pp. 46–9.

Digital Sources

https://ieeexplore.ieee.org/stamp/stamp.jsp?arnumber=7909880

https://france3-regions.francetvinfo.fr/

'Dunkirk 1940' directed by Bernard Claeys and broadcast on 29 May 1978 in the program 'Hexagonal, Histoire de France'.

INDEX